Models of Classroom Management

Third Edition
Principles, Practices and Critical Considerations

Jack Martin, Jeff Sugarman and John McNamara
Simon Fraser University

Detselig Enterprises Ltd.

Calgary, Alberta, Canada

Models of Classroom Management, Third Edition
© 2000 Jack Martin, Jeff Sugarman & John McNamara

Canadiana Information in Publication
Martin, Jack, 1950-
Models of classroom management

Includes bibliographical references.
ISBN 1-55059-177-0

1. Classroom management. I. Sugarman, Jeff, 1955-   II.
McNamara, John, 1969 III. Title.
LB3013.M37 2000   371.102'4   C99-911112-4

Detselig Enterprises Ltd.
210-1220 Kensington Rd. N.W.
Calgary, Alberta T2N 3P5
Phone: (403) 283-0900/Fax: (403) 283-6947
e-mail: temeron@telusplanet.net
www.temerondetselig.com

We acknowledge the financial support of the Government of Canada through the Book Publishing Industry Development Program (BPIDP) for our publishing activities.

ISBN: 1-55059-177-0
SAN: 115-0324
Printed in Canada
Cover Design by Dean Macdonald

Table of Contents

Preface

It has been 19 years since the first edition of *Models of Classroom Management* appeared in 1981, and 7 years since the second edition appeared in 1993. The 80s and 90s have passed, and the new millennium is underway. Our world, our society and our schools have witnessed incredible change during this time. Any such change inevitably necessitates adaptation. Adapting to change does not require that we abandon entirely those patterns of thought and action that have served us well in the past. Rather, sensible adaptation might best be considered as building upon and expanding our existing capabilities in ways that strengthen our overall repertoires of thought and action in light of changed circumstances, while retaining the possibility that some traditional practices may not be sustainable in dramatically altered societal and school contexts.

This third edition, *Models of Classroom Management III: Principles, Practice and Critical Considerations*, builds upon, critiques and expands those models and approaches to classroom management that were contained in the first and second editions. New material considers a range of socio-cultural theories and perspectives that have significantly affected how contemporary educators understand and practice their craft. This new context emphasizes the complex and diverse interactions among individual students and teachers, and the larger socio-cultural contexts in which they are embedded. In addition, all chapters have been updated and extended to reflect the most recent work in the areas of classroom management, interpersonal communication and teaching practice.

Models of Classroom Management III begins with a general discussion of the importance of classroom management in contemporary society and schools. Specific consideration also is given to relationships among theory, research and practice in the area of classroom management. The purposes of this first chapter are to establish the general context to which models of classroom management must apply, and to clarify what it is reasonable to expect from an enhanced knowledge of such models.

Following this introductory chapter are seven chapters that present different approaches to classroom management. Each of these chapters provides a unique perspective and emphasis. Chapter two presents approaches that consider classroom management to be a reflection of the quality of the communication that takes place between teachers and pupils. Chapter three presents an approach to classroom management that emphasizes the individual motivations and responsibilities of students in a democratic classroom context. In chapter four, the emphasis is on teaching methods associated with the effective management of classroom groups. Chapter five considers the modification of students' classroom behaviors when these behaviors are viewed as disruptive to the maintenance of positive environments for teaching and learning. In chapter six, the emphasis is on assisting students to acquire the cognitive strategies and dispositions required for appropriate levels of self-control and productive problem solving. Chapter seven presents three approaches to classroom management that emphasize the importance of effective school-wide, organizational practices in the promotion of appropriate, educationally-productive student conduct. Finally, chapter eight examines a number of contemporary socio-cultural approaches and perspectives concerning student and teacher activity and experience in classrooms.

Chapter nine departs from the focus on different models of classroom management, and attempts to help teachers construct their own approaches to classroom management. This chapter considers students' developmental levels, teachers' relationships with parents/guardians and colleagues, methods of coping with the ongoing demands of professional life, legal and ethical matters of direct relevance to teachers, and ways in which teachers can develop classroom management methods tailored to their own unique personal and pedagogical styles.

The substantive information in those chapters that present specific approaches to classroom management is organized in four main sections – *Overview and Rationale, Principles, Methods and Applications,* and *Critique*. The first introduces readers to the basic ideas on which the approaches to be discussed are based. The second summarizes assumptions and principles that define the approaches to classroom management that are being examined. The third offers a summary and description of the instructional methods and classroom applications that follow from these principles. The critique section in each of these chapters provides a brief evaluation of the possible strengths and limitations of the approaches under consideration.

While written directly to teachers, *Models of Classroom Management III* can be used by counselors, parents/guardians or anyone interested in examining current theories and practices relevant to assisting children and adolescents to develop positive personal, interpersonal and social attitudes and behaviors. The various principles and practices examined are presented clearly and openly, with as little bias as the authors' own, inevitably imperfect, attempts at balance permit. In this way, it is hoped that readers' legitimate rights to consider the various approaches presented in terms of their own particular contexts and personal styles/preferences will not be constrained unduly by the manner of presentation. Even the critique sections are presented in this manner, and are intended to provide an impetus to readers' own evaluations of the approaches discussed, rather than to stand as definitive assessments.

In preparing this new edition, Jeff Sugarman and I welcome John McNamara. His involvement, together with the welcome input of numerous teachers who have responded personally to the first and second editions, hopefully will help to make *Models of Classroom Management III* a better and more useful book than its predecessors.

Jack Martin, Ph.D.

Professor of Education

Simon Fraser University

Chapter One
Issues and Perspectives

This book is about classroom management. Classroom management refers to those activities of classroom teachers that create a positive classroom climate within which effective teaching and learning can occur. Numerous investigations of teachers' classroom actions consistently show that teachers spend approximately 50 percent of their time organizing students for instruction, dealing with misbehavior and handling individual problems (e.g., Gump, 1967; Wragg, 1984). However, the effective management of classrooms goes beyond these executive, disciplinary and counseling functions. In fact, effective classroom management cannot be considered independently of teachers' instructional activities (Doyle, 1986). The past decade of research has demonstrated the effectiveness of a variety of instructional techniques in controlling classrooms and enhancing achievement (Wang, Haertel & Walberg, 1993). The inevitable interdependence between management and instructional functions in classrooms is obvious when the effects of "good" teaching are considered. Motivated, involved and successful learners are less likely to present "management problems" than are students who are alienated and failing. To the extent that sound pedagogy enables the former, a clear link between effective teaching and effective classroom management is revealed. Consequently, it probably is pointless, and perhaps counterproductive, to attempt to disentangle effective classroom management from effective instruction.

The Problem

The notion that classroom management is a major problem in today's schools is both prevalent and well-founded. Jones and Jones (1998) summarize the results of several major surveys of American teachers, school administrators and citizens with respect to their perceptions of schools and student behavior. The 1994 Gallup polls of public and teachers' attitudes reveal that student behavior and discipline is now the most serious concern of the American public (Elem & Rose, 1995). Violence and fighting within the school environment was listed as the third most serious problem, while drug use was listed fourth. Further, 44 percent of teachers reported that student misbehavior significantly interfered with their teaching. Between 1990 and 1994, the National League of Cities reported that school violence increased 55 percent in large cities and 41 percent in cities with populations of 100 000 or more.

In Canada, recent reports by major teachers' associations, surveys of public attitudes and numerous position papers by educators and social scientists reveal a similar prevalence of concerns related to student behavior in schools. Clearly, classroom management remains a prominent concern of society, parents, teachers and students alike. In this respect the situation in today's schools is no less demanding of knowledge of principles and practices of classroom management than was the situation in 1981 when the first edition of this book appeared.

Problems of student drug abuse, school crime and student dropout continue at unacceptably high levels for the majority of North American educators and parents. There also appears to be a possible widening of violent student behavior, such that many school systems previously insulated from these incidents no longer enjoy such immunity (Kainz & Mangiacasale, 1992). Many of these more severe problems may be interactive with students' in-class behavior, and more general participation and sense of belonging in school classrooms and activities. For example, Finn (1989) summarizes a model of student disengagement from school that views dropping out of school as an extreme end on a continuum of school participation and identification. In Finn's view, dropping out of school may actually begin as a pattern of disruptive student actions or lack of positive engagement in ordinary classroom learning activities during the early elementary grades. In a 1993 report on violence and youth, the American Psychological Association indicated that the school system plays a pivotal role in addressing the issue of youth violence because of the potential for reaching a large number of children for early intervention and prevention and because teachers are ideally positioned to identify children who have social, emotional, behavioral and academic problems (Day, Golench, MacDougall & Beals-Gonzaléz, 1995).

Society and School

What is perhaps most disturbing about the continuation and possible widening of problems seemingly related to classroom management and instruction is that today's teachers probably are better educated and prepared than ever before. Theory and practice in classroom management have improved dramatically over the past decade (Jones & Jones, 1998). At the very least, it is extremely difficult to sustain the argument that contemporary difficulties associated with student in-school behavior are solely, or even predominately, problems created by teachers. With more than 55 percent of schoolchildren born in the 90s living in single-parent families, over 20 percent of schoolchildren living in poverty and increasing numbers of schoolchildren with extremely diverse linguistic/cultural backgrounds and physical/mental capabilities, the successful management of today's school classrooms can be an enormous job (Jones & Jones, 1998).

Contemporary life can be extremely demanding, not to say hectic, for both parents and teachers. Many parents, especially single parents, are hard pressed to find sufficient time to attend to the seemingly endless psychological, physical, recreational, educational and social needs of their children, while at the same time struggling to provide much more basic requirements in the way of food, shelter and clothing. Many teachers find themselves facing such challenges at home with their own children, before and after attempting to do their best to manage and facilitate the learning of pupils in their school classrooms. Consequently, it should come as no surprise that perhaps the single most significant change to models of classroom management that has occurred in the past decade concerns the forging of cooperative relationships (partnerships) between parents and teachers, and between home and school. Rather than casting blame at each other, as we sometimes are apt to do when confronted by seemingly intractable difficulties, joining together in a common effort to assist students to learn and develop is increasingly the choice being made by teachers and parents/guardians in many communities.

Nonetheless, whatever the proximal or distal causes of student difficulties, or the availability of systems of cooperation and mutual support, it is today's classroom teachers who must deal with increasingly diverse and demanding circumstances in the day to day operation of school classrooms. The various approaches to classroom management presented herein are intended to assist teachers to do exactly this. However, before turning to specific models of classroom management, a few comments are in order concerning the nature of relationships among classroom practice, theories of classroom management and instruction, and research that might support both theories and practice.

Theory, Research and Practice

This third edition of *Models of Classroom Management* discusses many different approaches to classroom management, including numerous variations within and across these distinct approaches. Each of the approaches presented consists of a set of principles and applications. The principles are derived from logical, moral and empirical analyses of human behavior and experience in social, interpersonal contexts. Sometimes these analyses are formalized according to various conventions of experimentation and inquiry. Such work typically combines the contributions of several theorists and researchers. Other times such analyses are less formally conducted, being more directly reflective of the personal beliefs, experiences and observations of a single individual. Whatever their origin, the principles and practices of any approach to classroom management are intended to guide the thoughts and actions of classroom teachers in an heuristic manner. What this means is that the principles and suggestions for practice that are discussed in this book do not have the status of universal laws that can be applied to any classroom situation with predictable effects. Classroom contexts and individual teachers and pupils display far too many complex variations and interactions to permit any such automatized, algorithmic application. Consequently, knowledge of the principles and practices discussed herein needs to be considered alongside more immediate knowledge of specific classroom contexts and the individuals within these contexts.

For example, the seemingly straightforward principle from behavior modification that desired student behavior can be strengthened if reinforced, offers a general guide to a teacher's thoughts and actions, not a recipe for a specific sequence of thought and action. Before a teacher might apply her knowledge of reinforcement theory and principles to a specific classroom situation, she must first determine what kinds of social interactions or responses actually function as positive reinforcers for the particular student in question, which of these are readily available in the classroom situation and what other classroom conventions or routines might interfere with the behavioral intervention being considered. There inevitably is a big gap between theory and practice. Even when theory (principles) is supported by research (experimentation or systematic inquiry), it still does not tell teachers exactly what to do in any specific classroom situation. The classrooms and other contexts within which research is conducted may vary in numerous important ways from the classroom contexts within which principles supported by research are applied. There can be no easy generalizations from research that will convey exactly what specific teacher actions will work with pupil X at time Y in situation Z.

Classrooms are complex social environments, a reality which receives more detailed attention in this third edition (see, for example, Chapter 8) than in the previous two editions of this book. Different students may possess quite different experiential histories, fostered by diverse cultural, social and economic contexts. Consequently, different students will perceive, interpret and understand classroom events (including the actions of teachers) in different ways. A teacher's mild admonishment may be received as such by one student, totally ignored by another student and interpreted as an extreme form of insult by yet another pupil. Further, the same student might respond to essentially the same teacher action in very different manners at different times, depending on recent experiences, mood and immediate situation. Complex interactions among student and teacher individual differences, and contextual variations within and across classrooms (including the different social, cultural and economic settings within which different schools and classrooms reside) mean that teachers must work constantly to adapt any set of classroom management principles to the general and current classroom situations that they confront on a moment by moment basis.

The inability of educational and social scientific theory and research to yield tight prescriptions for classroom practice may have very little to do with the quality or validity of such theoretical and empirical work. Even in areas such as physics, that generally are acknowledged to be mature, progressive sciences, the same general pattern of relationships among theory, research and practice holds. A physicist may know a great deal about the various forces that act on falling objects and yet be completely unable to predict or control the specific movements of individual leaves in a particular windstorm. Whenever theories and research findings are generalized to real-world contexts, such generalizations are constrained by the complex webs of interacting variables that inevitably define such settings. When the objects of study are the actions, beliefs and reactions of human beings, the situation becomes even more complicated given the obvious fact that humans differ from leaves, storms and trees by virtue of their capacities to actively determine their own responses and reactions to any set of externally-imposed conditions. In the final analysis, the actions of teachers (like those of weather forecasters, seismologists, farmers, business managers and economists) can be assisted by knowledge of good, relevant theory and research, but must still rely on personal, situational knowledge and analyses of relevant phenomena in the immediate action context.

At the same time, there can be little doubt that actions informed by knowledge of relevant principles generally are superior and more effective than actions divorced from any such knowledge base. Knowledge of the various principles examined in this book can assist teachers to view and understand classroom events and pupil behaviors and experiences in ways different from perceptions and understandings likely to occur in the absence of this knowledge. A good approach for teachers to adopt when studying classroom management is to experiment with different ways of adapting the principles discussed to their own classroom situations, gradually determining what set of principles best matches their own unique styles of teaching and the unique demands of their specific classroom settings. Teachers must discover for themselves what combinations of principle-driven classroom practices best serve their pedagogical needs and the learning needs of their students. This is a theme that will be reiterated and developed throughout this book.

As in the second edition, considerable emphasis is placed, in this newest edition, on encouraging readers to develop thoughtful, constructive, yet critical understandings of the various approaches considered in this book. Specifically to this end, chapters two to eight contain final sections devoted to the fostering of such informed, critical understanding. Our intent here is to help readers exercise their own informed judgments concerning the principles and practices under consideration.

References

Day, D.M., Golench, C.A., MacDougall, J. & Beals-Gonzaléz, C.A. (1995). *School based violence prevention in Canada: Results of a national survey of policies and programs.* Toronto, ON: Ministry of the Solicitor General of Canada.

Doyle, W. (1986). Classroom organization and management. In M.C. Wittrock (Ed.), *Handbook of research on teaching (3rd ed.)* (pp. 392-431). New York: Macmillan.

Elem, S. & Rose, L. (1995). Phi Delta Kappan/Gallup poll of the public's attitudes toward public schools. *Phi Delta Kappan, 77,* 41-55.

Finn, J.D. (1989). Withdrawing from school. *Review of Educational Research, 59,* 117-142.

Gump, P. (1967). *The classroom behavior setting: Its nature and relation to student behavior.* (Report No. BR-5-0334). Washington, D.C.: Office of Education, Bureau of Research. (ERIC Document Reproduction Service No. ED015515).

Jones, V.F. & Jones, L.S. (1998). *Comprehensive classroom management: Motivating and managing students* (5th ed.). Boston: Allyn and Bacon.

Kainz, A. & Mangiacasale, A. (1992). Students feel safe despite violence. *The Vancouver Sun,* March 2, 196.

Veenman, S. (1984). Perceived problems of beginning teachers. *Review of Educational Research, 54,* 143-178.

Wang, M.C., Haertel, G.D. & Walberg, H.J. (1993). Toward a knowledge base for school learning. *Review of Educational Research, 63* (3), 249-294.

Wragg, E. (Ed.). (1984). *Classroom teaching skills.* New York: Nichols.

Chapter Two
Communication Approaches

Overview and Rationale

A rather obvious, but frequently overlooked way to start thinking about classroom management is to focus on the communication that takes place between teachers and pupils. It is through such communication that teachers come to understand students' motivations, desires, beliefs and experiences. It is through classroom communication that students reach conclusions about teachers' capacities for fairness, trustworthiness, and caring, and teachers' general attitudes toward students and teaching. The approaches to classroom management discussed in this chapter all subscribe to the basic belief that a student's capacities for positive development and significant learning can be encouraged through respectful, empowering forms of teacher communication.

How a teacher communicates in the classroom reveals the teachers' attitudes and values. If students perceive that they are valued, respected and taken seriously as individuals with valid experiences and basic rights to self-expression, they will be more involved and less disruptive in classroom contexts. Further, specific methods and styles of communication that convey empathy and respect to students can be invaluable in better understanding and dealing with disruptive student behavior and the confusion or emotional turmoil frequently associated with it. The communication approaches to be examined in this chapter derive primarily from the work of Carl Rogers, Haim Ginott, Thomas Gordon and neo-Rogerians such as Robert Carkhuff, Gerard Egan and William Purkey.

Carl Rogers stresses the importance of the personal experiences and motivations of students in classrooms. He attaches great importance to a teacher's ability to comprehend the total experiences of students (particularly the affective or emotional components of these experiences), and to arrange conditions and facilitate an awareness which assists pupils in more totally sensing their own experiences. Unlike many approaches to classroom management, Rogers' approach is relatively devoid of specific teaching skills and techniques, although some of his followers (like Carkhuff and Gazda) have added a skill-based supplement to Rogers' basic model of human relationships. Rogers himself has much more to say about the kind of person a teacher must be, and the general styles and manners in which a teacher might ideally orchestrate classroom affairs.

While essentially a psychotherapist (Rogers, 1942; Rogers, 1951; Rogers, 1961), Rogers' work in, and devotion to, general education is well documented in his major texts for teachers – *Freedom to Learn* (1969) and *Freedom to Learn for the 80's* (1983). Rogers' central challenge to teachers is to trust, and positively regard students in classrooms, to the extent that students are permitted to actualize their own natural potentials for significant learning experiences. This chapter will attempt to trace the theoretical notions underlying this challenge, and to examine the role of the teacher as facilitator of pupil learning and growth (also see Egan, 1994; Purkey & Novak, 1996).

Rogers' work finds a natural extension in the work of Haim Ginott and Thomas Gordon, both of whom wrote at considerable length about the psychological effects of different styles of teacher communication on the self-esteem, emotional states and behavioral tendencies of students in school classrooms. Both Ginott and Gordon initially developed their ideas concerning communication between adults and children in the context of parent-child interactions (Ginott, 1965, 1969; Gordon, 1970). Buoyed by the widespread acceptance of his work by parents, and encouraged by many of these same individuals to convey similar notions to the teachers of their children, each of these men developed versions of his system of interpersonal communication for use by teachers in classroom settings. Several of the principles and applications presented later in this chapter are drawn from Ginott's (1972) volume, *Teacher and Child*, and from Gordon's (1974) book, *Teacher Effectiveness Training*. More recently, Egan (1994), Gootman (1997) and Purkey and Novak (1996) have made additional contributions to the practical application of many of these ideas.

The effective communication approach to classroom management emphasizes the importance of teachers' self-discipline and maturity as reflected in their ability to listen sensitively to students' communications, and to respond to students in productive ways. Productive, effective communication by the teacher accepts the validity of students' feelings, assists students to take appropriate responsibility for their actions, and helps both teachers and students to engage in styles of conflict resolution and problem solving that do not become mired in counterproductive, unnecessary personal struggles for power and respect, at any cost.

Principles

Rogerian theory.

A central philosophical assumption underlying Rogers' approach to classroom management is that all people (including students in classrooms) react not to some "real" or "pure" reality, but rather to reality as they (as individuals) experience it. The world in which we live is our experiential world. This reality is partly shaped by the environment, but is also a result of our active participation in the creation of our own subjective worlds. Before anyone truly can understand any of us, that person must be able to comprehend our subjective worlds.

According to Rogers, all humanity has but one basic motivational force – a tendency toward actualization. Our *actualizing tendency* is our inherent or natural disposition to develop all of our capacities in ways which maintain or enhance us as living organisms. This actualizing tendency is related to, and must be completely attuned to, our organismic valuing processes. Each of us is born with an *organismic valuing process* which allows us to value positively those experiences which maintain or enhance our lives, and to value negatively those experiences which would negate such growth. In short, our innate actualizing tendency motivates us; while our innate valuing processes regulate us. Most important in Rogers' conceptions of these innate, uniquely human endowments is that, if they are not interfered with, they can be trusted to serve us well. Rogers believes strongly that human beings have an inherent tendency toward "goodness," both for themselves and for others.

A very crucial part of our actualizing tendency is the differentiation of *self* and the development of *self-concept*. As we grow, we begin to perceive and comprehend the difference between experiences which are our own and those which belong to other people. Gradually, a very important part of our experiential worlds becomes that subset of perceptions characteristic of *I* or *me*. This concept of self must be closely aligned with the basic organism and its tendencies if we are to maximize fully our experiences in ways which promote personal and social growth.

If left to our own natural devices, our developing concepts of self would automatically be consistent with the basic experiences of our organisms. Unfortunately, as our awareness of self evolves, we develop a need for *positive regard*. When we experience the positive regard of significant others (e.g., parents, teachers), our concepts of self are enhanced. When our actions elicit negative regard from others, our concepts of self are weakened. In this way, the positive and negative regard of others translates into a set of *conditions of worth*. When we behave in some ways, positive regard makes us feel worthwhile; when we behave in other ways, negative regard makes us feel worthless. These conditions of worth become so powerful that they begin to rival our basic organismic valuing processes.

At a very early age, we learn to exchange our basic tendencies for actualization for the conditional love of others. In more dramatic terms, our emerging selves (dominated and regulated by conditions of worth) become incongruent with our basic organismic experiences (dominated and regulated by the organismic valuing processes). Such *incongruence* prevents us from being aware of our total experiences. Only when our experiences or behaviors fit our concepts of self (now heavily dependent upon the conditions of worth placed upon us by others) are they recognized and integrated into our self-structures. If incongruence between self and organism becomes severe or extreme, we actively work (often at a level just below conscious perception) to avoid our experiences and their implications; our self ideals bear little resemblance to how we are perceived by others; and our subjective realities may become increasingly remote from what our experiences are trying so desperately to tell us. When separated from basic organismic processes, our self-structures become very rigid, narrow and inflexible. We admit to awareness only those experiences that are in line with our "other-dominated" self structures, and reject or deny all experiences that are not. Consequently, we become "cut-off" from the totality of our experience in the world. Such denial of our own experiences severely limits our capabilities for effective, creative decision making, problem solving and action.

To prevent severe incongruence between self and organism from occurring, or to reduce it to functional levels once it has occurred, Rogers advocates an increase in the *unconditional positive regard* shown to the incongruent individual and a concomitant reduction or narrowing in the conditions of worth placed upon the individual. When more of a person's actions and experiences are unconditionally accepted by others, and when fewer conditions of worth act to separate the individual from basic organismic tendencies, self and organism become less split, more of a person's active experiences are permitted into conscious awareness, and the natural growth and learning tendencies of the person are released. The self-structure is integrated with the basic organism and is fluid and accommodating with respect to the majority of organismic experience.

The classroom teacher can facilitate congruence between the selves and organismic experiences of students by facilitating learning in an atmosphere of unconditional positive regard and freedom from threat. Free from the "shoulds," "musts," and "oughts" which characterize pervasive conditions of worth, students can be freed to explore themselves in relation to their total experiences. As pupils acquire more and more information about their experiences (affective and attitudinal information as well as knowledge and skills), they become increasingly aware of themselves as learners – how they learn as well as how they feel about their own learning. According to Rogers, such self-awareness cannot help but translate into more effective, self-directed and personally-significant learning.

In *Freedom to Learn* (1969), Rogers offers the following ten learning principles, the implications of which should be considered carefully by all classroom instructors. (These ten learning principles are reproduced here in slightly edited form with the kind permission of the publisher.)

[handwritten note in margin: 10 Learning Principles]

1. Human beings have a natural potentiality for learning.
2. Significant learning takes place when the subject matter is perceived by pupils as having relevance for their own purposes.
3. Learning which involves a change in self organization – in the perception of one's self – is threatening and tends to be resisted.
4. Those lessons which are threatening to the self are more easily perceived and assimilated when external threats are at a minimum.
5. When threat to self is low, experience can be perceived and learning can proceed.
6. Much significant learning is acquired through doing.
7. Learning is facilitated when the pupil participates responsibly in the learning process.

8. Self-initiated learning which involves the whole person of the learner – feelings as well as intellect – is the most lasting and pervasive.

9. Independence, creativity and self-reliance are all facilitated when self-criticism and self-evaluation are basic, and evaluation by others is of secondary importance.

10. The most socially useful learning in the modern world is the learning of the process of learning (a continuous openness to experience), and incorporation of the process of change into one's self.

Additional ideas of Ginott, Gordon and others.

One of the basic premises of classroom communication in terms of effective communication is that management is built from the "bottom up." Successful classrooms are not a direct result of the implementation of abstracted principles of teaching, learning, development or management. Rather, the successful implementation of any educational, psychological or administrative theories relevant to the creation of effective classroom environments ultimately depends on the quality of the moment by moment interactions that occur between teachers and their students. Effective communication is the "bedrock" on which productive teaching and learning are built.

A corollary of the foregoing principle is that classroom management is a series of "little victories," not the result of the implementation of some "grand strategy." In other words, the management of classrooms is a compilation of the host of communicative exchanges that occur between teachers and students throughout every school day. In order to implement successfully any system of classroom management, the ongoing communication between a teacher and the students in a class must be of a high quality. The attainment of effective communication is something that a teacher must work constantly to achieve. There is no substitute for establishing respectful, caring communicative relations with the students with whom a teacher interacts each and every school day. Children are more likely to be respectful when they themselves feel that they are respected (Kohn, 1996). Respect is an emotional need; and when met, children have the security of being able to meet other people's needs. This means that an educator is a person who should give and, at the same time, receive respect. Teachers' perceptions of students, as reflected in their own behavior, have the power to influence how students view themselves and ultimately how well they learn in school (Purkey & Novak, 1996). Caring interpersonal interactions are essential in establishing a feeling of safety, security, belonging and self-esteem (Jones & Jones, 1998).

The two most important ingredients of effective communication in the classroom are a teacher's own *self-discipline*, and a teacher's *communication style*. The former emphasizes the personal and inter-personal maturity of the teacher, while the latter emphasizes the interpersonal manner of the teacher. Both are extremely important for the establishment of effective classroom communication. Teachers must model the personal control and responsibility in their own communications and classroom behavior that they hope to foster in their pupils. To do so, they must learn to accept, understand and express their own perspectives and feelings in ways that respect, help and empower the children in their care. Such a communicative manner cannot possibly be achieved in the absence of considerable personal insight, self-awareness and self-respect on the part of the teacher. Put simply, to communicate in a caring, helpful manner requires a sustained level of personal maturity and sanity. [The term "sanity" is used here in the rather special sense in which Ginott (1972) uses the term. More will be said about this conception in the discussion of *sane messages* later in this chapter.] Jones and Jones (1998) describe positive student-teacher relationships as being open and caring. In open relationships teachers can share a wide range of personal concerns and values with students. Also, teachers and students can share their feelings about the school environment, with limited, appropriate sharing of more general life experiences.

The essential logic underlying the establishment of effective communication between teachers and learners as a basis for effective classroom management is that humans need to feel respected, understood and cared for if we are to achieve our potentials as learners and problem solvers. We must be able to take risks, to participate actively, to express our thoughts and feelings openly if we are to learn from our experiences with others in classrooms and other learning contexts. When we interact with others who treat us with respect, tolerance and understanding, we are much more likely to trust our own experiences, to avail ourselves of the experiences of others, and to reflect on the knowledge gleaned from these experiences in resolving conflicts, solving problems and setting learning goals.

Successful teachers recognize the importance of students' active, open participation in classroom learning. Purkey and Novak (1996) talk about the importance of viewing students as able participants. When teachers have positive views of students' abilities, students are more likely to respond in positive ways. Through their ongoing communications with pupils, such teachers *invite* students to cooperate in both teaching and learning functions in the classroom. Pupils who feel invited in this way come to view the classroom as their own, a place where they are respected, and in which their input is valued. It does not take much imagination to realize that students who perceive school classrooms in this way exert more positive, less disruptive influences on classroom life throughout the school year.

Methods and Applications

Rogers' instructional methods.

The central task that confronts each classroom teacher, from the viewpoint of Rogers' student-centered approach to teaching, is the creation of a facilitative, non-threatening (unconditional positive regard) classroom atmosphere within which students can develop concepts of themselves that are truly congruent with their full ranges of organismic experiences. In this way, pupils will come to see themselves more as they really are, as opposed to how they might idealize themselves as being. Their self-structures can embrace their total experiences in a congruent, integrated fashion. With such congruence, and the enhanced self-awareness and self-direction it fosters, truly significant learning becomes possible.

The two major instructional methods which Rogers advocates as necessary for facilitating the personal integration and growth of students in classrooms are:

1. Teachers should teach in ways which adopt the framework of their pupils. Before *significant learning experiences* (i.e., those experiences which enhance and elaborate the self-awareness of the learner) can be arranged, the teacher must comprehend something of the subjective worlds of students.

2. Teachers should teach in ways which clarify the attitudes, feelings, values and perceptions of their pupils. By interacting with students in ways that help them search and probe their experiences and self-concepts (particularly the relationships between the two) in supportive, non-threatening con-

texts, teachers can help students maximize their own natural tendencies for learning and growth.

In *Freedom to Learn*, Rogers offers the following ten guidelines to help the classroom teacher become a powerful facilitator of significant pupil learning. (These ten facilitator principles are reproduced here in slightly edited form with the kind permission of the publisher.)

1. The facilitator has much to do with setting the initial mood or climate of the group or class experience. If the teacher's own basic philosophy is one of trust in the classroom group and in individual pupils, this point of view will be communicated in subtle ways.

2. The facilitator helps to elicit and clarify the purposes of the individuals in the class as well as the more general purposes of the group. The facilitator must be able to permit a diversity of individual purposes to exist, and to be fostered in the classroom. Learners must be allowed to work toward their own personal objectives.

3. The facilitator relies upon the desire of each pupil to implement those purposes that have personal meaning, as the motivational force behind significant learning. The facilitator must help students motivate themselves, rather than motivating them through external means (e.g., threats, punishment, cajoling, bribing).

4. The facilitator endeavors to organize and make easily available the widest possible range of resources for learning. Every conceivable resource that students may wish to use for their own enhancement and for the fulfillment of their own purposes (writings, materials, psychological aids, persons, equipment, trips or audio-visual aids) should be obtained or arranged if at all possible.

5. The facilitator acts as a flexible resource to be utilized by the group. The role of the teacher encompasses counselor, lecturer, advisor, assistant or helper depending on students' needs.

6. In responding to expressions in the classroom group, the facilitator accepts both intellectual content and emotionalized attitudes, endeavoring to give to each the approximate degree of emphasis that it has for the individual student or the group.

7. As the acceptant classroom climate becomes established, the facilitator is increasingly in the role of a participant-learner, a member of the group who expresses personal views as those of one individual only.

8. The facilitator takes the initiative in sharing within the group – personal feelings as well as thoughts – in ways that do not demand nor impose, but represent simply a personal sharing that students may take or leave.

9. Throughout the classroom experience, the facilitator remains alert to student expressions indicative of deep or strong feelings. When feelings of conflict, pain, hurt and the like arise, the teacher tries to understand these from the pupil's point of view, and communicates empathic understanding directly to the student.

10. In functioning as a facilitator of learning, the teacher endeavors to recognize and accept personal limitations. The teacher must be genuine at all times.

Empathy, warmth and genuineness.

The primary reason that Rogers stresses broad guidelines for teacher classroom action, as opposed to specific skills, techniques and/or strategies, is that (for Rogers) successful and effective teaching results directly from the essential personality of the teacher and the many subtle ways in which this personality is manifested in the classroom. No skill or technical strategy, however well performed, can replace or override the pervasive effect of the teacher's personality or character.

Nonetheless, there are certain aspects of a teacher's personality that can be defined and observed. These aspects – empathy, warmth and genuineness – may be enhanced or further developed by practice and study, but they must exist to some degree in the basic personality structure of the effective teacher.

1. *Empathy* is the ability of a teacher to respond to student expressions in ways which indicate to the pupil that the meanings of, and emotions attached to, the students' behaviors have been understood. High levels of empathy also succeed in reflecting accurately the underlying meanings behind what a student is saying, thus assisting the pupil to explore more deeply private perceptions, beliefs and feelings.

Egan (1994) suggests that for effective communication of empathy, teachers should give themselves time to think and assimilate what the student is saying, they should use short and clear responses to promote dialogue, and they should direct their responses to the student while remaining themselves.

2. *Warmth* is the expression, on the part of a teacher, of non-possessive, unconditional acceptance of a pupil's experiences as a part of that pupil without imposing conditions, judgments, decisions or evaluations of any kind upon the students' experiences.

3. *Genuineness* is the ability of a teacher to know and accept himself or herself, to be open in interactions with students, and to permit students to perceive and understand the teacher as an individual human, complete with faults as well as virtues.

Egan (1994) discusses and suggests several ways to be genuine. Teachers should always attempt to clearly communicate their messages, while also listening intently to their students' messages. Genuineness may also be achieved through spontaneous and free communication between teacher and students. This can be done by avoiding the use of habitual and planned strategies. Finally, teachers should attempt to respond immediately to students' needs, and always be willing to commit themselves to all students in the class.

Obviously, there are degrees to which individual teachers possess and express the personality characteristics of empathy, warmth and genuineness. It is often difficult to say exactly how much each of these characteristics needs to be present in any individual teacher, or expressed in any given classroom situation or interpersonal context. Many factors influence such equations and make demands for precision impossible to meet – e.g., individual differences in pupils, differences in the social-cultural context of schools and classrooms, different teaching methods, different curriculum areas and important nuances in the depth of expressed feeling, honesty and commitment of individual students. Whatever the instructional context, the important thing to remember is that an effective teacher must possess the essential qualities of empathy, warmth and genuineness to sufficient extents to operate within the ten guidelines for facilitator behavior reviewed earlier in this chapter.

When teachers succeed in encouraging significant levels of self-awareness and self-directed learning on the part of their pupils, student disruptive behavior is minimalized. Students who feel respect-

ed and understood, who feel free to take risks and involve themselves wholistically (affectively as well as cognitively and behaviorally) in classroom learning are much less likely to contribute to
problems related to classroom management. When students are disruptive, a teacher's empathy, warmth and genuineness can help
these students to understand better their own emotions and motivations, and to discover alternate ways of dealing with, and channel-
ing them.

Inviting and sane messages.

Ginott (1972) and Purkey and Novak (1996) describe teacher
behaviors that extend empathy, warmth and genuineness to pupils
as *inviting*, in contrast to teacher actions that are *disinviting*. They
believe that much student alienation and disruption results from *disinvitation*, communicated through apparent teacher indifference and
failure to respond to students as unique individuals – real people
deserving of respect and capable of significant, positive self-direction. Ginott and Purkey are especially concerned with disinvitations
arising from teachers' intentional or unintentional ridicule, sarcasm,
displays of personal frustration and stereotyping.

Consider the following student expressions of disinvitation.

*"The teacher said I was just like my brother, and would end up just
like him."*

*"When I came to school, the teacher took one look at me and said, 'Oh
no, not another one'."*

*"When my teacher says she doesn't understand how anyone can be so
consistently 'out to lunch,' the other kids all laugh."*

Ginott urges teachers to invite cooperation rather than to
demand it. He considers disinvitations to occur when teachers lose
their own *self-discipline*. Teachers who maintain their self-discipline
do not lose their tempers (throw things, yell, employ verbal abuse);
behave in rude, cruel and insulting ways ("Just shut up. You're nothing but a trouble-maker who's too short on brains to know what's
right"); or threaten and over-react ("If I hear one more smart-alec
comment, you all will be in very big trouble.").

Ginott considers a particular form of disinvitation to be especially harmful. He labels as *insane* teacher communications that
attack a student's character rather than the situation that is creating
difficulties. For example, "You have no right to say those things to
me. You are nothing but a nasty little jerk. Now sit down and shut

up." Unlike insane messages, *sane* messages address the situation that needs addressing, express anger appropriately, acknowledge student feelings, and invite cooperation. For example, "I realize that you are angry, but it is important that we treat each other with respect. In this class, we talk about our problems and try to work things out. Please sit down and raise your hand when you are calm enough to discuss this further."

Neo-Rogerian skills.

In recent years, a number of educators and counselors have studied Rogers' concept of empathy, and have proposed specific interpersonal skills which teachers can employ in their classrooms to convey empathy, warmth and genuineness to *invite* their students (e.g., Carkhuff, 1987; Egan, 1994; Evans, Hearn, Uhlemann & Ivey, 1990; Gazda et al., 1991; Ivey, 1988; Purkey & Novak, 1996). Robert Carkhuff (1987) has been particularly active in this area. Carkhuff has operationalized three basic teaching skills – physical attending, content responding and affective responding which are basic to teacher communication of empathy. Sometimes these skills are referred to generically as *active listening* skills.

1. *Physical Attending* is a nonverbal skill of active listening by which teachers can communicate to students that they really are attending to what students have to say. In contemporary Western societies, good physical attending frequently involves sitting squarely and facing the speaking student, leaning slightly forward and maintaining eye-contact with the speaking student (without staring in a fixed manner). In other societies and cultures, appropriate, respectful listening postures may take rather different forms.

2. *Content Responding* is a verbal skill of active listening by which teachers communicate to students that they have heard and understood what students are saying. Content responding accurately paraphrases the substance of a students' comments.

   e.g., Pupil: "I disagree with Tom. I think the United Nations is a useful institution for maintaining world peace."

   Teacher: "You're much more optimistic about the ability of the U.N. to prevent major conflicts."

3. *Affective Responding* is a verbal skill of active listening by which teachers communicate to pupils that they understand some of the feelings being experienced by students.

e.g., Pupil: "Hilary always gets me into trouble, and then you get mad at me and don't even notice what she did."

Teacher: "You're pretty upset because you think I'm being unfair."

According to Carkhuff, Egan, Gazda, Ivey and others, intelligent and honest use of the preceding skills on a regular basis can help teachers to convey a quality of empathy to their pupils – a quality that, if perceived by pupils, can increase student comfort, interest, motivation and self-directed learning.

I-messages.

An important ingredient in a teacher's communication style is the ability to distinguish clearly between expressions of what the teacher is experiencing and what students are doing. As Ginott (1972) notes, when teachers lose their own self-discipline, they tend to communicate with students in ways that blame students for everything that is happening, even for a teacher's own feelings of anger and upset. Thomas Gordon (1974) describes a form of communication that permits teachers to express such feelings (as well as others) in ways that are *sane*, and do not blame students for things for which they are not directly responsible.

Gordon's *I-messages* might best be described as *responsibility-taking* messages. I-messages are teacher statements that clearly label the teacher's emotional reactions as belonging to the teacher, and leave the responsibility for the student's behavior with the student. As a result, such messages avoid the negative impact that accompanies messages in which teachers blame students for their own (i.e., the teachers') experiences (i.e., *You-messages*).

Consider the following conversation between a teacher and a student in which the teacher employs You-messages.

Teacher: You are late again. You are inconsiderate to everyone in this class. You interrupt us and make it impossible for us to work.

Student: Yeah. Well, I've got a busy schedule, and I can't always be on time.

Teacher: You have no right to distract me and everyone else by being late.

Student: What's the big deal?

Now, consider a similar conversation in which the teacher employs I-messages.

Teacher: When you come in late, I get distracted and interrupt what I'm doing. I find it frustrating when you aren't on time.

Student: Yeah. Well, I've got a busy schedule, and I can't always be on time.

Teacher: I see. I want to understand why it is difficult for you to be on time. Perhaps we can discuss this after class. In the meantime, I just want you to know that I get frustrated and distracted by having to interrupt my lesson.

Student: OK, sorry. I would like to talk with you later.

Obviously, there are no guarantees that when a teacher uses I-messages, these messages will work as well as they seem to have done in this example. On the other hand, it is easy to see that students are more likely to respond positively to a teacher's use of I-messages than to You-messages that blame them for a teacher's upsets.

Gootman (1997) describes two types of I-messages – one to disclose one's feelings or opinions, and the other to bring about change in another's behavior. When the speakers use the disclosure I-message, they just want to let someone else know how they are feeling or what they are thinking. Students who can express their feelings and opinions are developing their emotional intelligence and their sense of connectedness to others.

The goal of the I-message meant to bring about change in another's behavior is to facilitate positive change, without the verbal or physical "lashing out" that is sometimes used in an attempt to change behavior in the classroom. Gootman (1997) describes a three-part formula that can be modeled for students: (a) describe the unwanted behavior, (b) let the person know how the behavior makes you feel and (c) let the person know the consequences of the behavior for you. This method is intended to help the student who initiated the behavior to think about other's feelings and reactions.

Conflict resolution.

Communication skills like I-messages and content/affective responding can be invaluable to teachers when conflicts occur between students or between students and teachers. Consistent with the communication methods advanced by Rogers, Ginott, Gordon and others is a basic method of conflict resolution that makes use of several of the communication strategies described and illustrated in this chapter. This method consists of using I-messages, invitations and active listening to clarify the current experiences, understandings and desires of each party to a conflict.

If a teacher is involved directly in a conflict, the teacher simply uses I-messages to express openly and directly (and as briefly as possible) the teacher's personal reactions and interpretations, then invites the student or students involved in the conflict to do the same. Methods of active listening (content and affective responding) then can be used to help ensure that the teacher understands the positions of the students, and succeeds in communicating such understanding to them.

A teacher can employ this same strategy to facilitate the resolution of conflicts among students. Such facilitation may be accomplished by asking each student or student group (in turn) to use I-messages to describe their own personal experiences and interpretations of the conflict, and by asking the other student or student group involved in the conflict to listen attentively to these personal expressions. In facilitating such exchanges, teachers can provide clear communication guidelines to the students involved by outlining the process of conflict resolution (ensuring all parties that they "will get their chance to present their positions"), by demonstrating the kinds of I-messages and active listening responses that are appropriate, and by insisting that such a process and these communication methods be employed. It is particularly important that the teacher/facilitator ask students to use I-messages to communicate their own experiences and reactions whenever students begin to use You-messages that accuse, blame or malign the motives and actions of other parties to the conflict. For example, "Instead of telling us why Gregory did what he did, please tell us about your own feelings and reasons for doing what you did. Perhaps you might begin by saying, "I felt ... ," and continue on from there."

This simple strategy of conflict resolution helps to ensure that all parties to a conflict have an opportunity to express clearly their "sides" to the conflict, and to listen to (and hopefully, begin to understand) the other "sides." With these initial expressions and understandings in place, chances are much better that the parties involved will be able to take constructive steps to resolve or cope with the conflict or problem situation. [More will be said about specific methods of problem solving and resolution in chapter six of this book.]

An illustration.

The following conversation between Ms. Ashley and one of her grade eleven students provides an illustration of appropriate teacher communication in interacting with pupils whose current experiences, and reactions to them, pose difficulties related to the effective management of school classrooms. Note how the teacher responses in this illustration are inviting, sane, empathic and oriented to resolving problems and potential conflicts.

Ms. Ashley: "I thought you were having trouble following the lesson today, Philip."

Philip: "Well, yeah, I guess so. This stuff is so boring. How's a guy supposed to understand it?"

Ms. Ashley: "It's pretty hard to follow something you're not interested in."

Philip: "Well, sure. I mean, who cares about what happened 50 years ago. I've got more important things to think about."

Ms. Ashley: "Things more important than what happened years ago."

Philip: "Well, I'd say tonight's big game carries a little more weight than this (gestures towards his Social Studies notebook). I'm excited about the game, and so is the whole school."

Ms. Ashley: "When you're excited about something as important to you as a basketball game, concentrating on something like history doesn't make any sense."

Philip: "It's not that it doesn't make sense. It's just really hard to do."

Ms. Ashley: "At first, I thought you just didn't think history was important; but now it seems like you're saying that when you are thinking about basketball it's hard to concentrate in this class."

Philip: "Yeah, normally I don't mind this stuff, but today I'm really somewhere else, you know? I just can't help it. I'm sorry if I wasn't with it today. I guess I missed just about everything you said."

Ms. Ashley: "So, even though you're really 'keyed-up' about tonight's game, you don't feel very good about missing out on today's class."

Philip: "Well, I know I'll just have to catch up on this stuff later. So, in a way it's going to mean even more work for me now. It just seems like I have too many things to worry about."

Ms. Ashley: "You'd be less hassled if you had attended to today's lesson and didn't have to look forward to doing 'catch-up' work."

Philip: "Yeah, but I'm just so uptight about that basketball game. I can't help thinking about it. Everything else gets pushed out."

Ms. Ashley: "It would be nice to be able to control your excitement so that you wouldn't miss out on other things because of it."

Philip: "I'll say. The other thing is that the more I think about the game, the more uptight I get. Right now, I'm getting myself all worked up and it's not helping me in class or in preparing for the game."

Ms. Ashley: "It really seems like you're frustrated with your own inability to control your excitement, and that you'd like to do something about this."

Philip: "Yes, I would. I've always been pretty anxious about things like this; but lately, it's really getting out of hand." (looks at watch)

Ms. Ashley: "Well, I know it's time for you to go to Coach White's pregame meeting now, but I would really like you to do some thinking about how you can try to control your own excitement so that it doesn't interfere with the things you are doing. I'd be happy to talk to you about any ideas you come up with.

Philip: "O.K., I'd like that. Maybe we could talk about this again tomorrow. See you then?"

Ms. Ashley: "Sure, right after class will be fine. Good luck in tonight's game."

The teacher's style and manner, as revealed in the foregoing transcription, are critical in assisting pupils to explore, understand and act with greater awareness of their experiences. Such student-centered interactions keep communication open between teachers and students and help students to develop and grow in positive, self-enhancing directions. Typically, such conversations, when focussed on the unique problems and concerns of individual students, might best take place on a one-to-one basis, removed from the large group setting of the classroom during periods of active learning. Teachers' willingness and abilities to listen actively and respectfully to students' concerns and affective reactions can be especially important when teachers sense upsets in their students, especially if such upsets are related to current experiences of family problems, grief and loss, or significantly painful feelings of alienation, confusion and/or despondency. There often are no easy or obvious resolutions to many of the upsetting situations experienced by students in contemporary classrooms, homes and other social/personal contexts. However, knowing that it is possible to share concerns and difficulties with a teacher who will not stand in judgment, but who will attempt to understand such matters from the student's perspective, can at least help students to understand more of their own experiences and their reactions to them. Such understanding generally is indispensable to making the best of even the most difficult circumstances.

Critique

Since this is the first critique to appear in this book, a few words seem warranted concerning the intent of such critiques. The critiques provide brief, hopefully balanced assessments of the approaches to classroom management discussed in chapters two to seven, inclusive. Both strengths and weaknesses of these approaches are addressed as these are perceived by us, the authors of this book. However, the real purpose of the critiques is *not* to encourage readers to accept our assessments. Rather, it is to provide models of critical reflection that might stimulate readers to conduct their own assessments of each of the approaches presented. We hope that, through considering our assessments, readers will engage in thoughtful reflection concerning the possible advantages and limitations that might attend adoption and use of the various principles and methods of classroom management discussed in this book.

Turning now to an assessment of the communication approaches discussed in this chapter, it seems very reasonable to think about the quality of interaction between teachers and learners as providing a foundation for effective classroom management. Through appropriate communication with students, teachers can clarify classroom expectations and rules, extend caring and respect to pupils, and perhaps assist students to deal with their emotional reactions to classroom and extracurricular experiences that affect classroom behavior and learning. We are not quite as optimistic as Rogers that a teacher's communication of empathy, warmth and genuineness to students is sufficient to guarantee smoothly-running classrooms. However, it certainly would seem that the psychological environment in most classrooms would be improved if students felt understood and accepted by their teachers. Our own view is that effective communication probably is *necessary* but not *sufficient* for effective classroom management.

The specificity with which Ginott, Purkey, Carkhuff, Gordon and other communication theorists have described various types and skills of teacher communication can be extremely valuable. Information about exactly what is involved in active listening, inviting, conflict resolution and similar communication strategies can be very helpful to teachers. Without such specific information, it is unlikely that teachers would be able to experiment with these and other communication methods in their own classrooms. At the same time, it also should be emphasized that effective use of these strategies inevitably involves more than skill acquisition per se. Teachers must cultivate genuine dispositions to employ such methods with good, honest intent to help children gain more positive experiences in classrooms. Any communication method probably will fail if it is cultivated and used purely as a device with which to manipulate student compliance.

Further, the acquisition and effective use of communication methods such as active listening may require a reasonable amount of practice and effort on the part of teachers attempting to employ such methods for the first time. No matter how specific, concrete and well-illustrated discussions of these methods may be, if they are to be used effectively, teachers who use them must "make them their own." In other words, teachers must find ways and means of integrating such communication methods into their own personal and teaching styles. While standard phrases such as, "I hear you saying . . . " or "You are feeling . . . because . . . " sometimes are recommended as initial communication templates in certain communication skills training manuals, it is clear that over use of such "catch phrases" can make a teacher sound mechanical and overly scripted. A good deal of thoughtful practice and reflection usually is involved in acquiring personalized, fluid use of any communication skill or strategy.

Finally, it seems important to emphasize that no communication method is likely to guarantee positive results across all students and classroom settings. Human beings and interactive contexts are much too complex and multi-faceted to permit tightly deterministic, prescriptive relationships between what and how a teacher communicates and how students will react. In short, there are no guarantees that a teacher's efforts to communicate empathy and warmth to students always will be reciprocated by enhanced displays of trust and cooperation by students. A host of social, cultural and individual differences can affect perceptions and interpretations of and reactions to any communication method. The point of any approach to classroom management that emphasizes teachers' communications is that positive and productive student classroom responses are more likely if teachers develop and employ strong, varied communication repertoires. Only direct experience with particular student groups and classroom contexts will allow teachers to determine what works and what does not in their own work settings.

References

Carkhuff, R.R. (1987). *The art of helping VI*. Amherst, MA: Human Resource Development Press.

Egan, G. (1994). *The skilled helper* (5th ed.). Pacific Grove, CA: Brooks/Cole.

Evans, D.R., Hearn, M.T., Uhlemann, M.R. & Ivey, A.E. (1990). *Essential interviewing* (3rd ed.). Monterey, CA: Brooks/Cole.

Gazda, G. M., Asbury, F.R., Balzer, F.J., Childers, W.C. & Walters, R.P. (1991). *Human relations development: A manual for educators* (4th ed.). Boston: Allyn & Bacon.

Ginott, H.G. (1965). *Between parent and child*. New York: Macmillan.

Ginott, H.G. (1969). *Between parent and teenager*. New York: Macmillan.

Ginott, H.G. (1972). *Teacher and child*. New York: Macmillan.

Gootman, M.E. (1997). *The caring teacher's guide to discipline: Helping students learn self-control, responsibility, and respect*. Thousand Oaks, CA: Corwin Press, Inc.

Gordon, T. (1970). *P.E.T.: Parent effectiveness training*. New York: Wyden.

Gordon, T. (1974). *T.E.T.: Teacher effectiveness training*. New York: Wyden.

Ivey, A. (1988). *Intentional interviewing and counseling: Facilitating client development*. Pacific Grove, CA: Brooks/Cole.

Jones, V.F. & Jones, L.S. (1998). *Comprehensive classroom management: Motivating and managing students* (5th ed.). Boston: Allyn and Bacon.

Kohn, A. (1996). *Beyond discipline: From compliance to community*. Alexandria, VA: Association for Supervision and Curriculum Development.

Purkey, W.W. & Novak, J.M. (1996). *Inviting school success: A self-concept approach to teaching, learning, and democratic practice* (3rd ed.). Belmont, CA: Wadsworth.

Rogers, C. (1942). *Counseling and psychotherapy*. Boston: Houghton-Mifflin.

Rogers, C. (1951). *Client-centered therapy*. Boston: Houghton-Mifflin.

Rogers, C. (1961). *On becoming a person*. Boston: Houghton-Mifflin.

Rogers, C. (1969). *Freedom to learn*. Columbus, OH: Charles E. Merrill.

Rogers, C. (1983). *Freedom to learn for the 80's*. Columbus, OH: Charles E. Merrill.

Chapter Three
The Democratic Approach

Overview and Rationale

In this chapter, we will examine the classroom management system developed by Rudolf Dreikurs, and extended in more recent years by Don Dinkmeyer, Linda Albert and others. Dreikurs' theoretical system is based directly on the pioneering work of Alfred Adler in the area of individual developmental psychology. Unlike Freud, Jung and other prominent psychologists of his day, Adler emphasized individual development within a social context. Belonging to relevant social groups is a major goal of most human behavior. According to Adler (1938), individual differences in how people respond to similar situations can be traced to differences in the specific motives and methods they use to achieve a sense of social belonging. Learning to behave in manners consistent with the goal of accepting individual responsibilities within a *democratic* social context is a functional strategy for individual development. However, an individual's specific motivations may encourage social behaviors that attempt to achieve a sense of belonging in less functional ways, both for the individual and the larger social groups of which the individual is part.

The term *teleoanalytic* refers to an "analysis of purposes or motivations." In a teleoanalytic system, behavior is seen as a movement toward future goals. To change or alter behavior, it is necessary to change or alter the motivations or goals of behavior. To do this requires an initial understanding and analysis of existing motives. Dreikurs' democratic approach to classroom management (Albert, 1989; Dinkmeyer, Carlson & Dinkmeyer, 1994; Dinkmeyer & Dreikurs, 1963; Dreikurs, 1950; Dreikurs, 1957; Dreikurs & Cassel, 1972; Dreikurs & Grey, 1968; Dreikurs & Soltz, 1964; Dreikurs, Grunwald & Pepper, 1982; Kohn, 1996) attempts to give teachers the skills necessary to comprehend the motives and goals of children in classrooms; to alter motives, when necessary, to preserve the social and personal well-being of individual learners and the classroom group; and, by so doing, to facilitate classroom behaviors which are socially and academically productive and responsible in a democratic setting. To this basic democratic approach, Dinkmeyer and Albert have added an emphasis on enhancing students' self-esteem by assisting them to feel capable, "connected" (with others), and able to contribute cooperatively in the classroom.

This chapter commences with an examination of central Adlerian premises and concepts, and moves on to a discussion of procedures and methods of classroom management that Dreikurs, Dinkmeyer, Albert and others have developed based on these theoretical notions.

Principles

Basic Adlerian premises

Dreikurs' democratic approach to classroom management and discipline is based upon five psychological premises advocated by Alfred Adler (Dreikurs & Cassel, 1972). These five basic premises are:

1. Humans are essentially *social beings*, whose main need is the need to belong. Both adults and children share this basic social desire.

2. All behavior has the purpose of making the behaver belong – to be significant within that individual's social context. There are, of course, many ways to belong, and it is impossible to understand the behavior of another person without knowing the specific *"belongingness"* goal to which it is directed. When children or adults misbehave, it indicates that they have wrong ideas about how to belong and to be significant. Whatever the method chosen to achieve the goal of belonging, this method is selected early in life, and becomes the life style which characterizes the individual person.

3. Humans, in addition to being social animals, are *decision-makers*. They are not victims of heredity, environment, developmental or unconscious influences. Humans decide what they really want to do. The fact that we are sometimes unaware of our decision(s), does not negate or alter this essential truth.

4. Humans are *whole beings* who cannot be understood by analyses of partial characteristics. The whole is always

greater than the sum total of the parts. The best way to comprehend an individual is to observe entire patterns of behavior that indicate underlying motives or purposes.

5. Humans do not experience reality as it is, but only as they *perceive* it. Sometimes these perceptions may be mistaken or biased. The specific life style chosen by each individual acts as a subjective basis for interpreting all the actions of other people. Both Adler and Dreikurs go to great lengths to demonstrate and argue the importance of family position and constellation factors in the determination of individual life styles. The importance of familial factors in pupils' lives cannot be denied. However, specific claims made by Adler and Dreikurs with respect to the effects of "birth position" generally have not been supported in more recent research, and there is considerable debate concerning Adler's actual views in this regard (cf. Ferguson, 1984). Nonetheless, the "psychological positions" that children occupy in families can be particularly significant with respect to their overall development (Sweeney, 1981). Dinkmeyer and McKay (1976, 1983, 1989) and Albert and Popkin (cited in Albert,1989) offer useful counsel to parents based, in part, on such considerations.

The democratic teaching style

In many respects, Adler's emphasis on the social nature of humans and their central need to belong, was inextricably merged with his notion of democracy. In the classroom context, Dreikurs has continuously advocated a *democratic teaching style*. For Dreikurs, effective teaching "stimulates children from within," as opposed to "pressuring them from without." Autocratic teaching that employs power, pressure and punishment to demand cooperation; that takes away student responsibility and keeps all decision-making in the teacher's hands; and that imposes, dominates, criticizes and finds fault is definitely out. Today's discipline problems can be largely overcome if teachers turn away from the obsolete method of demanding submission and accept a new order based on principles of freedom and responsibility. Teachers should be neither permissive nor punitive. They should be democratic. By emphasizing teaching processes of stimulation, encouragement, cooperation, guidance, helping, suggestion and acknowledgment of student achievement, teachers can become a match for their students – wise in their ways and capable of guiding them without letting them run wild, or alternately, stifling them.

Linda Albert (1989) advocates a cooperative, democratic form of classroom teaching (not to be confused with the approaches to cooperative teaching and learning discussed in the next chapter) based on the work of Dreikurs, Dinkmeyer, McKay and Dinkmeyer (1980), and Dinkmeyer, Carlson and Dinkmeyer (1994). Inside democratic classrooms, where teachers are less controlling and more inclined to include children in decision making, students are more self-confident and more interested in learning for its own sake (Kohn, 1996). Consistent with Adlerian theory, Albert's approach is based on three foundational, democratic principles: (1) students choose their behavior, (2) the overall goal of student behavior is to meet the need to belong and (3) most (approximately 90 percent of) student misbehavior can be understood in terms of four immediate, but mistaken, goals that students pursue in attempting to belong.

Goals of misbehavior

When students choose misbehavior over positive behavior, they still are attempting to belong, but have become frustrated in their more positive attempts to belong, or simply have not learned more positive ways of belonging. Consequently, they opt for attaining more immediate gratification of their need to belong by choosing inappropriate behaviors guided by more immediately attainable, mistaken goals. It is imperative for teachers to understand that a misbehaving child is only a discouraged child trying to find a place to belong. Children often act on the faulty logic that misbehavior of various kinds will give them the social acceptance they desire. Once a teacher can come to understand the goals of student classroom behavior, the teacher can practice effective methods of correction. Modifying behavior must involve modifying motivation for the behavior (Dreikurs & Cassel, 1972). Dreikurs has identified *four basic goals of children's misbehavior* – attention-getting, power, revenge and display of inadequacy (or *avoidance of failure*). These four goals, in this sequence, represent increasing degrees of behavioral disruption and discouragement in the classroom. Although the maladaptive goal is generally purposeful, students are not always aware of the negativity of the goal. Consequently, a teacher's or fellow student's reactions are sometimes a better indicator of the initial goal (Dinkmeyer, Carlson & Dinkmeyer, 1994). The descriptions of the four goals that are provided below are supplemented with descriptions drawn from the recent work of Linda Albert (1989).

1. *Attention-getting* – Behavior is intended to have an impact on others. The purpose of behavior is to attract attention (Dinkmeyer, Carlson & Dinkmeyer, 1994). Attention-getting children work on the faulty premise that only if people pay attention to them do they have a place in the world. Unfortunately, getting attention cannot take the place of making useful contributions which result in the development of self-confidence and self-reliance. Therefore, the attention-getter may quickly develop an insatiable appetite for attention; requiring ever-increasing amounts of it to guarantee a personal place in the classroom group. These students engage in all kinds of behavior that distracts the teacher and classmates from whatever they are doing. Such behavior clearly is influenced by the reactions of teachers and classmates. The attention-getting child will temporarily cease misbehaving when reprimanded or given attention. In the final analysis, although misguided in their efforts to secure it, attention-seeking children want a relationship with teachers and classmates.

2. *Power* – Power-seeking children want to be in charge. These children become angry, provoked or even withdrawn when they feel as though their integrity or authority is threatened. They operate from the faulty premise that "If you don't let me do what I want, you don't love me," or, "I only count when you do what I want you to do." In constant battle with authority, power-seeking children will tend to escalate their misbehavior when reprimanded. While these children can be disruptive and confrontational, they often can be pleasant, even agreeable, so long as things are going their way.

3. *Revenge* – Revenge-seeking children feel so beaten-down that they no longer seek to win power struggles, but seek only to retaliate. These children feel deeply hurt and become so discouraged that they work from the faulty premise that only by hurting others, as they have been hurt, can they find their place. Openly hostile and vicious or defiant, revenge-seekers make themselves hated, and retaliate directly to the agent of any perceived threat. They can be alternatively hurtful and sullen, refusing overtures of friendship. Nonetheless, such

Nonetheless, such children at least show a "spark of life" in attempting to protect themselves from further hurt.

4. *Display of inadequacy (Avoidance of failure)* – These children are so deeply discouraged that they have essentially given up all hopes of significance (expecting only failure and defeat), and seek only to avoid any situation that may occasion embarrassment or humiliation. With very little self-esteem, these children use their inability to shield what little self-worth remains. The inadequate student's discouragement is contagious, and teachers often are tempted to accept his or her mistaken plea of "You can't do anything with me so leave me alone and give-up." These children generally procrastinate, withdraw and occasionally may display "frustration tantrums" when the pressure to succeed becomes too great.

Attention-getting mechanisms

In addition to recognizing the four goals of misbehavior, Dreikurs identified four types of *attention-getting mechanisms (AGMs)* or *patterns of misbehavior,* some or all of which are employed in relation to each of the four goals of misbehavior. The four AGMs are derived from combinations of two bipolar factors. Maladjusted children may be classed as *active* or *passive,* and they may use *constructive* or *destructive* methods. The combination of the active-passive factor with the constructive-destructive factor gives rise to four distinct AGMs – (a) *active-constructive,* (2) *active destructive,* (3) *passive-constructive* and (4) *passive destructive* (Dreikurs & Cassel, 1972). Once again, the sequence as presented is based upon the actual progression of maladjustment.

A complete picture of child misbehavior may be obtained by associating each of the four goals of misbehavior with one or more of the four patterns of misbehavior (AGMS). This picture is represented in Table 3:1.

Table 3-1: AGMs

(Based somewhat upon Dreikurs and Cassel, 1972)

Goals	Passive Destructive	Active Destructive	Passive Constructive	Active Constructive
Attention-getting	'Idler' (untidy, disorgan-ized, unpre-pared)	'Class clown' (makes minor mischief)	'Charmer' (excessively pleasant-teacher's pet)	'Self-centred succeeder' (especially good, but not cooperative with class-room group)
Power	'Refuser' (stubbornly forgetful and disobedient)	'Rebel' (openly ar-gumentative and bad-tempered)		
Revenge	'Violent sulker' (sullen and deficient)	'Juvenile delinquent' (violent and hurtful)		
Display of inadequacy	'Complete failure' (hopelessly inept-inferiority complex)			

As may be seen from Table 3:1, all four AGMs may be active at the first goal level of attention-getting, two AGMs may be active at the goal levels of power and revenge, and only one AGM (the passive destructive) can typify the fourth goal level of display of inadequacy. The descriptions contained in Table 3:1 are intended to provide general means of identifying various types of misbehaving children. The stereotypes and labels associated with the various descriptions in table 3:1 are intended for diagnostic purposes only, to help teachers determine the mistaken goals of troubled children in their classrooms. They are not to be used to restrict inappropriately teachers' views of children and their potentials. More recent work in this area by Albert (1989) eschews entirely such labels.

Logical and natural consequences

Because of the importance of the democratic teaching style, teachers must learn to distinguish *logical* and *natural* consequences from punishment. It is quite permissible for the democratic teacher to employ logical consequences, or to permit natural consequences, following upon pupil misbehavior. It is not permissible to use autocratic punishment (Brophy & Putnam, 1979). Dreikurs defines punishment as any hurtful action taken by a "superior authority" as a means of coercing an "inferior being" to do the bidding of the authority.

Punishment is rarely corrective in nature, but it is usually retaliatory. It is thus almost impossible to avoid punishment (in the Dreikurian sense) unless a classroom operates as a true democracy in which a status of social equality is granted to everybody, and the authority of one over others is refuted.

Natural and logical consequences take the place of punishment in the democratic classroom. Natural consequences are based on the natural flow of events, and take place without adult interference. They are the unavoidable consequences or inevitable reactions entailed by a child's actions when no one interferes to prevent these consequences from occurring. Thus, a small child receives scraped knees as a result of running too quickly on concrete, children quickly learn from experience that hot things should not be handled and so forth.

Logical consequences, on the other hand, involve adult interventions. However, while logical consequences are structured and arranged by the adult, they must be experienced by the child as logical in nature. Logical consequences are often associated with the violation of classroom rules that are fully understood by the misbehaving pupil. If a child is not listening in a reading lesson, a logical consequence would be to let the child miss a turn for oral reading. If a whole class of youngsters is inattentive, the teacher may go and work at her own desk saying, "Children, when you are ready to work, you can ask me to teach you." For a child who cannot sit in a chair, or who constantly tips it, a logical consequence might be to remove the chair and allow the child to stand. To be logical, the consequence administered should be directly related to the misbehavior in question.

Encouragement

Another distinction that is crucial for the operation of a democratic classroom is that between praise and *encouragement*. According to Dreikurs (1957), praise alone (e.g., "Well done!" or "Keep up the good work" or "That's absolutely great") often serves different purposes from what the teacher intends. Such statements, rather than conveying to pupils that their skills and activities are recognized as valuable to the social and academic order of the classroom, are often interpreted (by the child) as meaning that the child's personal worth depends upon external assessments of him or her as a person. The unfortunate aspect of this kind of interpretation by the student, is that it translates directly into the following logic – "If I am praised, my personal worth is high; if I am scolded, I am bad; if I am ignored, I am worthless." When this child becomes an adult, personal effectiveness and ability to cope and function with daily tasks is likely to depend too much on an estimation of how she or he "stacks-up" in the views of other people. "How do I measure up" takes precedence over "What needs to be done in this situation – how can I help."

The crucial distinction between praise and encouragement is that praise recognizes the actor, while encouragement acknowledges the act. To illustrate this distinction, consider the differences between the following praise statements ("Aren't you smart to be able to do this!" "I'm so proud of you for getting good grades." "I thought your performance at the recital was exquisite.") and their encouragement parallels ("How nice that you could figure that out for yourself; your skill is growing." "The most important thing is that you enjoy learning." "It's good to see that you are enjoying playing the flute. You deserve to be very proud of the job you did.").

Notice that where praise gives an external evaluation of the actor, encouragement assists the actor in valuing and appreciating personal skills and actions.

Kohn (1996) points out that when a child is praised, the praising teachers or parents include "I" in their statement of commendation. For example, "I thought your performance at the recital was exquisite." In this situation, the student is not encouraged to reflect on how he or she acted. Rather the emphasis is on what the teacher or parent thought about what was done. Such praise can lead to approval or attention-seeking behavior. Kohn refers to this type of encouragement as "control through seduction." The unwanted effects of this kind of praise may become even worse when the praise is offered in front of others, thus creating competition amongst classmates.

The three Cs

In extending Dreikurs' work, Linda Albert (1989) has discussed in considerable detail students' needs for belonging. In classrooms, the need to belong may be interpreted as a desire to feel significant and important, to find a satisfying place in the classroom groups where students spend at least six hours each school day.

The "three Cs," if satisfied, result in students achieving a strong sense of belonging. To belong, students must feel *capable* of completing academic and other school tasks, they must believe that they can *connect* successfully at an appropriate personal level with teachers and classmates, and they must think they can *contribute* in a significant way to the group.

Three factors affect students' abilities to satisfy the three Cs: (1) the quality of the relationship between students and teachers; (2) the classroom climate, especially with respect to opportunities for cooperation and success; and (3) the appropriateness of the classroom structure with respect to encouraging contributions from all students.

Building self-esteem

Intervening to redirect student misbehavior associated with mistaken goals into more positive forms of classroom behavior that help students to belong, is a major objective of the Adlerian, democratic approach to classroom management. However, according to Albert (1989) and Dinkmeyer, Carlson and Dinkmeyer (1994), such intervention must be accompanied by consistent attempts to build the self-esteem of children in classrooms. Teachers only can influence students. It is students themselves who have the power to choose to behave in ways that will facilitate their belonging to the classroom group in positive ways. The likelihood that students will make such positive choices is enhanced greatly if they develop healthy levels of self-esteem in the classroom context. Teachers can develop self-esteem in their students by fostering feelings of independence and responsibility for their own learning (Dinkmeyer, et al., 1994). Classrooms almost always should be structured as to increase students' motivation to think and act for themselves.

Methods and Applications

The Four Goal Technique

Consistent with the teleoanalytic emphasis on the goals or motives of behavior, Dreikurs and Cassel (1972) present a system called *"The Four Goal Technique"* that consists of a series of classroom applications for modifying the motivations behind the misbehaviors of young students. (Note that Dreikurs and Cassel address their techniques to students up to the age of 10. For the correction of older children and adolescents, they claim that "The Four Goal Technique" is not always sufficient.) Nonetheless, neo-Adlerians, such as Albert (1989) and Dinkmeyer, McKay and Dinkmeyer (1980) have found steps one, two and five of the Four Goal Technique, as described below, to be generally effective for working with adolescents in classroom settings. The Four Goal Technique consists of five steps.

1. *Step 1: Observe the Child and the Child's Goals.* Not surprisingly, the first step involves a detailed observation of the behavior of the disruptive or troubled student. Assuming that the teacher is familiar with the four goals of misbehavior, and with the theoretical descriptions of the student behaviors and attention-getting mechanisms that characterize each of the goal levels, it is usually not a difficult task to place the misbehaving child accurately at one of the goal levels. This initial placement allows the teacher to comprehend the meaning of the child's actions.

2. *Step 2: Observe Your Own Reactions.* In order to verify the assessment of the child's goal arrived at in step 1, the teacher should attend to his/her own immediate responses to the child's actions. Indeed, according to Dreikurs and Cassel, a teacher's recognition of his/her own reactions to a student is probably the most accurate and reliable method available for confirming a child's mistaken goals. This is so because the immediate response of the teacher is usually in line with the child's expectations. Thus, if the teacher feels annoyed or "hassled," this is usually an indication that the child who elicits these reactions or feelings is operating at the goal-level of attention-getting. If the teacher feels defeated or threatened, power is the goal that is indicated. If the teacher feels deeply hurt, revenge very likely will be the child's motive.

Finally, if the teacher feels helpless, the teacher probably is responding to a child operating in terms of the mistaken goal of "display of inadequacy." In matters of classroom behaviors manifesting mistaken goals or motives of misbehavior, a teacher's own feelings when interacting with the child are the best gauges.

3. *Step 3: Confront the Child with Possible Motives.* Once the teacher has a firm suspicion of the child's mistaken goal, it is most important to confront the child with this knowledge. Such confrontation will disclose and confirm the mistaken goal to the child. (Remember that, while each individual acts according to personal decisions with respect to goals or motives, one is not necessarily totally aware of the essential nature of such decisions or goals.) The disclosure of motive must be done in a friendly manner, without criticism. Confrontation should occur in a relaxed classroom discussion period or in a private teacher-pupil session. It should not be attempted during times of conflict. The easiest, and probably best, approach for the teacher to take when confronting a misbehaving pupil with a mistaken goal is to simply (and calmly) ask the child if s/he knows why s/he did X. After hearing what the child has to say ("No" is probably the most common response), the teacher should proceed by asking the child if s/he would like to know, and if s/he would be willing to listen to some ideas the teacher has that might be helpful. Once the child's interest has been aroused, the teacher should (in a non-judgemental and unemotional manner) go through the following sequence of questions (always in this order and always completing all four questions), carefully noting the child's verbal and nonverbal reactions to each guess.

a) Could it be that you want special attention?

b) Could it be that you want your own way and hope to be boss?

c) Could it be that you want to hurt others as much as you feel hurt by them?

d) Could it be that you want to be left alone?

All four questions always are asked sequentially, regardless of the child's responses. This is to cover the possibility that a child may be operating on more than one goal at a time.

4. *Step 4: Note the Recognition Reflex*. When a teacher accurately guesses the child's present intentions and motives, this disclosure will produce a "recognition reflex" in the child' facial expression. The *recognition reflex* indicates with certainty the correctness of the teacher's interpretation and the child's recognition of this "correctness." It consists of a roguish smile and peculiar twinkle of the eyes or twitch of a facial muscle. Sometimes the child will even go so far as to cover his/her face and/or burst forth with laughter. Even if the child says nothing, or even says "No," the recognition reflex is unmistakable and gives him/her completely away.

5. *Step 5: Apply Appropriate Corrective Procedures*. Having ascertained and communicated the child's mistaken goal, the teacher is now in a firm position to apply classroom corrective procedures. Since these procedures differ depending upon the goal-level to which they are directed, it perhaps will be best to consider each goal separately.

a) If the child's goal is *attention-getting*, the basic strategy is to ignore the child when bidding for attention (remember that nagging, punishing, advising and so forth are all forms of giving attention), and to give lots of attention at other times. In doing this, the teacher should make every effort to avoid showing annoyance. Distracting students from attention-seeking rituals (without providing undue levels of attention), and moving them to less "stimulating" or central locations in the classroom also might prove worthwhile.

b) If the child's goal is *power*, the teacher should not fight, but should not give in either. Power struggles may be avoided by recognizing that the child has power. Rather than threatening the child, the teacher may appeal for help, even saying "I cannot make you do it and I know I can't." By withdrawing from power struggles, the teacher can take the wind out of the child's sails, and disarm the child. At the same time, the power-seeking child should be given power in situations where it can be used productively. By respecting the child, enlisting the child's aid and by reaching common working agreements, the mistaken power motive can be rechanneled into more productive social and personal goals. If necessary, negotiated, logical consequences, including use of time-out (see chapter five), can be employed in response to student misbehavior associated with the mistaken goal of power.

c) If the child's goal is *revenge*, the teacher must never appear to be hurt by the often brutal and vicious behavior of the child. The revenge-seeking child needs lots of encouragement. It helps a great deal if the teacher can convince this child that s/he is liked. The teacher can do this directly, and also can arrange special forms of group encouragement through enlisting a "buddy" or through classroom group discussions. The teacher must, of course, be very alert to the possibility of the group making things worse by "turning against" the revengeful child. The teacher must promote and model mutual understanding and help. All forms of punishment should be avoided. Natural consequences will work for the revengeful child; but logical consequences only work if the child really cares, and must therefore await the acceptance of peer and teacher approval on the part of the child. If such acceptance is present, negotiated, logical consequences in the form of loss of privileges and time-out (again, see chapter five) may be applied to the misbehavior of the child who mistakenly seeks revenge.

d) If the child's goal is to *display inadequacy* or *avoid failure*, the teacher must devote a major effort to making the child feel worthwhile. Encourage such children when they try; tell them that you will not give up on them; get the class to cooperate with special help from selected peers; avoid any support for the inferiority feelings; and most importantly, avoid being discouraged yourself. In particular, when working with these children, teachers should make consistent efforts to build the students' self-esteem by using some of the methods discussed in the very next section of this chapter.

In summary, according to Dreikurs and Cassel (1972), the most discouraged student can be helped by an informed teacher and class. Such children must be shown and helped to feel that they belong. By not playing into their ploys, by using logical and natural consequences where appropriate, and by encouraging and respecting all learners, the classroom teacher can help students overcome mistaken goals, correct misbehaviors and become happy and enthusiastic learners.

Building students' self-esteem

Linda Albert (1989) and Dinkmeyer, Carlson and Dinkmeyer (1994) are quick to point out that intervening to redirect students' disruptive classroom behavior spawned by mistaken goals is only part of the overall democratic solution to problems of classroom management. Before students can choose more positive forms of classroom behavior as a means of belonging to the classroom group, they must feel capable, "connected" and confident in their ability to contribute in the classroom context. Albert (1989) offers specific suggestions for helping students achieve these three Cs.

Examples of strategies that may help teachers to assist students to feel more *capable* include the following.

1. Helping students to understand that it is alright to make mistakes. Teachers can talk about mistakes as being a vital part of learning. They can equate mistakes with effort, and generally attempt to minimize any negative effects that might be associated with making mistakes.

2. Building the confidence of students by focusing on improvements, noticing contributions, acknowledging strengths and generally showing faith in students. The difficulty of many school tasks can be recognized explicitly, and teachers can try to ensure that students are not left to fail at tasks for protracted periods of time.

3. Past successes that students have experienced can be recalled and lauded. In particular, tangible aids that assist students to recognize their accomplishments can be provided. Examples include accomplishment albums in which students keep examples of past work that has been done successfully, and checklists of skills or flowcharts of concepts that "track" students' progress by recording and displaying what they have learned.

4. Recognizing success by providing opportunities for students to acknowledge their own and others' accomplishments. Occasionally assisting students to run their own award assemblies, and providing positive time-outs (i.e., opportunities for self-congratulation and selection of self-rewarding activities) are good examples.

Examples of strategies for assisting students to *"connect"* with the teacher and their classmates include the following.

1. Accepting students by distinguishing between the deed and the doer (e.g., "I like you very much, but I am not pleased with what I just saw you do."), and by showing a willingness

to accept differences in students' personal styles (e.g., personal idiosyncrasies in dress, habits or mannerisms).

2. Attending to students by greeting them warmly, listening to them actively (see the previous chapter), and helping them to ask for attention in appropriate ways when they desire it.

3. Appreciating students' efforts to contribute positively to the classroom group, and to their own and others' learning. Explicit statements of appreciation (oral or written) can acknowledge a student's actions, the teacher's own positive feelings about these actions and the benefits created when students act in responsible ways.

4. Showing appropriate affection to students, especially when such affection is not contingent on any sort of accomplishment per se, or when students are upset or troubled by events in their lives inside and outside the classroom.

Examples of strategies that might help students *contribute* include the following.

1. Encouraging students to contribute to the class by inviting their help with daily tasks, requesting them to make choices and express "input" with respect to classroom practices and curriculum, and requesting their participation in classroom discussions.

2. Encouraging students to help each other through peer tutoring, peer counseling and peer recognition (applause, displays of appreciation). If methods of peer tutoring or counseling are adopted, students should be given specific assistance and information relevant to their roles in such helping relationships.

By helping students to feel capable, to connect and to contribute, teachers can help build the self-esteem of students so that students will be more likely to pursue their goals of belonging in positive ways that will benefit themselves and others in the classroom.

Involving parents as partners

Adlerian psychology long has advocated working closely with parents in helping children develop their potentials in ways that will benefit them and society at large. Continuing in this tradition, Albert (1989) makes several potentially useful suggestions for involving parents in cooperative efforts aimed at enhancing the classroom experiences and behaviors of students. In particular, she stresses the importance of keeping parents informed about classroom activities, policies and expectations. Disseminating written policies and newsletters, making introductory telephone calls early in a school year, arranging presentations to groups of parents, and facilitating parent and parent-teacher study groups are common ways in which information can be shared across home and school. Additional information pertinent to developing effective working coalitions between parents/guardians and teachers will be discussed in the final chapter of this book.

Classroom discussions

Because of Dreikurs' continuous emphasis upon the need for children to belong to the classroom social group, it is natural that he should view the *class discussion period* as a primary preventive and remedial vehicle for classroom management problems. Any child with problems is a problem for the whole class, and solutions to such problems must grow out of the helpful involvement of all class members. A democratic classroom eschews teacher authority in favor of classroom cooperation.

Ideally, a 30-minute discussion period should be structured into the weekly timetable of the classroom. Group discussions help children understand themselves and others, and develop cooperative motives. It is suggested that class discussion periods begin as soon as the teacher becomes acquainted with the class in September. Initially, the teacher may chair the discussion, but over time pupils can rotate through this position. The chair ensures that only one person speaks at a time while others actively listen. No disturbances are acceptable. If disruptions occur, the discussion stops until order is established. Rules for the classroom discussion periods, and for the classroom as a whole, may be advanced by any group member; and, providing they are logical and understandable, may be approved by consensus, associated with logical consequences, and posted on the chalkboard or bulletin board.

The topical format for classroom discussions will vary, but agendas including such items as (1) good things of the past week, (2) ways in which we can improve this week, (3) personal problems, (4) responsibilities and (5) future plans commonly are employed.

In Dreikurs' model of classroom management, the classroom discussion period serves three purposes: 1) everybody learns to listen, 2) children learn to understand themselves and each other and 3) all students are encouraged to help each other (Woolfolk, 1990).

When leading classroom discussions in the democratic tradition it is essential that the teacher invites and encourages the participation of all pupils. This may be done in a variety of ways. A very good illustration of some of the discussion leading techniques which may be used in this regard is provided from a transcript of a discussion period held in Mr. Kinhara's grade four classroom. In what follows, many of Mr. Kinhara's comments are grouped together under headings indicative of different strategies associated with effective leadership of classroom discussions.

1.   Invite the participation of the quiet children.

e.g., "What do you think about this Sandy?

"We need to hear what some others have to say. What's your opinion, Tomi?"

"I saw you nodding while Paul was talking, Jean. What were you agreeing with?"

2.   Encourage student to student exchanges.

e.g., "That's a very novel idea, Tracy. What do you think of Tracy's suggestion, Luigi?"

"You've raised an interesting point, Kim. How would you answer that question, Meridith?"

3.   When unsure of what has been said, seek clarification.

e.g., "So, you're not in agreement with Joe. Is that right?"

"I thought I heard you say that you wouldn't have done what Sandra did, but I'm not absolutely sure that's what you said."

"I'd like to repeat what you said Susie . . . . Did I hear you correctly?"

4.   Pause after questions and after pupil statements.

e.g., Mr. Kinhara was very careful to pause after he asked a question so as to give students a chance to think of a response, and then to make a statement to the group.

Mr. Kinhara was also careful not to jump in too quickly when a student stopped speaking. This helped him to ensure that he would not be interrupting if the same student wanted to continue speaking, or if another student wanted to respond to what the previous speaker had said.

When Mr. Kinhara paused after his own questions and after pupil statements, he gave himself time to look around the class group and to assess the reactions of the students to what was going on. In this way,

Mr. Kinhara kept himself alert to pupil expressions of confusion, interest, excitement, boredom, and other reactions.

5. Encourage pupil participation.

e.g., "I can see that you're all very excited about all the good ideas you've been expressing. You really are very good problem-solvers."

"I've learned a lot from you today. Many of the suggestions you made were ones that I had not thought about at all."

Unlike the four goal technique, classroom discussions or meetings can be employed effectively with students of all ages. While such discussions typically occur in classroom groups, special group meetings also can be organized in which students from different classrooms and grade levels might participate. Such "groups" might be organized by a school counselor, resource room teacher, or regular classroom teacher with special knowledge and skills in areas such as helping students to discuss and deal with issues related to drug and alcohol abuse, sexuality, grief and loss, or interpersonal difficulties. In all such groups, Dreikurs' overriding concern is that all students be respected as unique, worthwhile individuals with the right to express their own legitimate views. In this manner, students can be helped to achieve their goal of belonging to the classroom group without resorting to the pursuit of "mistaken" goals such as gaining attention, power, revenge or displaying inadequacy.

By developing legitimate social interest and responsibility in a democratic context that respects their rights as individuals, children in classroom groups can acquire styles of interpersonal and personal behavior that benefit themselves and society as a whole. In a recent extension of Adlerian principles applied to school contexts, Barbara Colorosa (1990) advocates democratic principles and practices that extend beyond individual classrooms to the overall organization and management of the total school environment as it affects pupils, teachers, parents/guardians and school administrators.

Critique

The democratic approach to classroom management appears to be generally well-suited to the classrooms of the future. Greater flexibility and diversity in school organization, classroom practice, curriculum content, teaching methods and pupil background make appropriate a strong emphasis on individual rights within complex, multifaceted settings such as today's school classrooms. The general view of classrooms as democratic societies in miniature may be both apt and functional.

At the same time, the multifaceted nature of contemporary classroom groups (e.g., multiple ability levels, diverse social-cultural backgrounds, increased variety in extracurricular experiences and circumstances) makes it unlikely that all students who are experiencing difficulties adjusting to life in classrooms will fit readily into the categories of goals/motives and patterns of misbehavior identified by Adler, Dreikurs and their followers. While Albert (1989) claims that as much as 90 percent of students' classroom misbehavior can be understood within this framework, it must be remembered that advocates of particular approaches to classroom management are likely to render such judgments on the basis of personal perceptions that are influenced strongly by their theoretical and practical attachments to their favored approaches.

Teachers probably can use these categories and the suggested classroom practices associated with them as general aids to conceptualizing pupils and their patterns of classroom behavior. However, overly rigid adherence to such conceptualizations may produce its own difficulties. For example, it may be unfortunately easy to confuse the understandable upset or reticence expressed by children from different linguistic and cultural backgrounds, when adjusting to mostly English-speaking, North American classrooms, with behavioral displays indicative of motives like revenge or inadequacy. In such cases, teachers must be able to conceptualize and understand students' classroom behaviors in ways other than those provided by Dreikurs and his colleagues.

The potential problem of overly-rigid categorical understanding and classroom intervention may be exacerbated by the types of labels found in Table 3:1, despite the various cautions frequently associated with their use. The intent of labels such as "idler" and "rebel" is to facilitate ready understanding of the behavioral patterns being described. However, any such labels are double-edged swords, and teachers must be careful to balance their own prior conceptions of these labels with careful, "objective" observations of what children actually do. Taking time to talk with individual children, perhaps by developing some of the communication methods advocated in the previous chapter, might assist teachers in gaining a more valid assessment of students' classroom motives.

The various suggestions made by Albert (1989) with respect to enhancing students' self-esteem seem generally sensible and desirable. It is unlikely that students will feel a sense of belonging in classroom settings where they do not believe that they can contribute, connect with others and demonstrate their capabilities. Further, it seems possible that increased student self-esteem and belonging might flow from a teacher's adoption of the types of strategies advocated by Albert. However, it also is important to remember that a great deal of student self-esteem inevitably flows from the acquisition of skills, knowledge and attitudes embedded in a good school curriculum, and promoted by good teaching. To be most effective, it probably is necessary to couple instructional and management strategies targeted at the enhancement of students' self-esteem with instructional methods and strategies conducive to enhanced student learning of the knowledge, skills and attitudes embedded in a sensible, relevant and challenging curriculum. Without such a context, it is doubtful that strategies targeted specifically at enhancing students' self-esteem will succeed in convincing learners that they are capable contributors to either the academic or social aspects of classroom life. More will be said about the contributions of good teaching to classroom management in the very next chapter in this book.

The purposes and suggestions for classroom discussions advocated by Dreikurs, Dinkmeyer, Ferguson, Colorosa and others seem particularly useful. In our view, any time that teachers can find to encourage cooperative exchanges of information, viewpoints, ideas and suggestions is time well spent. It seems reasonable to assume that pupils in classrooms likely will participate in and identify with the values and goals implicit in learning and other classroom activities to the extent that they believe they have legitimate input into the society of the classroom. In this sense, school children and adolescents probably are no different from us adults in our identification with, and participation in, the groups and organizations of which we are part. Recent work on the problem of students who drop out of school (Finn, 1989) suggests that students' sense of belonging to school (defined as participating in school and school-related activities, and identifying with values consistent with schooling and learning) is the best predictor of whether or not they will continue to attend school past the age of mandatory attendance. Thus, while some of the diagnostic categories and intervention plans suggested by Dreikurs and others may need to be modified to suit the demands of contemporary classrooms, the overall theme of encouraging genuine student participation in democratic classroom and school contexts seems as important now as it ever has been.

References

Adler, A. (1938). *Social interest*. London: Faber & Faber.

Albert, L. (1989) *A teacher's guide to cooperative discipline: How to manage your classroom and promote self-esteem*. Circle Pines, MN: American Guidance Service.

Brophy, J.E. & Putnam, J.G. (1979). Classroom management in the elementary grades. In D.L. Duke (Ed.) *Classroom management: The seventy-eighth yearbook of the National Society for the Study of Education*. Chicago: The University of Chicago Press.

Coloroso, B. (1990). *Kids are worth it* (Videotape series). Littleton, CO: kids are worth it! Publications.

Dinkmeyer, D. & Dreikurs, R. (1963). *Encouraging children to learn*. Englewood Cliffs, NJ: Prentice-Hall.

Dinkmeyer, D.C., Carlson, J. & Dinkmeyer, D. Jr. (1994). *Consultation: School mental health professionals as consultants*. Muncie, IN: Accelerated Development Inc.

Dinkmeyer, D.C. & McKay, G.D. (1976). *Systematic training for effective parenting (STEP), Parent's handbook*. Circle Pines, MN: American Guidance Service.

Dinkmeyer, D.C. & McKay, G.D. (1983). *Systematic training for effective parenting of teens (STEP/TEEN), Parent's guide*. Circle Pines, MN: American Guidance Service.

Dinkmeyer, D.C. & McKay, G.D. (1989). *Parenting young children: Helpful strategies based on systematic training for effective parenting (STEP) for parents of children under six*. Circle Pines, MN: American Guidance Service.

Dinkmeyer, D.C., McKay, G.D. & Dinkmeyer, D. Jr. (1980). *Systematic training for effective teaching (STET)*. Circle Pines, MN: American Guidance Service.

Dreikurs, R. (1950). *Fundamentals of Adlerian psychology*. New York: Greenburg.

Dreikurs, R. (1957). *Psychology in the classroom*. New York: Harper.

Dreikurs, R. & Cassel, P. (1972). *Discipline without tears*. New York: Hawthorn Books.

Dreikurs, R. & Grey, L. (1968). *A new approach to discipline: Logical consequences*. New York: Hawthorn Books.

Dreikurs, R., Grunwald, B.B. & Pepper, F.C. (1982). *Maintaining sanity in the classroom (2nd ed.)*. New York: Harper & Row.

Dreikurs, R. & Soltz, V. (1964). *Children: The challenge*. New York: Hawthorn Books.

Ferguson, E.D. (1984). *Adlerian theory: An introduction*. Vancouver, BC: Adlerian Psychology Association of British Columbia.

Finn, J.D. (1989). Withdrawing from school. *Review of Educational Research, 59*, 117-142.

Kohn, A. (1996). *Beyond discipline: From compliance to community*. Alexandria, VA: Association for Supervision and Curriculum Development.

Sweeney, T.J. (1981). *Adlerian counseling: Proven concepts and strategies (2nd ed.)*. Muncie, IN: Accelerated Development Press.

Woolfolk, A.E. (1990). *Educational psychology for teachers (4th ed.)*. Englewood Cliffs, NJ: Prentice-Hall.

Chapter Four
Group Management Approaches

Overview and Rationale

Many difficulties in classroom management can be prevented by effective teaching that holds students' interest, does not engender frustration and confusion, and moves students from one activity to another in an organized manner. Learning to work effectively with groups of students in school classrooms constitutes a major part of a teacher's competence. If teachers can learn effective ways of organizing the classroom, presenting information and motivating students, classroom behavior problems will be greatly reduced. An effective group management system will prevent small problems from becoming bigger problems, and moderate size problems from becoming a classroom crisis. Systematic group management is not just for treatment, it is good prevention (Cipani, 1998).

The approaches to classroom management discussed in this fourth chapter are primarily, although not exclusively preventive in nature. All emphasize: (a) the importance of arranging the classroom and planning for instruction, (b) ways of instructing and interacting with groups of learners and (c) methods of responding to disruptive behaviors of individual students without losing control of the classroom group. A further characteristic common to the group management approaches discussed is that each approach is supported by empirical research conducted in actual classroom settings.

Kounin's group managerial approach to classroom discipline is based on the classroom teacher's successful acquisition of a variety of basic teaching skills. These skills help ensure that the social learning interactions that occur between teachers and students in classroom groups will be productive and responsible. Kounin's is the first of the classroom management approaches discussed in this book that is less concerned with what to do when disruptive classroom behaviors occur, than with what to do to prevent disruptions from occurring in the first place. Kounin's own research studies (Kounin, 1977) into the associations between teacher actions and student disruptive behavior revealed that there are a number of specific teacher actions that appear to be correlated highly with increased student work involvement and with decreased deviant or disruptive student behavior. Kounin's entire approach is devoted to a clear description of these *teaching skills* so that they may be understood and practised by teachers anxious to promote more positive learning environments in their classrooms.

The *systematic* approach to group management advocated by Robert Spaulding (1983a, 1983b) emphasizes the importance of a teacher's control over a variety of classroom variables that can be employed differentially in response to various classroom *coping styles* exhibited by students. Such variables include the number of choices given to students, the amount of direction and supervision provided, the size of classroom work groups, and the location and use of classroom work stations. To assist teachers in keeping track of their intentional use of these variables as a means of appropriate group management, Spaulding advocates the use of instructional *calendars* through which teachers can plan, organize and implement their strategies of group management.

A final set of recommendations for group management discussed in this chapter is drawn from research on *teaching effectiveness* that has attempted (as have Kounin and Spaulding) to identify classroom teaching practices that are associated empirically with higher levels of student learning and engagement, and lower levels of classroom disruption. A rather wide range of teaching methods has been identified in such research, depending on what specific criteria have been adopted for assessing effectiveness. *Direct instruction* is a synthesis of teaching practices that has been shown to correlate highly with student achievement, defined as the successful learning of rules, procedures and basic concepts in traditional curriculum areas. *Cooperative learning* is a synthesis of teaching and learning practices that is thought to correlate with enhanced student interest, motivation, positive social interactions and possibly creativity. Both direct instruction and cooperative learning will be presented as examples of approaches to classroom teaching and group management that claim to be supported by research on teaching effectiveness.

Principles

The basic assumption behind the approaches to classroom management and discipline discussed in this chapter is that 'good' teaching (the kind of teaching which keeps students interested in, and involved with, classroom learning activities) solves most classroom behavior problems before they start. In other words, if students are motivated and involved, disruptive behavior will be largely absent. The main principle stemming from this assumption is that teachers concerned with classroom management should spend more time learning strong general teaching skills (which will prevent most disruptive behaviors from occurring), than specific techniques to use in reaction to disruptive behaviors only after they have occurred. More simply, "an ounce of prevention is worth a pound of cure."

Good and Brophy (1997) describe three characteristics of this proactive approach: (1) it is preventive rather than just reactive, (2) it integrates management methods that encourage appropriate student conduct with instructional methods that encourage student achievement of curricular objectives and (3) it focuses on managing the class as a group, not just on the behavior of individual students.

The specific teaching skills that make up many of the instructional variables examined by Kounin in his research on classroom management have been shown to possess strong positive associations (correlations) with high levels of student work involvement, and low levels of disruption. The statistical and practical significance of these associations attests to the validity of Kounin's claims. For more detailed information about these experiments and results, the reader is directed to Kounin's 1977 text, *Discipline and Group Management in Classrooms.* Similarly, Spaulding (1983a, 1983b; Spaulding & Spaulding, 1982) reports results from his research program that indicate strong positive correlations between students' engagement in academic tasks, students' "on-task" behavior, students' "self-motivated" time, and teachers' use of the various classroom management strategies he advocates.

To assist the reader in understanding the implications of such work for instructional practice, it is useful to conceptualize teaching at three levels of action. All the things that teachers do in classrooms may be subsumed under the labels of *teaching skills, strategies, attitudes* and *styles* (Martin, 1981; Good & Brophy, 1997).

Teaching skills

Teaching skills are discrete and specific behaviors that are employed for some immediate instructional purpose. Asking a factual question ("Where does coffee come from?"), praising a student's work ("That's a very well written sentence Tommy."), giving clear instructions, pausing after a question so as to give students time to respond, pacing the speed with which information is given and redirecting one pupil's comment to another pupil ("That's an interesting idea, Bill. What do you think of Bill's suggestion, Jane?") are all examples of specific teaching skills. Such skills may be acquired with effort and continuous practice. They form the foundation of effective teaching, in the same way that mastery of the specific skills of forehand, volley, lob, backhand and serve form the foundation for an effective game of tennis.

Teaching strategies

Teaching strategies are series of skills that are arranged (or 'orchestrated') purposefully in terms of some longer-range instructional objectives. Just as the tennis player may put together a strategy of "deep, hard serves, followed by rapid approaches to the net and slashing cross-court volleys," to enable him/her to defeat a strong opponent who lacks a good lob or passing shot; so the teacher can put together a number of specific teaching skills to assist different learners in the acquisition of a range of skills and information in a variety of subject-matter areas. Thus, when teachers wish to teach specific facts, they may employ a strategy consisting of information-giving, factual questioning, informational feedback with corrections and descriptive praise for correct responding. When they wish to assist students in discussing information and arriving at their own opinions, teachers may employ a different series of teaching skills consisting of open-ended questioning, redirection of pupil comments to other pupils and responses to student comments which ask them to further probe and/or extend their ideas. By purposefully arranging carefully selected teaching skills into a number of teaching strategies, the classroom teacher can develop an extensive repertoire of such strategies appropriate for a wide range of pupils, curriculum areas and instructional settings.

Teacher attitudes

Certain key attitudes and personal qualities must be present if principles of classroom management are to be applied successfully. Positive attitudes will make the teacher someone students will respect and want to please, not merely obey. Good and Brophy (1997) and McCaslin and Good (1996) found that teachers must: (1) earn the respect and affection of their students by developing personal relationships with individual students and demonstrating enjoyment of and concern for students and their individual welfare, (2) be consistent and, therefore, credible and dependable, (3) assume responsibility for seeing that their students learn and (4) value and enjoy learning and expect their students to do the same.

Teaching styles

Teaching styles go beyond specific teaching actions and their purposeful arrangement, and describe all of those things which characterize individual teachers as unique human beings. Thus, individual teachers may appear to be warm, open, sincere, friendly, stern, business-like, democratic, etc. Since teaching styles are reflections of what teachers are, as much as of what they do, styles are not as easily acquired or altered as are skills and strategies. While the acquisition and employment of specific skills and strategies can affect the style of a teacher, individual teaching styles can also determine the effectiveness with which a particular teacher can use different skills and strategies. In a very real sense, development as an effective teacher may be characterized by the continuous, effortful and appropriate matching of specific skills and strategies to individual teaching styles. Just as the shorter, slower tennis player would be ill-advised to select a "serve and volley" strategy as his/her bread-and-butter tactic, many teachers would be ill-advised to center their instructional efforts around skills and strategies incongruent with their own physical, social and emotional make-ups. This is not to say that teachers should not experiment with different skills and strategies, but to say that such experimentation should be encouraged and the criterion of appropriate strategy-to-style match used to adjudicate the effectiveness of the instructional results yielded by such experimentation (Martin, 1981).

A vivid illustration of the importance of harmony across an individual teacher's skills, strategies, **attitudes** and style can be obtained with reference to this book. Some of you will undoubtedly find some of the approaches (strategies) of classroom management discussed in the book more or less suited to your own personal teaching styles, than others. This is fine and natural. Make sure, however, that you take the time to determine and acquire some of the teaching skills which make up the different management strategies. You cannot always determine whether or not a particular strategy is congruent with your own teaching style, until you experiment with it. Often our present perception of our own styles may not be entirely accurate. Such experimentation can make us more aware of what our styles really are, in addition to providing us with extended teaching repertoires (strategies and skills).

Acquisition of teaching skills

Acquiring teaching skills is hard work, but such effort may be minimized if expended with an understanding of the essential ingredients of successful skill acquisition programs. The acquisition of teaching skills requires, (1) clear *specification* of the skill, (2) ample opportunity to practice the skill in realistic settings and (3) precise and specific *feedback* to the teacher who is practicing the skill. Teachers may obtain precise definitions and demonstrations of skills through a variety of sources. Books, such as this one, are useful in describing many potentially useful teaching skills, but by far the most powerful skill specification medium is the direct observation of another teacher effectively employing the skills being examined. Practice of teaching skills should be done, as much as possible, within the regular classroom setting. Microteaching, role-plays, simulation and peer-teaching may provide useful approximations to regular classroom settings during the early stages of skill practice, but eventually (if the skill is to be transferable to the regular classroom setting) there is no substitute for 'real' learners in 'real' classrooms. Finally, precise feedback to skill practice may be facilitated through the use of collegial observation and supervision, video- and audio-tape, and teaching skill-observation grids or checklists. For extended examples of the skill-acquisition programs currently available for teachers (both pre- and in-service), the reader is directed to such sources as Borg et al. (1968), Brown (1975), Cipani (1998), Cooper et al. (1977), Martin (1981), Rosenshine and Stevens (1986), Weinstein (1996), and Weinstein and Mignano (1993).

In the next section of this chapter, the various teaching skills, strategies and styles advocated by Kounin, Spaulding and other researchers of teaching effectiveness will be examined more specifically.

Techniques and Applications

Kounin's teaching variables

Perhaps the most important teacher variable described and documented by Kounin is *with-it-ness*. With-it-ness refers to a teacher's behaviors that demonstrate knowledge of what is going on in the classroom. More precisely, Kounin defines with-it-ness as "a teacher communicating to the children by her actual behavior that she knows what the children are doing." Teacher behaviors that demonstrate that a teacher knows what is going on in the classroom tend to increase students' work involvement and decrease deviant or disruptive pupil behavior. In Kounin's study (1977), he found a correlation of .62 between teacher with-it-ness and students' work involvement, and a correlation of .53 between with-it-ness and absence of student deviant behavior. These relationships are high enough to indicate that teacher with-it-ness is an important factor in keeping learners on-task and reducing misbehavior in the classroom.

It should be noted that a study by Irving and Martin (1982) failed to replicate Kounin's positive findings for teacher with-it-ness, and raised questions about Kounin's definition and measurement of this teaching variable. The general pedagogical method that Kounin referred to as with-it-ness can be described more specifically by a brief examination of four teaching skills thought to demonstrate with-it-ness in classroom settings. These skill descriptions are taken from Borg (1973).

1. *Desist* – Teachers may demonstrate with-it-ness by telling students to stop deviant, off-task behaviors. To be effective however, such desists must be timely (i.e., administered before the deviant behavior spreads or becomes more serious) and on-target (i.e., directed at the student who initiated the deviant behavior). If desists include timing or target mistakes, they will not be effective.

2. *Suggest Alternative Behavior* – When deviant behavior occurs, a teacher may demonstrate with-it-ness by diverting the attention of a disruptive student to an alternative behavior (e.g., "O.K. Bill, instead of getting angry, let's see if you can solve the problem by carefully following the four steps we just talked about.").

3. *Concurrent Praise* – The teacher may avoid direct confrontation with a student who is displaying deviant or off-task behavior, and still demonstrate with-it-ness, by using such behavior as a cue for concurrently praising the non-deviant behavior of other students.

4. *Description of Desirable Behavior* – The teacher describes, or has the off-task student describe, the desirable behavior that

the pupil usually exhibits or should exhibit in place of the on-going deviant or off-task behavior (e.g., "What is the classroom rule about talking loudly during seat-work periods?").

By using one or more of these four skills, teachers can demonstrate to their students that they know what is going on in the classroom, and that certain behaviors simply are not acceptable.

Smoothness of Transitions is another very important Kounin teaching variable. The classroom management techniques used by teachers can facilitate or interfere with the smooth transition from one classroom activity to another. In Kounin's (1977) study, the ability of a teacher to deal with classroom disruptions in ways which did not interfere with ongoing classroom activities, and which led to smooth transitions between different topics, correlated .60 with pupil work involvement and .49 with freedom from deviancy.

Smoothness of transitions may be demonstrated by three important teaching skills (Borg, 1973).

1. *Delayed response* – In order to avoid problems of *stimulus boundedness* in which the teacher is deflected from the main classroom activity and reacts to some external stimulus unrelated to that activity, the teacher delays responding to an unrelated stimulus until a natural break occurs in the classroom activity (e.g., "I'll get your permission slip after we solve this problem, Ilene," as opposed to "Ilene, what is this? Oh, it's a note from home giving you permission to go on the field trip. You know I said to have these in yesterday. In the future would you please try to get your permission slips in on time?").

2. *Timely Interjection* – The teacher demonstrates smoothness by introducing information in a manner that minimizes interruption to the students' activity. This is to avoid sudden *thrusts* into the ongoing activities of learners that might indicate a complete disregard for students' concentration (e.g., During the middle of a class discussion of Canadian history, the teacher says "Oh, by the way, that reminds me. We still don't have a volunteer speaker for next week's public speaking forum. Can I please encourage you to consider this? O.K., now back to the Riel Rebellion.").

3. *Smooth Transition* – The specific skill of smooth transition refers to a teacher's actions in fully completing one activity

before moving on to the next (e.g., "So, we've seen how the norms of a particular society stem from the basic concerns for individual and species preservation. That concludes the discussion portion of today's social studies class. I'd like you now to apply the information we were just discussing to the 'think questions' contained in yesterday's hand-out."). Smooth transitions prevent *flip-flops* that occur if a teacher starts a new activity without bringing the original activity to a close, and then returns to the original activity (e.g., "Right, let's start today's 'think questions.' Oh, by the way, before you do that, I'll need to tell you a bit about different kinds of societies . . . . O.K., now let's get back to the 'think questions.'").

The principle underlying *Group Alerting*, a third important Kounin teaching variable, is that teacher behaviors designed to keep students alert will increase on-task behavior and reduce deviant behavior in the classroom. Kounin (1977) found that group alerting skills correlated .44 with freedom from deviant behavior during recitation (question-answer discussions between teacher and pupils) lessons.

The three specific teaching skills that contribute most to the demonstration of group alerting are positive questioning technique, positive recitation strategy and alerting cues (Borg, 1973).

1. *Positive Questioning Technique* – The teacher frames a question, pauses (3-5 seconds on the average) and then calls on a reciter. This ensures that all students think through the question. If a specific pupil is called upon before the question is framed, other students may tend to 'turn-off' and not attempt to reflect upon the question themselves.

2. *Positive Recitation Strategy* – The teacher calls on reciters at random, as opposed to using a predetermined sequence. If students know exactly when they will be called upon, they can 'turn-off' during safe times. Another disadvantage of predetermined questioning sequences is that more anxious students may tend to get very upset as they watch the often slow and painful approach of their turns. Teachers should be able to ensure that all pupils participate without adopting an inflexible talking pattern within the classroom.

3. *Alerting Cues* – Alerting cues include anything a teacher does to alert non-performers that they may be called upon (e.g., "Now, I want everyone to think about this as I might ask any

one of you to give the answer," or "Be thinking of other ways to do this, because you may get your chance after Terry has finished.").

Learner Accountability is the fourth major Kounin teaching variable that will be discussed in this chapter. The concept of learner accountability is based on the idea that when a teacher uses specific strategies to hold students accountable for their classroom activities, these management strategies will increase students' work involvement and reduce the overall frequency of disruptive behavior in the classroom. In Kounin's (1977) study, accountability skills correlated .49 with work involvement and .39 with freedom from deviancy during classroom recitation lessons. Both correlations were statistically reliable.

Three specific teaching skills that demonstrate learner accountability are goal-directed prompts, work showing and peer involvement (Borg, 1973).

1. *Goal-Directed Prompts* – The teacher asks questions that focus on a student's goal by asking about work plans or work progress (e.g., "Now, what is the first step, Sally?" or "Remember, you've done this before. What was the problem-solving plan you used then?" or "First of all, you must decide what it is you wish to do.").

2. *Work Showing* – The teacher holds students accountable for their work by having them show work or demonstrate skills or knowledge (e.g., ."Harry, let me see your work." or "Susan, come up to the board and show us how you worked the problem." or "I'd like you to tell the rest of the class what your library research revealed.").

3. *Peer Involvement* – The teacher involves students in the work of their peers by having them respond to another student's recitation or work activity (e.g., "O.K., Hal, what did you think of Teresa's answer? Can you add anything to it?" or "Joe's point seems to me to be a bit at odds with something you were saying a while ago, Kelvin. Do you see any inconsistencies in your positions?").

Before leaving this section, the reader should be acquainted briefly with three additional Kounin teaching variables – overlapping, momentum and variety. While these three variables are not as readily translated into specific teaching skills as are the four major Kounin variables of with-it-ness, smoothness, group alerting or learner accountability, their descriptions should help to guide the general group managerial performances of teachers in classrooms.

1. *Overlapping* refers to a teacher's ability to deal with two matters at the same time. According to Kounin, a teacher must be able to keep all pupils on-task while dealing with the disruptive actions of an individual student. Signaling a student reciter to continue, while delivering a 'soft' reprimand (a brief admonishment delivered quietly and directly, with physical proximity) to an off-task pupil, is a very simple example of overlapping.

2. *Momentum* may be defined as the absence of slowdowns in the forward motion of a learning activity. Teachers must learn to avoid overdwelling on substantive or procedural points when the giving of additional information or extended 'nagging' are not necessary to ensure that pupils can complete classroom tasks. Most learning activities lose their power if their natural momentum is severely disrupted (Arlin, 1979).

3. *Variety* refers to the programming of variations in classroom routines, lessons and activities. Using a variety of instructional strategies, assignments and curriculum materials can help avoid boredom and saturation; and can therefore increase work involvement and decrease deviancy. (Note that variety must be purposeful and instructionally sensible. Variety for variety's sake, which may be completely unrelated to instructional objectives, is not recommended.)

The following example illustrates the potential utility of Kounin's teaching skills in managing classrooms.

Wanda knew she could be a good teacher, but just couldn't seem to get things going smoothly in the grade eight classroom to which she had been assigned for her student teaching practicum. Her lesson plans were meticulously prepared, and Wanda's knowledge of the grade eight curriculum in her subject areas was excellent. Unfortunately, her lessons never seemed to go the way she had planned them, because students were often confused about what was expected of them and what the lesson was all about. They would often find themselves working at one thing when Wanda had already moved on to something else. The frustration felt by the pupils was starting to manifest itself in a variety of uncooperative, disruptive classroom behaviors. When Wanda's cooperating teacher described what she saw happening in the classroom, she and Wanda decided to do something about it right away. With her sponsor teacher's help, Wanda studied Kounin's and Borg's suggestions for making smooth transitions from one lesson activity or topic to another. Following a detailed discussion with her cooperating teacher of how the specific teaching skills of delayed response, timely interjection, and smooth transition could be used in the grade eight classroom, Wanda began to work these skills into her lesson plans, and to practice using them in actual class periods. The difference that her acquisition and use of these few basic skills made to the classroom learning environment was amazing. In just two or three days, student frustration and misbehavior had all but disappeared; pupils were actively engaged in classroom activities; and, most importantly from Wanda's point of view, Wanda was teaching with increased confidence, to the point where she was relaxing and interacting with the students in a generally more positive, encouraging manner.

Spaulding's systematic methods

According to Robert Spaulding (1983a, 1983b), teachers must learn to adapt their teaching strategies and styles to the *coping styles* of pupils in classroom contexts. From observations of over 1000 K-12 students, he has identified seven common and distinctive classroom coping styles exhibited by pupils in school classrooms. For current purposes, it is enough to know that four of these coping styles present obvious difficulties with respect to the promotion of student learning and the maintenance of appropriate classroom environments. Students who are *active aggressive* ("acting out"), *passive aggressive* ("delaying," "off-task"), *withdrawn* ("avoidant," "dreamy") and overly *peer dependent* ("distractable") do not learn well in typical classroom settings. Spaulding's goal in classroom management is to move children who present these coping styles to alternative forms of classroom behavior. In particular, Spaulding wants to promote student coping styles that are *socially integrative* ("assertive and task oriented") and *self-directed* ("self-motivated and task oriented"). Because some pupils may require considerable time to attain either or both of these desired classroom coping styles, a third less problematic style, *attentive* ("teacher oriented and compliant"), may be encouraged as a stepping stone to the two desired styles, especially in teacher-directed settings.

In order to assist pupils who currently are exhibiting any of the four maladaptive coping styles to acquire one of the three more adaptive coping styles, Spaulding suggests that teachers employ specific *treatment schedules*. Different treatment schedules are recommended for each type of pupil maladaptive coping style. Good and Brophy (1997) emphasize the need to build different assignments around common themes to allow students who differ in ability, achievement and behavior to address the same content at varying levels of sophistication. The treatment schedules vary with respect to such variables as the academic and social choices given to students, the location of work stations, the size of instructional groups, the amount of direct teacher supervision and the manner of the teacher's response to students' acting out, resistance and delay, day-dreaming and manipulation, as well as to students' socially acceptable and on-task behaviors. For example, active aggressive students are given no academic or social choices, and work alone at work stations or with a small number (1 to 5) of peers in instructional groups, all under close teacher supervision. Acting out and manipulative behavior directed at peers results in "time out," where the student is removed for a brief, set period of time to a quiet corner in the classroom or to an appropriately-supervised location outside of the classroom if necessary. Resistance, daydreaming and attempted manipulation of the teacher are ignored until they cease, and socially acceptable, on-task behavior is praised.

Peer dependent students are subjected to a similar treatment schedule, with the exception that they are permitted some limited social choices. Withdrawn pupils also are given some social choices, and their less severe acting out and manipulative behaviors are simply ignored. Passive aggressive students, on the other hand, are given some academic but no social choices, more subtle forms of teacher supervision, and have their socially acceptable and on-task behaviors noted rather than praised explicitly. Otherwise, they are treated similarly to active aggressive students.

Because classrooms contain many students, Spaulding suggests that once groups of students that exhibit specific coping styles have been identified, the delivery of appropriate treatment schedules to each of these different student groups be controlled through the use of *calendars*. Calendars show academic assignments, due dates, topics of study, upcoming activities, work locations and extra-credit options. The amount and type of direction, supervision and instruction to be provided by the teacher to each group of students also is indicated on the calendar, as are size of work groups, and amount and type of choice to be given. Each student is given a copy of the calendar under which he or she is operating. In primary grades, daily calendars are common. By grade four, weekly calendars are manageable, and by grade seven or eight, monthly schedules typically can be managed. The idealized result of appropriate use of such calendars is described by Spaulding (1983b).

> *After using such calendars for several years, students who exhibit [appropriate] coping styles will develop sufficient self-control, self-management skills, and motivation to be permitted to work in the school library or at other work stations outside the classroom – subject always to the loss of the privilege of choices for a day or a week if they fail to fulfill their academic obligations. These students become models for other students, who see the rewards that accrue to these responsible and task-oriented peers. Since the privilege of making choices requires self-control, self-management, completion of work in a timely fashion, and respect for the rights of others, rather than the attainment of a specific level of performance, any student who wishes to qualify for this privilege can do so.*

A very important use of calendars is that they can be shared with parents/guardians so that they too can understand more specifically the nature of the school experience proposed for their children. Such documents often can become important facilitators of productive exchanges between teachers, students, and parents/guardians.

Suggestions from research on teaching

A final set of recommendations for group management in classrooms to be considered in this chapter comes from the general research on teaching effectiveness. Such research, as has been seen in the work of Kounin and Spaulding, attempts to identify teaching skills, strategies and styles that are associated with high levels of student achievement, creativity and socially acceptable, educationally-productive classroom behaviors. In recent years, more experimental research has been conducted in which teachers have been taught to employ such methods in actual classroom contexts, and the achievement, creativity and/or classroom behaviors of children in these experimental classrooms have been compared to those of children in regular classrooms. While there inevitably is heated debate concerning what should count as desired achievement and so forth, research of this sort gradually is producing (subject to variability associated with different subjects, grade levels and student composition) a reasonable degree of consensus about the kinds of teaching methods and approaches that seem generally to promote high levels of student achievement and involvement, together with relatively low levels of disruption and management difficulties. One set of instructional methods frequently associated with the promotion of academic achievement and orderly classroom conduct commonly is referred to as *direct* or *explicit instruction*. A second set of instructional methods frequently associated with the promotion of academic achievement and orderly classroom conduct, especially when new subject matter is being presented, is referred to as *clarity*. A third set of instructional methods frequently associated with the promotion of pupil creativity and socially effective interactions goes under the general rubric of *cooperative teaching and learning*.

Direct instruction is described by Rosenshine and Stevens (1986) as most applicable to classroom lessons in traditional curriculum areas where the objective is for students to master a body of knowledge or learn a skill that can be taught in a step-by-step manner. It is least applicable to classroom lessons in which content to be learned is "ill-structured," or where the skills to be learned do not follow explicit steps. The major components in direct instruction include clear, explicit demonstrating/explaining of skills or content in small steps, with student practice after each step, guiding or coaching students during their initial practice attempts, and ensuring that all students obtain a high level of successful practice.

In direct instruction, teachers perform six basic instructional *functions* (Rosenshine & Stevens, 1986).

1. *Review*, check previous day's work (and re-teach if necessary).

2. *Present* new content/skills (providing objectives and overviews, clear descriptions and explanations, demonstrations, examples and highlights of important points) in small steps.

3. Arrange *guided* student *practice*, during which pupils are called upon to demonstrate their understanding in response to direct teacher questions, worksheets and brief practice exercises.

4. Provide correctives and *feedback* to student practice, giving additional informational feedback and explanations where required and descriptively praising appropriate student responses.

5. Arrange *independent* student *practice* during which students work alone or in small groups, and are held accountable for the seatwork or group work they accomplish.

6. Provide weekly and monthly *review* that involves systematic summaries of previously learned material, homework, frequent tests and re-teaching of material missed in tests/homework.

Brophy (1987), Good and Brophy (1997), Rosenshine and Stevens (1986) and others provide detailed discussions of direct instruction and its positive effects on both student achievement and classroom behavior. In particular, they point out that (within the subject matter limitations mentioned above) direct instruction is, for most students, one of the most effective means of ensuring appropriate student conduct in the group setting of the school classroom. When students are on-task and learning effectively, they are much less inclined toward disruptive, dysfunctional behavior. Popular manuals for teachers that provide specific instruction in the kinds of teaching skills and strategies that comprise direct instruction include those by Madeline Hunter (1981) and Carol Cummings (1980).

Clarity is described by Evertson, Emmer, Clements and Worsham (1994) as communicating information and directions in a clear, comprehensible manner that helps students learn faster and more successfully. Clarity helps students to understand teachers' directions and expectations for behavior. Clear instruction can result from the organization of information into coherent sequences, the use of an adequate number of illustrations or examples, precision and concreteness of expression, keeping in touch with student comprehension and the provision of enough practice to ensure mastery.

Evertson et al., (1994) illustrate five ways in which teachers can be clear in their instruction.

1. *Communicating lesson objectives* by telling students what they will be accountable for knowing or doing, and then reviewing key points or objectives at the end of a lesson.

2. *Presenting information systematically* by outlining the lesson sequence and sticking to it, summarizing previous points, breaking complex content into manageable portions and giving step-by-step directions.

3. *Being specific* by providing a variety of illustrations, using words students understand and (whenever possible) referring to concrete objects. Being specific also means stating what is and is not correct and why.

4. *Checking for understanding* by asking specific questions or obtaining work samples to be sure that students are ready to

move on, asking students to summarize main points to verify comprehension, and re-teaching content that students
find unclear.

5. *Providing for practice and feedback* by ensuring that students
have adequate practice so that critical objectives are mastered, checking work regularly, re-explaining needed concepts, and re-teaching when appropriate.

Cooperative teaching and learning is a general label that has been
applied to a variety of instructional methods that promote responsible, productive student learning in small group contexts. Working
cooperatively with peers appears to enhance positive attitudes
toward both subject matter and school in general, create positive
peer relationships and enhance students' self-esteem and creativity
(cf. Johnson, 1979, pp. 149-151). Three variants of cooperative learning now are commonly employed in many Canadian and American
classrooms. All are thought to contribute to effective classroom management to the extent that they make school learning more engaging
to many students, thus reducing the likelihood of disruptive behaviors in the classroom. These three types of cooperative learning are
(a) Spencer Kagan's (1990) *simple structure activities,* (b) Robert
Slavin's (1983) *extended structure approach* and (c) Johnson and
Johnson's (1985; Johnson, Johnson & Johnson-Holubec, 1990) *process
approach.*

Kagan's (1989) simple structure activities are exactly what they
claim to be: simple group activities that can be adapted to almost
any relatively open-ended curriculum content (i.e., material for
which there is no one correct response). In activities such as
"Roundtable," the teacher sets an open question (e.g., "List possible
causes of Canada's current constitutional crisis." or "What kinds of
feelings do you experience when you look at this painting by
Monet?"). Students in mixed-ability groups of three to five pupils
work together to respond to such questions by following prescribed,
structured steps. For example, in Roundtable, students make a list of
possible responses on a single sheet of paper, with each student contributing one response before passing it to the left. In another activity, called "Stars," students in study groups develop questions about
content previously presented by the teacher, then attempt to respond
to these questions by forming "quiz groups" consisting of students
from different study groups.

Robert Slavin's (1983) extended structure activities combine
cooperation and competition in game or tournament activities. In

"Team Games Tournament," the teacher presents material to the entire class, students then study the material in mixed-ability groups of four or five students, preparing for an end-of-the-week tournament. At the end-of-week tournament, students respond to questions on cards or ditto sheets prepared by the teacher, earning points for their team. Teachers try to ensure that groups, activities and rewards are arranged to maximize opportunities for success for all students.

While the activities proposed by Kagan, Slavin and others provide useful classroom structures for cooperative teaching and learning, the most extensive work in this area has been conducted by David Johnson and Roger Johnson at the University of Minnesota. The Johnsons' process approach describes a series of steps that teachers can follow to implement cooperative learning with almost any subject matter. They emphasize four basic elements in the process of cooperative teaching and learning.

1. *Promoting positive interdependence* by ensuring that students must be concerned about the performance of all members of the group. For example, in "Jigsaw," each member of a cooperative group is given one vital fact, clue or direction that must be considered together with other "parts of the puzzle" in order for the group to accomplish its task.

2. *Encouraging individual accountability*, through quizzes and other "calls for demonstration," so that each student is responsible for mastering the material.

3. *Fostering face-to-face interaction* among students in cooperative groups by arranging the physical structure of the groups so that all students can see, and interact directly with, all members of their group.

4. *Teaching collaborative skills* such as stating assignments and tasks, monitoring time limits, assigning group roles, and summarizing and evaluating group activities, so that students will have the necessary "process tools" to work together effectively.

Cooperative learning environments all incorporate the use of independent and interdependent group contingencies (Kauffman, Mostert, Trent & Hallahan, 1998; Smith & Laslett, 1993). A reinforcement contingency refers to a happening or occurrence in a classroom that is likely to influence student behavior. Reinforcement contingencies may focus on individuals or groups. Any group reinforcement contingency will involve some sort of peer pressure. However, peer pressure can be positive and encourage appropriate behavior. Kauffman, et al. (1998) describe three types of reinforcement contingencies that can be useful in managing classroom behavior.

Independent group contingencies are those that apply uniformly to each student regardless of the performance of a group. In this case, individuals who exhibit appropriate behavior will be appropriately rewarded with, for example, five minutes of free conversation time. This is a group contingency in that it applies to the entire class, yet it is independent in that one student's behavior does not affect any other student's consequences.

Dependent group contingencies are those under which rewards are available for all group members only when requirements are met by one member or a small subset of the group. This is often successful for hyperactive or overly-disruptive students, in that disruptive students may earn a reward for the entire class by paying attention and behaving appropriately. By using a dependent group contingency, a teacher can create a positive peer atmosphere where students may behave appropriately because they have something to gain by doing so – the approval of their peers and increased social status. A possible disadvantage to this approach is that the target student(s) may feel peer harassment from the other members of the class who may think that they are being denied an entitlement when the student fails to achieve the target behavior. This possibly may be controlled by considering carefully the nature of the group, the target student and the appropriate contingency.

Interdependent group contingencies are those in which a specific requirement for a reward applies to all members of the group, but in which the reward depends on the combined or total performance of the group, as well as the behaviors of individuals. Team sports are typically interdependent group contingencies, in that individuals contribute to the team's success, but it is the team that wins. In the same way, a teacher may allow the class to participate in a special activity after each student in the class completes an assignment successfully.

Although the preceding group contingencies all can encourage positive peer pressure, if not properly implemented, they also can result in negative peer pressure and coercion. Kauffman et al. (1998) suggest five ways to avoid negative peer pressure: (1) be certain that the performance standard you set is not too high for the target student or group, (2) emphasize reward for appropriate performance rather than punishment for undesirable behavior, (3) keep the group competition fair, (4) when using interdependent group contingencies, encourage everyone to participate, but do not require it and (5) make allowances for those who do not work well as part of any group that is constructed.

Cooperative teaching and learning, like direct instruction, is an approach to the effective teaching and management of classroom groups that has evolved from research on teaching that has been conducted over the last four decades. These approaches, like those of Kounin and Spaulding, assume that classroom disruptions and management difficulties will be minimized if students are actively engaged in the intellectual and social life of the classroom. To promote student engagement, teachers must develop teaching skills, strategies, attitudes, styles and routines that enable them to perform such teaching functions as setting clear, appropriate tasks, promoting and monitoring student engagement, reacting appropriately to student disengagement, and moving smoothly from one classroom activity to another. Hopefully, some of the descriptions of teaching methods contained in this chapter will provide a framework within which teachers can develop and refine that part of their classroom management repertoires that consists of good, basic teaching abilities.

Critique

As with other approaches to classroom management discussed in this book, the central premise undergirding group management approaches is sensible enough. It seems obvious that a "good" teacher is more likely to maintain student interest and enthusiasm, and that interested, enthusiastic students are less likely to disrupt classroom teaching and learning. The fact that Kounin, Spaulding and others have provided specific descriptions of some of the teaching skills and strategies that have been associated empirically with teaching success in a variety of real-life classroom settings lends clarity and ecological validity to their proposals for effective teaching and classroom management. Further, experimental tests, in which the classroom learning and behavior of students taught by teachers who employ such methods have been compared to the learning and behavior of students taught by teachers who do not employ such methods systematically, tend to support many of the claims made by these advocates of effective teaching and student group management.

Perhaps the most significant difficulty in implementing the teaching methods advocated by Kounin and others relates to the general absence of an overall theoretical framework for these methods. Whereas previously-encountered approaches to classroom management (like those of Rogers or Dreikurs) advocated classroom practices that were linked clearly to specific theories of human learning and educational development, the group management approaches considered in this chapter are essentially atheoretical. Aside from obvious propositions associating effective classroom management with effective teaching, there is little theoretical support for the variety of teaching skills, strategies and routines described. Rather than being derived from theory, these methods have been taken solely from empirical observations of classroom teaching and learning. While empirical support is clearly desirable, the ideal role of empirical work in psychology and education is to test theory. When no theories are tested, the results of empirical work come across as sets of largely disconnected pieces of information that may be difficult to integrate. Thus, teachers who read this chapter may attempt to develop and use a wide variety of empirically-supported classroom teaching and management methods, ranging from Kounin's with-it-ness to Spaulding's treatment schedules. However, without a theoretical framework consisting of principles that attempt to explain the underlying mechanisms by which such methods foster students' educational development, implementation of these methods may amount to little more than an attempt to learn and practice teaching skills without understanding why and how they might relate to the educational enterprise.

A particularly undesirable consequence of the atheoretical nature of the group management methods just discussed is a prescriptive fallacy that might attend attempts to use these methods in classroom contexts other than those in which they have been observed to work. Because a teaching method seems to be associated with desired pupil achievement and engagement in several classroom contexts in no way ensures that it will show similar associations in other classroom contexts. Classrooms differ dramatically in terms of student composition and abilities, teacher personalities and styles, social-cultural settings and so forth. Any of these variables, singly or in interaction, may prevent or alter relationships between teaching methods and student learning and behavior. When teaching methods are embedded in theoretical contexts, classroom teachers can use their understandings of relevant theoretical principles to determine the exact ways in which they should act in their classrooms so as to be consistent with these theoretical formulations. In the absence of such formulations, teachers have little choice but to attempt to do exactly what was done in classrooms in which prescribed teaching methods were developed and tested. If the classrooms of application differ in important ways from the classrooms of development, there is no reason to expect that results associated with the methods employed will be similar across these classrooms. For example, a teacher with a quick, bright classroom style might be able quickly to suggest an alternative behavior to a disruptive student (Kounin's with-it-ness) without drawing other students' attention away from an ongoing classroom lesson. On the other hand, a teacher with a less spontaneous style working in a special classroom with a group of highly distractable learners might need to develop other means of being "with-it." Unfortunately, in the absence of a set of theoretical propositions that attempt to state the principle of "with-it-ness," explain how it functions, and illustrate the variety of ways in which it might be implemented, it probably will be difficult for this second teacher to determine what practical teaching methods to employ. This is why some educators, including the authors of this book, continue to believe that "there is nothing more practical than good theory."

Nonetheless, so long as teachers who attempt to make use of the various suggestions for classroom management contained in this chapter understand that they inevitably will need to tailor these methods to their own classroom contexts, and develop understandings of the methods proposed that help them to perform such tailoring in sensible ways, the methods described may be quite helpful. The key is for teachers to treat such suggestions as illustrative possibilities rather than tight prescriptions for "good" teaching that can be copied without regard to contextual and other more philosophical (e.g., moral) considerations.

References

Arlin, M. (1979). Teacher transitions can disrupt time flow in classrooms. *American Educational Research Journal, 16*, 42-56

Borg, W.R. (Project Director) (1973). *Protocol Materials.* Utah Protocal Materials Project, Utah State University.

Borg, W.R., Kallenbach, W.W., Kelley, M.L. & Langer, P. (1968). *The minicourse: Rationale and use in the inservice education of teachers.* Paper presented at the meeting of the American Educational Research Association, Chicago.

Brophy, J. (1987). Synthesis of research on strategies for motivating students to learn. *Educational leadership, 45*, 40-48.

Brown, G. (1975). *Microteaching: A programme of teaching skills.* London: Methuen.

Cipani, E. (1998). *Classroom management for all teachers: 11 effective plans.* Upper Saddle River, NJ: Merrill.

Cooper, J.M. et al. (1977). *Classroom teaching skills: A handbook.* Lexington, MA: D.C. Heath.

Cummings, C. (1980). *Teaching makes a difference.* Edmonds, WA: Teaching Publishing.

Evertson, C.M., Emmer, E.T., Clements, B.S. & Worsham, M.E. (1994). *Classroom management for classroom teachers.* Englewood Cliffs, NJ: Allyn and Bacon.

Good, T. & Brophy, J. (1997). *Looking in classrooms (7th ed.).* New York: Harper and Row.

Hunter, M. (1981). *Increasing your teaching effectiveness.* Palo Alto, CA: Learning Institute.

Irving, O. & Martin, J. (1982). With-it-ness: The confusing variable. *American Educational Research Journal, 19*, 313-319.

Johnson, D. (1979). *Educational psychology.* Englewood Cliffs, NJ: Prentice-Hall.

Johnson, D. & Johnson, R. (1985). *Cooperative learning warmups, group strategies, and group activities.* Edina, MN: Interaction Book Co.

Johnson, D., Johnson, R. & Johnson-Holubec, E. (1990). *Cooperation in the classroom.* Edina, MN: Interaction Book Co.

Kagan, S. (1990). *Cooperative learning: Resources for teachers.* Laguna Niguel, CA: Resources for Teachers.

Kauffman, J.M., Mostert, M.P., Trent, S.C. & Hallahan, D.P. (1998). *Managing classroom behavior: A reflective case-based approach (2nd ed.).* Boston, MA: Allyn and Bacon.

Kounin, J.S. (1977). *Discipline and group management in classrooms.* New York: Kriegar.

Martin, J. (1981). *Mastering instruction.* (1981). Boston: Allyn and Bacon.

McCaslin, M.M. & Good, T.L. (1996). *Listening in Classrooms.* New York: Harper-Collins College.

Rosenshine, B. & Stevens, R. (1986). Teaching functions. In M.C. Wittrock (Ed.), *Handbook of research on teaching (3rd ed.)* (pp. 376-391). New York: Macmillan.

Slavin, R. (1983). *Cooperative learning.* New York: Longman.

Smith, C.J. & Laslett, R. (1993). *Effective classroom management: A teacher's guide.* New York: Routledge.

Spaulding, R.L. (1983a). A systematic approach to classroom discipline, Part 1. *Kappan*, September, 48-51.

Spaulding, R.L. (1983b). A systematic approach to classroom discipline, Part 2. *Kappan*, October, 132-136.

Spaulding, R.L. & Spaulding, C.L. (1982). *Research-based classroom management.* San Jose, CA: Maple Press.

Weinstein, C.S. (1996). *Secondary classroom management: Lessons from research and practice.* New York: McGraw-Hill.

Weinstein, C.S. & Mignano, A.J. (1993). *Elementary classroom management: Lessons from research and practice.* New York: McGraw-Hill.

Chapter Five
Behavior Modification

Overview and Rationale

Behavior modification is the practical application of the principles of operant learning to the task of aiding human change. It is undoubtedly the most researched, debated and discussed approach to classroom management. Literally hundreds of articles (see journals such as *Behavior Modification, Journal of Applied Behavior Analysis, Behavior Therapy*), scholarly texts (e.g., Jones & Jones, 1998; O'Leary & O'Leary, 1977; Thoresen, 1973) and "how-to" books (e.g., Alberto & Troutman, 1990; Cipani, 1998; Kazdin, 1989; Maher & Forman, 1987; Stone, 1990; Wielkiewicz, 1986) have appeared over the last four decades reporting the logic, principles, applications and effects of behavior modification in classroom settings.

The general aim of this chapter is to introduce readers to the basic principles of operant learning theory and the techniques of behavior modification in classrooms. It should be clear as the chapter unfolds, that behavior modification is a learning-teaching approach which possesses many elements essential for good classroom management. You do not have to be a "card-carrying" behaviorist to appreciate and use many of the ideas and techniques discussed. Methods of behavioral modification can be used to help teachers better understand students' behavior and improve it by applying consistent positive and logical consequences (Jones & Jones, 1998).

In gaining an understanding of the theoretical underpinnings of various practices of behavior modification it is necessary to consider the question, "What is learning?" This question is among the most complex encountered by educational psychologists and despite widespread disputation, there are points of agreement. Most educational psychologists would agree that learning is a change in behavior, thought or feeling that is due to experience. However, there is far less accord on how learning occurs. This chapter is devoted to one perspective, that of operant learning theory. As a matter of emphasis, operant learning theory examines and explains factors which affect behaviors. Thoughts and feelings are de-emphasized in the hope of providing an analysis of human learning that is easily observed and verified.

Principles

Operant learning theory

All learning theories attempt to explain how humans change as the result of experience. In operant learning theory, it is held that learning results from the interaction between behavior and environment. *Behavior* refers to all actions a human being can perform. Thus, unlike other learning theories, the operant model makes no real distinctions between thoughts, motor behaviors and emotional responses. Thoughts and feelings are not ignored in the operant model, but neither are they viewed as essentially different from other forms of behavior (Creel, 1980).

Environment refers to all events, activities and situations which precede or follow upon the emission of a behavior. Environment, in the operant sense, not only includes inanimate objects such as desks, pens, watches, red socks, kitchens and circular shapes, but also the behaviors of other persons, such as smiles, frowns and comments. In classrooms, among the most influential sources of events that precede or follow students' behaviors are the behaviors of the teacher and fellow students. Such events comprise the social environment of classrooms and, in operant learning theory, are presumed to contribute to the rich and varied context that *shapes* the behaviors of individual students.

The relationship between behavior and environment can be thought of as a three-member sequence (or contingency): "A, B, C." "A" refers to the antecedent environment before a behavior occurs, "B" refers to a single occurrence of a specific behavior, and "C" refers to the environmental consequences produced by the behavior. Behaviors change environments. When a person does something, the situation after the behavior occurs is somewhat different from the situation present prior to the behavior. The word *operant* conveys the notion that behaviors operate directly on the environment to create changes.

The consequences that arise following behavior are very important in determining what happens to the operant (operating) behavior in the future. Some consequences strengthen behavior (make it more efficient and frequent); other consequences weaken behavior (make it less efficient and more infrequent). The change in behavior which results from the consequences that behaviors produce is called *learning*. In operant learning theory, learning is synonymous with behavior change.

The interaction between environment and behavior that engenders learning is *reciprocal*. Operant behavior is behavior that both creates consequences and is determined by the consequences it creates. In this sense, behavior is a function of environment, but environment is also a function of behavior. One could not exist without the other. Rather than being passive individuals controlled entirely by external environment, operant learning theory views human beings as active creators of the very environments that exert control upon them. The interaction between behaviors and environments is reciprocal (Bandura, 1978).

The reinforcement of behavior

Consequences that strengthen behavior are called *reinforcers*, and the learning process of behavior strengthening itself is called *reinforcement*. There are two kinds of reinforcement: (a) *positive reinforcement* and (b) *negative reinforcement*. Both kinds of reinforcement strengthen behavior. Reinforcement occurs when behaviors produce consequences that make those behaviors more likely to occur in the future. In *positive reinforcement*, the consequences produced are additions to the environment (most often of a pleasant variety). For example, a correct student response (behavior) that results in a friendly smile and comment from the teacher (environmental consequence) may increase the likelihood of the same student again responding correctly. If this is so, the teacher's smile and comment are positive reinforcers for the student's behavior of "correct answering," and the strengthening (learning) process involved is one of positive reinforcement.

In *negative reinforcement*, the consequences produced by behavior involve the removal of some aspect (usually aversive) of the environment. When a student who is being teased by other students withdraws from a peer group, the consequence of the withdrawal behavior is escape from a taunting environment. If this consequence increases the frequency of the student's withdrawal behavior, the cessation of the taunts by the student's peers may be viewed as a negative reinforcer, and the strengthening (learning) of withdrawal behavior involves the process of negative reinforcement. The key feature of negative reinforcement is that a behavior increases because it functions to avoid or escape an aversive situation.

When talking about positive and negative reinforcement, it is important to focus on the word reinforcement rather than upon the adjectives "positive" and "negative." All reinforcement operations strengthen behavior (increase its frequency and efficiency). Negative reinforcement is not to be confused with punishment. Negative reinforcement removes aversive environmental elements, therefore it tends to be perceived by the learner as a positive experience. Remember that the words "positive" and "negative," when used to describe types of reinforcement, have nothing to do with our everyday use of these words.

Extinction and punishment

Behavior may be weakened (reduced in its frequency and efficiency) by the learning processes of *extinction* and *punishment*. *Extinction* is simply the non-reinforcement of behavior. When behaviors consistently produce no discernable effects upon external environments, they are eventually discontinued. The weakening effects of extinction can be illustrated by considering an example of the attention-seeking behavior of an elementary school student who constantly interrupts with calls of "Teacher, teacher!" Usually, these interruptions will gradually decrease if the teacher completely ignores such calls and proceeds with the instructional duties at hand. The typical reinforcer for such behavior is immediate teacher attention. When this is withheld, the behaviors fail to produce reinforcers, and become weaker and weaker, eventually disappearing altogether.

Punishment also serves to weaken behavior. There are two kinds of punishment. *Punishment type 1* occurs when the consequences produced by behavior are additions to the environment (usually aversive) and function to weaken the behavior that produced them. A high school student who answers several questions in class may be ridiculed by fellow students. If such peer derision results in a decrease in the student's responses to future questions, then the peer derision is acting as a type 1 punishment.

Punishment type 2 occurs when the consequence produced by behavior leads to the removal of some aspect of the environment (usually pleasant) that weakens future behavior. In the previous example of the high school student, if the peer group had not openly ridiculed, but had simply withdrawn any friendly contact with the student, the weakening process involved would be punishment type 2. Rather than aversive elements being added to the environment as a consequence of the student's behavior (punishment type 1), the peer group has withdrawn its friendship as a consequence (punishment type 2).

While both punishment and extinction weaken behavior, the more general impact of these operations on the learner can be quite different. Punishment can produce emotional side-effects that are quite incompatible with a positive learning program. This aspect of punishment will be more fully explored in a subsequent section of this chapter.

Having described the general operant learning processes that create behavior change (either weakening or strengthening behavior), it is important to point out that operant learning is very individualized. While processes of reinforcement, extinction and punishment operate on the behaviors of all of us, they do so in very different ways. What constitutes a reinforcer for one individual does not necessarily constitute a reinforcer for a second person, let alone a third or a fourth. Similarly, punishers differ across people. While positive reinforcers are always perceived as pleasant or positive for the individual, likes and dislikes vary across different individuals. The same attention of a teacher may be highly reinforcing for one child, and highly punishing for another. Further, we all react differently at different times. Sometimes the watchful eye of a mother is very reinforcing for the "clowning" behavior of a child; at other times that same watchful eye may interfere and reduce significantly the exploratory behavior of the child.

Due to the great differences in environmental preferences across different people, and within the same person at different times and places, operant learning does not prescribe specific behavioral consequences that always act as reinforcers for all people at all times. Operant learning theory simply details general principles of learning that may assist teachers in examining the effects of their behavior on the behaviors of students (Alberto & Troutman, 1990; Wielkiewicz, 1986). By careful observation and recording of individual reactions and behaviors, teachers can develop effective management strategies for individual students. Teachers must be aware, however, that the formal elements of such strategies (the specific reinforcers employed) will vary across time, contexts, and students. An important skill in the successful implementation of behavior modification rests with analyzing what consequences produce what effects for which students.

Types of reinforcers

There are many different classes of reinforcers. *Material or tangible reinforcers* include such things as food, drinks and toys. *Social reinforcers* encompass the behaviors of other people such as smiles, laughs, physical contact and conversation. *Activity reinforcers* consist of such things as games, special lessons, free-play times and trips. Finally, *token reinforcers* are general reinforcers such as check marks, money, gold stars, trading stamps or poker chips that acquire reinforcing properties by association with material, social or activity reinforcers for which they can be exchanged. All of these types of reinforcers may be employed in classrooms for a variety of purposes.

Activity reinforcers are particularly useful in classrooms since they can be made to be instructional in nature. It is possible for children to acquire many skills and concepts while engaging in reinforcing activities as opposed to simply receiving smiles, gold stars and so forth. While material and token reinforcers in particular may sometimes be needed initially to bolster the reinforcing value of instructionally-relevant activity and social reinforcers, the former should generally be used on short-term bases and then only with learners for whom social and activity reinforcers are not effective.

Activity reinforcers can be determined by applying an heuristic known as *Premack's Principle* (Premack, 1965). Premack's principle states that any high-frequency activity can be used as a reinforcer for any lower-frequency activity. If, for example, Rochelle spends a great deal of her time listening to music, but very little time studying algebra, the activity of music-listening can be made contingent (dependent, in the sense that it will follow) upon periods of studying algebra. If this is done properly, according to Premack's principle, the music-listening activity will act as a reinforcer that will increase the frequency of Rochelle's studying behavior. Premack's principle provides teachers with a guide to determining effective reinforcers for individual students.

Shaping behavior

An operant learning principle central for teaching purposes is *shaping* or *successive approximation*. As the name suggests, *successive approximation* involves the learning of complex behaviors one small step at a time. The instructional principle which stems from successive approximation is "Teach for success." More formally, *shaping* is the gradual reinforcement of increasingly more complex forms of behavior. For example, children in grade one are often expected to sit quietly for periods of up to 20 minutes. Since children at this age typically have not learned to sit still for such periods of time, they cannot be expected to do so immediately. Requiring them to do so is almost bound to fail. What's worse is that when failure occurs, there is nothing to reinforce (no positive behavior to increase), and therefore little learning is possible.

The application of the shaping principle resolves such dilemmas by breaking down the complex behavior required into a series of smaller, more manageable steps. Children may be required initially to sit for only five minutes before being allowed a few minutes of free-play (the "free-play" activity is the reinforcer). Gradually, free-play can be made contingent upon progressively longer periods of quiet behavior – 7 minutes, 15 minutes, etc. – until the goal of 20 minutes is achieved. Gradually increasing behavioral requirements over time insures that reinforcers will be obtained and that their impact upon the learning of "quiet behavior" will be maximized.

When using successive approximation, it is important that teachers have clearly communicated what final or target behavior is desired (Wolfgang, 1995). Teachers then can reinforce students' behavior at each step as it gradually moves towards the target behavior. Pacing the successive approximation is important, in that it should not be too slow nor too fast. In this respect, students' behavioral responses are often the most reliable guide.

Shaping is a very flexible instructional principle (e.g., one good way to teach a child how to tie shoes is to set up the laces of 10 shoes in various degrees of tie-completion, and to permit the child to finish each tie moving from the "almost completed" shoe to the "not-even-started" shoe). It is basic to effective classroom behavior modification. In the final analysis, nothing reinforces like success. Experiencing success will lead students to raise their expectations and to set higher goals, whereas failure often leads to lower expectations and a reduced motivation to re-attempt learning tasks. Jones and Jones (1998) suggest that when students are monitored and assisted by a teacher, a success rate of 70 to 80 percent is desirable. However, when students work individually, a success rate of 95 to 100 percent is desirable. Of course, all of this implies that learning should be adjusted so that such rates of success are possible. Having said this, it is extremely important that learning tasks gradually are increased in difficulty and complexity to the point where reasonable, appropriate curriculum goals eventually are achieved.

Schedules of reinforcement

It would be difficult to apply operant learning principles to classroom management if every single occurrence of a desired behavior had to be reinforced in order for learning to occur. In classrooms of 30 children, such individualized instruction seldom is possible. Fortunately, behaviors can be learned in accordance with various schedules of reinforcement.

There are two broad classifications of reinforcement schedules: (a) *continuous* and (b) *intermittent. Continuous schedules* provide reinforcers for every single emission of a behavior – "one response, one reinforcer" is the rule.

Intermittent schedules provide reinforcers on the basis of response ratios or intervals of time. In a *ratio schedule*, a teacher might respond positively to a child who answers several arithmetic problems correctly – the greater the number of correct problem responses to a single social reinforcer, the higher the ratio schedule. In an *interval schedule*, a teacher may reinforce a child for several minutes of good classroom conduct – the longer the time interval required, the greater the interval schedule. Intermittent schedules, whether they are ratio or interval, may be either fixed or variable. In *fixed schedules*, the ratio of responses to reinforcers, or the length of time interval required for reinforcement, is static (e.g., 8 problem responses to 1 reinforcer; 20 minutes good conduct required for 1 reinforcer). In *variable schedules*, ratios or time intervals vary over time and are unpredictable. In the case of variable schedules, ratios or time intervals are expressed as averages (e.g., an average of 8 problem responses to 1 reinforcer; an average of 20 minutes good conduct required for 1 reinforcer).

Different schedules of reinforcement produce different long-term effects on behavior. New behaviors that are reinforced on a continuous schedule will be learned more quickly. Unfortunately, such behavior also extinguishes quickly when reinforcement is removed. Conversely, new behaviors that are reinforced on an intermittent schedule are learned more slowly, but are also less likely to extinguish rapidly when reinforcement is removed. The different effects of various schedules of reinforcement have important implications for teaching practices. When attempting to teach students new behaviors, reinforcement should be used continuously. This will help ensure rapid acquisition of the target behavior. Once the behavior is firmly in place, teachers should move to an intermittent schedule of reinforcement. This will enhance the permanence of the newly acquired behavior (see Baer, Blount, Detrich & Stokes, 1987, and Wolfgang, 1995, for examples of the effects of different schedules of reinforcement).

Techniques and Applications

From the perspective of behavior modification, the essential task of management in classrooms involves the strengthening of socially and academically productive ("on-task") behaviors through the use of positive reinforcement. An equally important task for the teacher is systematically to weaken disruptive or inattentive ("off-task") behaviors by the use of extinction or mild punishment. The specific on-task or off-task behaviors addressed by any behavior modification program are called *target behaviors*.

Differential reinforcement

The most common type of behavior modification program combines positive reinforcement and extinction contingencies. When used in this combined form, the strategy is called differential reinforcement. In order to teach a specific classroom behavior using this basic strategy, teachers attend positively to the behavior they wish to occur more often, and systematically ignore the occurrence of competing off-task behaviors. For example, in order to maintain a positive learning environment, teachers usually insist that students raise their hands and wait to be called upon during classroom discussions, as opposed to blurting out responses that interrupt the responses of others. A teacher can achieve these targeted behavior goals by interacting positively with those students who raise their hands, and by completely ignoring interrupting behaviors. If the teacher is consistent in this approach over time, the positively-reinforced behaviors should increase in frequency while the ignored behaviors should decrease.

It is interesting to note that by reacting negatively to certain behaviors such as "interrupting," in the previous example, teachers often end up unintentionally reinforcing the very behaviors they wish to discourage (Becker, Englemann, & Thomas, 1971). Teacher attention, even if intended to be negative and punishing, is often very reinforcing. Indeed, if students are able to receive more attention, or to produce a greater reaction on the part of the teacher (which their peers may find amusing) by behaving disruptively rather than productively, they will tend to do so. What are generally considered to be "negative" reactions by a teacher can still function as positive reinforcers. It is unfortunate that sometimes teachers, in their very efforts to solve behavior problems in their classrooms, may actually promote them.

The key to differential reinforcement, sometimes called an *attention-ignorance strategy*, is to attend systematically to on-task behaviors and to ignore off-task behaviors. When such a strategy is implemented, it often means doing exactly the opposite of what a teacher is presently doing. Teachers often find themselves (without necessarily intending to do so) interacting with children when they are misbehaving, and ignoring them when they are "being good" (Jones, 1980). This course of teacher action is to some extent understandable; students are more noticeable when they disrupt classroom activities. Despite this quite natural tendency of teachers, it should be remembered that it is far better to catch students behaving in the way you desire, than to allocate the majority of your attention to inappropriate behavior. "Catch them being good" is a useful motto.

In order for teachers to attend to behaviors important to efficient learning, and to ignore behaviors incompatible with this goal, they often must learn to be most active when "things are going well" and least active when "things are mildly disruptive." (Very serious forms of disruptive behavior are excluded from this basic attention-ignorance strategy. Methods for dealing with these behaviors will be discussed later.)

An important teaching skill in attending effectively to appropriate student behavior is the ability to employ *descriptive praise* contingent upon on-task behavior (Becker, Englemann, & Thomas, 1971; Good & Brophy, 1997; Wolgang, 1995). Teachers who use descriptive praise verbally describe the appropriate or on-task behavior of a student and explain why it is appropriate by linking it to its consequence. For example, when children give correct answers, responses such as "That's right, you've remembered to add the columns from right to left and to carry-over the second digit in each of the column totals" or "That answer really shows that you understand how Shakespeare was influenced by the social-political context of his times," are useful descriptive praise responses. Notice that, while comments such as "Great," "Wonderful," or "Excellent" may sometimes function as reinforcers, descriptive praise provides more specific information and feedback about target behaviors to the student and consequently is more reinforcing for most learners. Wolfgang (1995) suggests that praise must be descriptive and specific. Comments such as "good work" or "nice job" are too vague. A teacher's comments should directly address the target behavior – e.g., "You did an excellent job remaining on task while I was working with the others. Keep it up"!

Praising techniques may also be used differently when teaching primary as opposed to secondary students (Wolfgang, 1995). Students in primary classrooms may require frequent praise that is public and genuine, whereas praise within secondary classrooms probably should be given less publicly and more quietly, out of the hearing range of peers so as to reduce possible embarrassment.

The effectiveness of descriptive praise may be contingent on two factors. First, correlations between teachers' rate of praise and students' learning or behavioral gains are not significant enough to be of practical importance (Good & Brophy, 1997). This may imply that the key to the effectiveness of praise as a reinforcer lies in its quality and appropriateness rather than in its frequency. Second, the purpose of descriptive praise should be to draw attention to the students' efforts and accomplishments rather than to their role in pleasing the teacher. Such praise will help students to establish an internal attribution for their successful learning or behavior and may lead to increased intrinsic motivation.

Despite the common-sense appeal of using descriptive praise in classrooms, research suggests that many teachers are infrequent and imprecise in their praise of students (see Anderson, Everston & Brophy, 1979; Brophy, 1981; Wyatt & Hawkins, 1987). From the perspective of behavioral learning, ambiguity induced by non-contingent and non-specific use of praise impedes, if not undermines totally, student learning.

Teachers' ignoring off-task learner behaviors is, like descriptive praise for on-task responses, a definite teaching skill. Ignorance reactions completely fail to recognize the behaviors to which they are directed. When in the act of ignoring, a teacher simply continues with what he or she was doing prior to the occurrence of the off-task behavior. Such complete lack of response takes practice and a good deal of self-control, but is essential if extinction of off-task behavior is to occur as a result of using the basic attention-ignorance strategy.

Teachers' use of ignoring strategies is often put to considerable test by students. It is not unusual for students to increase momentarily the intensity or frequency of their inappropriate behavior when teachers begin to ignore the behavior. In common terms, students often want to "up the ante" when extinction is first used. In psychological language, this phenomenon is called an *extinction burst*.

Extinction bursts present a number of problems for teachers. First, teachers may abandon extinction procedures when they encounter an initial increase in inappropriate student behavior. If this occurs, an otherwise effective long-term strategy will have been thwarted by the student. Second, and perhaps more importantly, teachers who begin to attend to a student following an extinction burst will reinforce a higher rate of inappropriate behavior. Teachers who give into extinction bursts communicate that even higher rates of misconduct are necessary before teacher attention is given (Jones, 1987).

Obviously, not all things students do in classrooms can be ignored. When behaviors are self-injurious or physically harmful to other students, or when behaviors are so frequent as to be overly disruptive to the entire class, extinction by ignorance is not the teaching strategy of choice. When such behaviors occur, the strengthening-weakening process of behavior modification can best be achieved by combining positive reinforcement of on-task behavior with mild punishment of extreme off-task behavior (Smith & Laslett, 1993; Walker, 1979). This reinforcement-punishment strategy should, however, only be used under special circumstances, and then only in a careful and sensitive manner. Smith and Misra (1992) suggest that the use of extinction in combination with social reinforcers that facilitate acquisition of appropriate alternatives is a particularly effective strategy.

The limits of punishment

In order to understand fully the problems associated with a reinforcement-punishment strategy, it is necessary to examine the practical effects of punishment. There are four side-effects of punishment, particularly punishment type 1, which demand that its use be restricted.

1. Punishment, while it may teach students what they should not do, does not teach students what they should do. It is often assumed that if we punish students for leaving their seats during work periods, they will learn to work productively in class. This is not necessarily so. Effective punishment of out-of-seat behavior may teach students not to leave their seats, but it will not teach them to sit down, attend to tasks and complete them satisfactorily. Punishment alone is not a positive learning strategy. The real danger here is the assumption that if we punish disruptive behaviors, productive actions automatically will occur. Productive actions must be taught directly through the use of positive reinforcing strategies. Learners must be taught what to do. Punishment may simply lead to student inactivity and withdrawal, or behaving appropriately only when the teacher is present and there is a chance of being punished. These side-effects are hardly justifiable educational goals.

2. Punishment will often generalize to the agent and setting of punishment. Thus, a second problem with punishment, especially when employed in the absence of positive reinforcement for on-task behaviors, is that it can make the teacher and classroom aversive to the learner who receives it. When people are punished, they learn to avoid people and places associated with punishment (Thomas, 1980). Avoidance of the teacher and classroom (whether through actual tardiness and absenteeism, or through more subtle forms of daydreaming and inattention) makes learning almost impossible.

3. Punishment models aggression. It teaches (if it teaches anything other than passivity) subjugation by force. Students who observe punishing interactions tend to be more punitive in their personal relationships. An overemphasis on punishment as a means of solving problems can prevent the teaching of more positive forms of social interaction and problem-solving.

4. Punishment may teach students to avoid getting caught. Students who have been punished may suppress their behavior only in the presence of the teacher who administered the punishment (Smith & Laslett, 1993). The undesired behavior may, in fact, resume in another classroom or other environment. Furthermore, students may also engage in

lying and deception in order to avoid both punishment and responsibility.

In a more pervasive way, the consistent use of punishment soon leads to the creation of a coercive social system in the classroom. Teachers who use punishment are reinforced by the immediate compliance of students. Students, as they witness the punitive acts of the teacher, may imitate such acts in their interaction with other students. This of course, leads to further use of punishment by the teacher, which further models aggressive social interaction. As these elements of aggressive teacher and student behavior interact, the social system becomes one based primarily upon mutual coercion.

Despite the problems associated with the use of punishment, it is, nonetheless, sometimes necessary under conditions of physical danger and excessive disruption. In such circumstances, teachers must intervene in order to safeguard the welfare of all the learners under their charge. Such interventions most often involve consequences that are somewhat punishing in nature. The point here is to ensure that the punishment used is as mild as possible (usually type 2), that it is never used without concomitant positive reinforcement of appropriate behaviors when those occur, and that it is never used without a warning signal which gives students the opportunity of avoiding the actual onset of punishment (Becker, Englemann & Thomas, 1971).

Faced with a dangerous or excessively disruptive action, the teacher should remain calm and deliver a clear command that such activity is to stop immediately. If this warning is not heeded, the teacher should proceed very calmly and professionally to take preventive actions that may involve such punishers as the removal of the student from the classroom. The mildest, acceptable forms of punishment that are effective should be employed. [Teachers always should be informed thoroughly about school, ethical and legal constraints relevant to their use of any such punishers.] The teacher should always follow the pattern of warning first (including a brief pause afterward to give students time to comply) and punishing only after noncompliance. Strong type 1 punishers such as slaps, abrasive language and loss of temper should always be avoided (Walker, 1979). The avoidance of such punishers lessens the negative side-effects associated with any punishment strategy. The advantages of warnings and punishers such as "time-out" (removal of the student involved from the immediate situation to a previously agreed upon quiet, non-stimulating area in or outside the classroom), and "loss of privileges" (e.g., loss of "free time," loss of points in a token system, etc.) are that these do not model undue aggression. They are unlikely to induce avoidance of the teacher, and are mild enough to avoid the creation of a negative learning environment.

Two final points on the effective use of punishment should be noted. First, the teacher and class all should know what the punishing consequences are for particular behaviors. Second, the teacher, once a warning has been issued, should follow through with the administration of the consequence if the aversive behavior continues. Consistency, clarity and calmness on the part of the teacher are key elements in effective classroom management.

Time-out procedures

Time-out is one form of punishment that deserves particular attention because of its mildness and overall effectiveness. The term "time-out" is derived from the longer phrase, "time-out from positive reinforcement," and is a form of punishment type 2. The process itself is defined as the removal of access to reinforcement following an unacceptable behavior. In classroom situations, time-out usually consists of isolating an excessively disruptive student for a short period of time following the occurrence of the disruption. In order for the time-out procedure to be effective, the classroom in which the disruptive behavior occurred must be reinforcing for the disruptive student in question. However, there are some children, perhaps those who are overly shy, dependent or frightened, for whom classroom settings, and the social interactions they contain, are not reinforcing. In these cases, time-out makes little sense because there is no positive environmental situation to remove contingent upon disruption.

A second condition that must be met if time-out is to achieve its intended effect of weakening behavior is that the time-out area itself must be relatively free of potential positive reinforcers. This does not mean that time-out areas need be done in "dungeon decor," but rather that relatively private, uncluttered, self-contained areas are preferable for this function to exciting interest centers, playrooms or hallways full of exciting passers-by.

To set up a time-out procedure, the teacher should designate a quiet area that meets the foregoing requirements, clearly specify to the student the relationship between this area and certain forms of unacceptable behavior, and follow the standard "warning-conse-quence" routine when disruptions of the stated type occur.

Students should be led as quietly and professionally as possible to the time-out room, and told that they are to stay there until they can settle down and behave in a manner appropriate for the class-room. After a set period of time, providing disruptive behaviors have subsided and the child is now calm, the child should be allowed to return to the classroom. Usually, the duration of time-out ranges from 5 to 10 minutes of silence, but the choice of time depends upon the severity of disruption, and the specific child and teacher involved. If disruptive behavior continues in the time-out area, the five or ten minute interval generally begins only after silence and calmness have been attained (see MacDonough & Forehand, 1973, for a detailed account of time-out procedures).

As a student requests to be readmitted to the classroom, or the time-out period has ended, teachers should offer a clear invitation to re-enter the classroom and rejoin the class activities (Good & Brophy, 1997). The previously emitted, undesired behavior should be forgot-ten, and the student's future efforts should be monitored. Here, the focus shifts from punishment of maladaptive behavior to reinforce-ment of positive effort.

Quiet reprimands

When giving warnings or implementing mild classroom punish-ers, the teacher should remain calm and collected. Quiet reprimands (quietly spoken but firm teacher commands directed to specific stu-dents) are much superior to loud, boisterous, angry teacher threats. Quiet reprimands not only prevent an unfortunate escalation and modeling of conflict, but also help ensure that the actions a teacher takes toward disruptive classroom behaviors do not inadvertently reinforce the very behaviors they are intended to weaken. Reprimands should also be brief (Abramowitz, O'Leary & Futtersak, 1988; Smith & Misra, 1992). Short reprimands often result in less off-task behavior, whereas "putting on a big show" can be a great rein-forcer for troublesome behavior, even if its tone is generally aversive.

When using quiet reprimands (see O'Leary & O'Leary, 1977), a teacher should move close enough to the offending child to ensure the reprimand is heard, and that there can be little mistake on the part of the child receiving the reprimand as to whom it is directed.

Selecting reinforcers

It should be clear from the foregoing discussions of punishment and ignorance procedures that all behavior weakening strategies, if they are to be effective, depend upon the presence of a good deal of positive reinforcement for on-task behaviors. Positive reinforcement is the essential ingredient of behavior modification. It teaches students what to do in a positive, supportive fashion. It is therefore of tremendous importance that teachers provide both, through their own behaviors and in the social and physical environment of the classroom, a great variety of positive reinforcers. Finding positive reinforcers is not difficult, but it must be done conscientiously and continuously.

Selection of reinforcing materials can be facilitated by asking children what curriculum items they like, and by observing learners' activities both inside and outside the classroom. By systematically observing the frequency and intensity of students' actions and the settings in which these occur, teachers can apply Premack's Principle to assist in the planning of reinforcing environments and programs. Material reinforcers such as games, puzzles, books, instructional magazines and pictures should be readily available for learners who satisfactorily complete academic tasks within appropriate social limits. Likely activity reinforcers such as field trips, free-time, student-planned periods or special classroom projects may be made available contingent upon set amounts of academic and social progress.

Classroom programs rich in special materials and activities allow teachers consistently to vary the type and amount of reinforcement. This makes it more likely that effective reinforcers will be available for individual children, and that learners will not become so bored or satiated with the same reinforcers that these lose their effectiveness. A second advantage gained from special activities in particular, is that when excessive disruptive behaviors occur, a mild form of punishment type 2 can be employed that involves loss of privilege (e.g., loss of ten minutes of a free-time period, loss of part of a game). The advantage of using punishment type 2 is that it does not involve an aversive addition to the learner's environment, and it is possible to set up systems where privileges can be regained as a consequence of appropriate on-task behavior. This latter point, in particular, ensures that punishment never occurs without positive reinforcement for appropriate and productive student actions (O'Leary & O'Leary, 1977).

Occasionally, a teacher is confronted with a student for whom potential activity or social reinforcers do not function as positive reinforcers. In other words, unlike most students, the productive behaviors of this particular learner are not strengthened by positive social interactions and activities. Reasons for this state of affairs may be numerous and varied, and in cases where a learner is particularly regressed, hostile or hyperactive, teachers are strongly advised to consult professional school psychologists, counselors, special educators or other resource specialists. In many cases, however, the student in question simply needs to learn the reinforcing nature of positive social contact. This often can be taught by pairing social attention and instructional activities with token reinforcers associated with more basic material rewards.

Token reinforcement

Due to the individual nature of reinforcers, and the practical difficulties associated with reinforcing the on-task behaviors of an entire classroom of students, the use of token reinforcers (that can be exchanged for a variety of material or activity reinforcers) is a viable strategy for implementing behavior modification in classroom contexts. The use of tokens permits efficient and effective use of classroom time and effort (Woolfolk & Nicolich, 1980). Tokens can be administered quickly, and the numbers of tokens earned or lost, as a result of various on- and off-task behaviors, may be recorded easily to provide the teacher with a record of individual students' progress. The removal of tokens contingent upon off-task behaviors (*response cost* – a form of punishment type 2) is an effective means of controlling disruptive activity (Kazdin, 1972). Once lost, such tokens can be earned back by appropriate on-task responses. Exchanges of tokens for other reinforcers can be confined to special times and places compatible with the timing of a solid classroom activity schedule or routine. In many respects, tokens operate much like currency operates in the everyday world outside the classroom.

While the literature on token reinforcement programs is extensive (e.g., Kazdin, 1977; Becker, 1986; Jones & Jones, 1998; Smith & Laslett, 1993: Smith & Misra, 1992) and should be consulted for specific assistance in designing such behavior modification systems, the general procedures are relatively straightforward. During the initial stages of a token program, tokens (chips, points, etc.) that can be traded in at specified times for appropriate material reinforcers (perhaps inexpensive toys, pictures, brightly-colored crayons, etc.) are given to the learner following the emission of specifically targeted on-task behaviors. It is crucial that tokens are never given without first giving descriptive praise. By consistently *pairing* the token reinforcement with social attention in the form of descriptive praise, the behavior of the teacher gradually will take on the reinforcing value of the token. Over time, as students learn the reinforcing value of such social interactions, the tokens gradually can be eliminated. Fading out tokens can be facilitated by gradually reducing the frequency of the praise and token reinforcement. As stated previously, reinforcement should be continuous at first, gradually becoming more intermittent. Notice in the foregoing discussion that the central purpose of the token system is to assist learners in acquiring social and academic interactions and reinforcers. If tokens are used in any other way, they seriously conflict with the overall goal of education to create effective, self-directed learners. The dependency involved in a token system should be seen as a temporary instructional aid to be discarded as quickly as possible (Bates, 1979).

Peer reinforcement

Applying the logic of behavior modification in group contexts like classrooms involves utilizing peer pressures to enhance, rather than detract from, a positive, well-managed learning environment (Woolfolk & Nicolich, 1980). To accomplish this end, teachers must learn to understand and to capitalize upon the potent influence learners exert upon each other's behaviors through the processes of peer reinforcement. In terms of the basic properties of determining reinforcement effectiveness, immediacy and quantity, peer reinforcement is perhaps the single most powerful instructional force available to the teacher.

There are many ways in which a teacher can make use of the behaviors of classmates to support individual behavior modification programs. Three such methods are particularly worth noting.

1. It is often essential to the success of an attention-ignorance strategy, for classroom peers to cooperate with the teacher in systematically ignoring disruptive off-task behaviors. Obviously, it will do little good for the teacher to ignore the "clowning" antics of a particular student if others around this individual are laughing and grinning at his or her every move. If approached in a reasonable and open fashion, students are generally quite willing to cooperate in accordance with the contingency arrangements of an individual modifi-

cation program. Classroom discussion strategies discussed in Chapter 3 are excellent vehicles for eliciting *peer coopera-tion*. Once students become familiar with the general nature of behavior modification programs, discussions can be left more open-ended and peers can have a greater hand in devising learning plans to assist each other. All plans to elic-it peer cooperation should be discussed openly and honest-ly with all learners in the classroom (Schonewille, Martin & Winne, 1978).

2. An important and useful way of motivating the kind of peer cooperation advocated in the preceding point is to arrange *group activity reinforcers* as the ultimate reinforcers for indi-viduals' programs. This approach, together with continued teacher praise for the cooperative teaching behavior of class-room peers, is particularly effective in avoiding possible jeal-ousies or hurt over the special attention temporarily given to learners with individual programs. When target behaviors are met or surpassed by individuals, the entire class partici-pates in a special event planned by the teacher and individ-ual program student. In this way peers are rewarded for their efforts to assist specific students in reaching their class-room learning goals, and successful individual program stu-dents obtain the special privilege of planning an event for the whole class.

3. *Peer tutoring systems* are also a useful means of deploying peer reinforcement to support individual learning programs. For certain tasks, learners may be assigned to work in pairs designed to operate as one-to-one teaching-learning sys-tems. Within each of these dyads, "teaching" students (already competent in the relevant tasks) can be taught to praise and attend positively to the successful on-task per-formances of their "student" partners. Tutoring systems are excellent ways to maximize the teaching potential of stu-dents. It often is desirable for learners to have individualized programs within which they can succeed in small, step-by-step units. It is not necessary for all students to be doing the same thing at the same time. Peer tutoring systems can turn a classic teaching problem – "too many students" – into a very workable solution – "all kinds of teachers."

Targeting reinforcement

A central concept in behavior modification is that teachers should react to specific behaviors rather than to the learner as a whole. While this may sound odd at first hearing, think for a moment of how most children, and adults for that matter, react to praise or criticism of their actions. In our society, it is extremely difficult for any of us to avoid associating praise or criticism of what we do with praise or criticism of what we are. When a teacher tells a student that they have given a good answer, it is not unusual for the student to interpret this as meaning that they are good. While such generalized effects of praise are not terribly amiss, confusion between criticism of a single action and criticism of the person are likely to be of more concern. It is fundamentally imperative that teachers learn to differentiate between the specific actions of learners and learners as individual people. If a teacher reacts consistently to learner behaviors with descriptive praise, as opposed to more generalized, non-specific statements such as "good," "bad," "correct," or "wrong," learners are helped to understand that while some of their actions may be inappropriate, they are always worthy of respect and affection.

When reprimanding or imposing behavioral penalties, teachers should act in ways that communicate to the learner that such consequences follow from certain inappropriate actions, not from their status as worthwhile people. One of the most important, and yet difficult, ways for teachers to convey this understanding is for teachers to react to specific behaviors rather than to specific students. A teacher must be able to administer a mild punishment (such as "time-out" or "loss of privilege") to a student who has been extremely disruptive at one moment, and to turn around and give the same student positive attention when the student is on-task. A teacher cannot afford to carry personal grudges against specific students. Learners should not be punished when they are behaving productively. To avoid this, teachers must recognize that their own temporary emotional reactions to students (particularly negative feelings) must be put aside and not allowed to interfere with the ongoing task of positively encouraging productive learning activities. It helps if the teacher can understand that most often when students misbehave, they are not purposefully being obnoxious or troublesome to the teacher, they simply have not learned more appropriate and agreeable interpersonal skills.

Contingency contracting

Contracting is a viable way for teachers to implement many of the principles of operant learning theory. Contingency contracting entails drawing up a written agreement between teacher and student. A contingency contract specifies student behaviors to be changed and consequences that will be earned when contract goals are met. The purpose of contracts is to establish and detail the contingent relationship between student behavioral change and consequences for behavioral change.

A carefully constructed contingency contract can be very effective in promoting positive change in students' behaviors (Homme, 1972). Unfortunately, many contracts fail to achieve this desired aim because they are constructed haphazardly or applied inconsistently. Caution should be taken when using contingency contracts to ensure that such arrangements act as rewards for doing something worthwhile, and are not perceived as bribes for not doing something inappropriate (Smith & Laslett, 1993). These and other common pitfalls can be avoided by proper planning and adherence to some general guidelines for developing contingency contracts with students. Contingencies can be implemented with groups of students. Teachers can reward a specific group of students for a certain group behavior (e.g., co-operative task completion). Both verbal and written contracts may be used. However, a written contract is often useful in that it can help students and teachers to remember terms of, and commitments to, their contract. It is helpful to view contracting as a three stage process: pre-contract planning, contract implementation, and behavior maintenance.

1. *Pre-contract Planning* – Without clear goals, little predictable change in student behavior can be expected through the use of contingency contracts. A necessary first step is for teachers to specify the aims of the contract. Teachers usually know in a general sense that some student behavior requires change. For example, they may recognize that Peter needs to work harder or that Mary must study more. These global descriptions, however, are not specific enough to serve as useful objectives in a contingency contract. They have to be *pinpointed*, that is, refined into specific targets for student change.

Pinpointing involves describing the physical features of the behavioral targets set in the contract. For example, a teacher interested in increasing on-task behavior, must specify what constituent behaviors indicate when a student is on-task. Without a clear idea of what behavioral change will look like, teachers are unlikely to recognize its occurrence. Similarly, students are unlikely to know how they should change their behavior to meet the objectives of the contract.

Complete definitions of target behaviors include the *locus of behavior* – what the behavior is directed toward. For example, in specifying appropriate social behavior, reference should be made to whom the behavior must be directed. In a similar way, when defining on-task behavior, it should be noted to what specific things (textbooks, worksheets and the like) the behavior is to be applied.

Other features of behavior may also require elaboration in clearly specified targets for change. Sometimes, the magnitude or intensity of the behavior must be stated. If, for example, a contract is developed to enhance a withdrawn student's verbal interaction with fellow students, it might be necessary to specify that the verbal interaction must be sustained and display a social intent, rather than merely being a perfunctory gesture.

Although clarity and specificity are hallmarks of a well-stated target behavior, other factors should be kept in mind. Contract goals ought to focus on positive behaviors that need to be increased, rather than negative behaviors that require reduction. Stating behaviors in positive terms gives the student something to work toward. Also, students are likely to experience more success with contracting if contracts specify a few target behaviors, rather than a long litany of behavior. As the student progresses through a series of contracts, the teacher can add new target behaviors to replace those achieved.

Perhaps the most difficult and critical element of pinpointing involves the setting of a realistic performance criterion. Expecting too much change in target behaviors usually results in frustration both for student and teacher. As a general rule, the performance criterion specified for target behaviors should ask for no more than a 20% change. For example, if the target behavior is assignment completion and the student currently completes 5 assignments per day, a realistic performance goal would be 6 assignments. Over a series of contracts, the performance criterion changes, but the rate of change should remain the same. In this way, the teacher employs the principle of shaping closer and closer approximations to the desired level of performance.

Another contract planning task involves selecting a reinforcement that can be given to the student when the terms of the contract are fulfilled. The simplest way to determine effective reinforcers is to ask the student what he or she would like to earn during the contract. Applying the Premack Principle may also be helpful in selecting a suitable reinforcement. Whatever method is used, it is advisable to select rewards that are natural to the classroom, such as free time.

2. *Contract Implementation* – With a clear target behavior in mind and a reinforcement selected, the teacher is in a position to draw up the contract. The contract need not be overly legalistic or formal, but should clearly specify the target behavior, reinforcer and contingent relationship between the two. It is advisable that some negotiation about the terms of the contract take place between student and teacher. This will enhance the student's commitment to the contract. Of course, the teacher may well have to place limits on such negotiation.

Contracting should not be viewed as a static technique. When the student has fulfilled the contract goal for three consecutive days, the contract should be renegotiated and a new performance criterion set. During renegotiation, the teacher should praise the accomplishments of the student. Remember that the eventual goal is to replace contracts with the naturally occurring rewards of appropriate classroom behavior, such as teacher praise and the pride of accomplishment. In addition, the teacher should attempt to move from a continuous to an intermittent schedule of reinforcement to help ensure that the new behaviors are more permanent.

3. *Behavior Maintenance* – Few teachers, parents or principals would wish that contracting was a permanent part of every classroom. Most would agree that the best state of affairs occurs when students are self-directed and do not need the external support present in contingency contracting. Thus, a major challenge confronting teachers who use contracting with their students is the reduction and eventual elimination of students' reliance on contracts.

Once a student has achieved the terminal goal of a series of contracts, the major concern becomes one of behavior maintenance, that is, maintaining behavioral gains made during contracting. Many of the procedures recommended earlier will help maintain student behavior. Teachers who praise students' accomplishments during contracting will enhance behavioral maintenance. In addition, as contract goals are met, many of the natural contingencies of the classroom come into play. For example, with increasing on-task behavior, the student will experience many favorable consequences, such as higher achievement, parent and teacher recognition, and an enhanced feeling of mastery.

Behavioral maintenance also can be aided by teaching students to self-monitor and reward their own behaviors. This entails a form of self-contracting, in which students set goals, monitor their own progress and self-reward when goals are met. It should also be recognized that techniques such as self-contracting are valuable personal management skills. They mark the sorts of self-direction and autonomy that are major educational aims.

Guidelines for implementing behavior modification programs

Contingency contracting provides a useful curriculum device for implementing behavioral management approaches in classrooms. It represents but one of many kinds of behavior modification programs. Despite the diversity of behavior modification programs, all adhere to the following set of general principles for guiding their implementation.

1. Define the on- and off-task behaviors to be strengthened and weakened in precise behavioral terms. Avoid vague definitions such as "inattention" in favor of more exacting definitions such as "lack of eye contact with the teacher during classroom instructional periods." If all behaviors are defined very specifically it is much easier to discern when they are occurring and when specific consequences should be administered.

2. Select a small number of on- and off-task behaviors to be modified. Try to select those behaviors that are most fundamental to more advanced learning behaviors. For example, if a child doesn't attend and doesn't answer questions correctly, it is likely that incorrect answering follows from poor attention. In this case, the program should attend first to the prerequisite task of strengthening attentive behavior. This is a most efficient strategy since correcting a fundamental behavior will often render future modification of more sophisticated behaviors unnecessary. In this example, strengthening attention may lead directly to correct answer-

ing behavior without requiring an additional formal modification program.

3. Once target behaviors have been selected and defined, they should be observed and recorded systematically prior to the formulation of the specific modification program itself. Such careful monitoring and recording can yield invaluable information about the current frequency of target behaviors (called *baseline* frequency), the environmental contexts within which target behaviors occur, and potential reinforcers.

The accurate observation and recording of target behaviors demands considerable skill, diligence and practice. However, the time taken to obtain this information will result in a much more effective, individually-tailored program than would otherwise be possible, and usually saves time and effort in the long-run. Some target behaviors can be defined in ways that permit recording their occurrences as discrete events (e.g., "talking out of turn"). In these cases, the teacher (or an assistant) can make a single tally mark on a specially-constructed observation grid that indicates the occurrence of a single response. Response frequencies per observation session are obtained by adding the number of such tallies within each specific target behavior category used. These frequencies then can be graphed (plotting number of occurrences per session along the vertical axis, and observation sessions along the horizontal axis) to provide a clear visual representation of the baseline rates (strengths) of target behaviors. Observation sessions should be set after an initial determination of the approximate time periods during which target behaviors generally occur (e.g., some off-task behaviors will be limited to specific subject matter periods or times of day), and should be long enough to permit the collection of representative data. The total number of observation sessions spread across days should normally be five to ten, or enough to provide a stable indication of the pattern of the behavioral frequency.

In addition to collecting data on baseline rates of behavior, it is often useful to observe and note the actions of other students and the teacher before and after target behaviors occur. This information often can indicate what actions of others consistently precede and follow, and thus possibly cue and reinforce, targeted behaviors. Knowing what cues and reinforces off-task behaviors is the key to weakening them. Finally, general observations of individual student activities throughout the day can, by invoking Premack's Principle, give the teacher additional information about what potential reinforcers are effective for specific students and behaviors.

4. Having defined, selected and collected data on target behaviors, the teacher is in a position to plan the specific behavior modification intervention. The teacher now knows exactly what behaviors are to be dealt with, has a good idea of what reinforcers or punishers might be effective, and possesses information about the current strength of target behaviors against which the effectiveness of the intervention strategy can be determined.

At this stage, the teacher must consider whether an attention-ignoring or reinforcement-punishment system is most appropriate in a given situation. The teacher then must use the information that has been collected to set specific classroom rules, to decide on specific shaping schedules and to determine specific reinforcers and punishers appropriate to the learner. Specific goals (in terms of desired frequencies or number of occurrences of target behaviors for the program) also should be set at this stage.

5. The next step is to implement the modification program. All learners should be clearly informed of the nature, rationale and goals of the program, and how they might be able to assist (e.g., perhaps by not attending to disruptive behaviors of a classmate). Such information should be provided in language learners can comprehend readily, and any questions or misunderstandings should be discussed thoroughly and patiently. The overall goal of helping each other become effective learners should be emphasized, and cooperating students should be thanked sincerely for their assistance. Keeping everything "up-front" is always the best policy.

6. Finally, the teacher should periodically monitor the effects of the program by spot-checking and recording the occurrences of target behaviors. When specified goals are met, the teacher should reassess the situation and, if necessary, select a new and more advanced set of target behaviors for modification. If the program, after two weeks or so, is not producing the desired effects, go back over your program planning and implementation procedures, and analyze them in relation to the principles discussed in this chapter. In most cases, with a minimal amount of trial and error, changes can be made which will improve the program's efficacy.

Example

A practical illustration of how the foregoing sequence of steps can assist the classroom teacher in constructing behavior modification programs is provided in the following example.

Since the beginning of the current school year, Mr. Levine had become increasingly concerned with the troublesome classroom behaviors and lack of achievement demonstrated by one of his students – a 9-year-old boy named Randi. During lessons, Randi seemed inattentive, talked softly but incessantly to himself, "doodled" with pens and papers, and seldom began, let alone completed, assignments. Mr. Levine had often interrupted lessons to ask Randi to pay attention, had given Randi small tasks of reduced difficulty, and had often stood beside Randi's desk softly reminding him to pay attention and to make even the smallest attempt to work on assignments.

Outside class periods, Mr. Levine had tried to befriend Randi and to talk to him about his likes and dislikes, his attitudes toward school, and his perceptions of his own classroom behavior. When all of these efforts failed to lead to any improvements in Randi's classroom behaviors and work, Mr. Levine decided to become more systematic about his interactions with Randi.

Mr. Levine's first step was to observe carefully what Randi was presently doing, noting both off-task and on-task behaviors. Even though on-task behaviors seemed to occur infrequently, Mr. Levine tried to note any action on Randi's part that might be associated with productive learning. The following lists resulted:

Current Off-Task Behaviors:

1. muttering to self
2. playing with pens, papers, etc.
3. lack of eye contact with classroom speakers
4. non-compliance with task instructions ("doesn't begin assigned tasks")

Current On-Task Behaviors:

1. sometimes sits quietly
2. occasionally glances at teacher when he is speaking
3. very infrequently takes an initial look at a class assignment and/or begins to work at it.

Next, Mr. Levine selected two on-task behaviors for strengthening that he thought were most fundamental to effective classroom learning. Given Randi's current repertoire of classroom behaviors, Mr. Levine decided if Randi could maintain eye contact with the teacher when task instructions were being given, and could more consistently begin and complete very brief task assignments (which had been reduced in both length and difficulty), that reasonable initial progress would have been made. For the time being, Mr. Levine decided to ignore Randi's "muttering" and "doodling," because he felt if Randi was paying more attention, and was busier with task assignments, there would be less opportunity to engage in these other, off-task activities. Mr. Levine was also anxious not to attempt to do too much at once and run the risk of setting Randi up for failure.

Before deciding on the specific behavior modification strategy, Mr. Levine wanted to determine the current frequency with which Randi engaged in the target behaviors of "eye contact during task instructions," and "assignment initiation and completion." Mr. Levine asked the school counselor to help collect data on Randi's current performance of the targeted behaviors. The school counselor observed Mr. Levine's class for one hour (half an hour before morning recess, and half an hour following afternoon recess) each day for five consecutive school days.

In addition to recording the frequency of Randi's targeted on-task behaviors, the counselor tried to observe what Mr. Levine was doing when he gave task instructions, and subsequently when students were expected to work at task assignments. The counselor's observations confirmed that Randi seldom engaged in the targeted on-task behaviors. However, to the surprise of Mr. Levine, the counselor's recordings showed that Randi would often start task assignments, but would discontinue them almost as soon as he started. Consequently, assignment completion became a more important focus than assignment initiation. The counselor also observed that Mr. Levine often "nagged" at Randi to "get to work," and that when he did this, Randi would most often end up doing nothing (even though he might very briefly attend to the task immediately after being told to do so).

Mr. Levine now felt that he was in a position to plan an initial behavior modification program for himself and Randi. The specific objectives of the program would be (a) to increase Randi's attention (eye contact with the instructor) during task instructions, and (b) to increase Randi's rate of assignment completion (Mr. Levine realized that assignment completion assumed assignment initiation and now understood that Randi had little trouble beginning, but a great deal of trouble continuing and finishing). Reviewing what he now knew about the classroom interaction between himself and Randi with respect to these objectives, Mr. Levine decided to adopt a basic attention-ignorance strategy. He decided to refrain from "nagging" Randi when Randi was inattentive or not completing assignments. On these occasions, Mr. Levine felt that he could help himself to ignore Randi's off-task behaviors if he actively looked around the room to find another student who was paying attention and completing assigned work. This simple technique might help him to attend constructively to the productive learning behavior of another student and at the same time prevent him from "nagging" at Randi. The second step in Mr. Levine's basic attention-ignorance strategy was to attend to Randi with descriptive praise whenever Randi was maintaining eye contact during task instructions or actively working to complete assigned tasks. With respect to task completion, Mr. Levine decided to make a special point of breaking complex tasks down into series of smaller tasks so that he could descriptively praise Randi upon the completion of each step.

Before beginning the program, Mr. Levine discussed the plan with Randi. Mr. Levine described the target behaviors and how he would help Randi learn these behaviors so that he could become an more effective learner. Mr. Levine then explained the importance of attending to task instructions and completing task assignments to the class as a whole, and said that he would be making a special effort to help Randi and others in the class to learn to follow instructions and to complete assignments. After the program had begun, the school counselor continued to record Randi's target behaviors for an hour every other day. When the school counselor was unavailable, Mr. Levine recorded his own observations using a small wrist counter (borrowed from his golf bag) to keep track of total frequency counts.

Both Mr. Levine's own observations and those of the counselor helped Mr. Levine to evaluate his own performance in relation to the planned program. At first, it was very difficult for him to refrain from nagging Randi. However, with some practice and feedback from the counsellor Mr. Levine was able to become more consistent in offering his attention only when Randi was on-task.

After four weeks, it was obvious that the frequency of Randi's on-task behaviors had increased to the point where he was now attending to task instructions regularly and completing over 50% of his assignments. Encouraged by these changes, Randi and Mr. Levine talked together about where they could go from here. It was agreed that they would continue to work together to improve the completion of slightly more complex tasks. Coincidentally, Randi's "muttering" and "doodling" had almost disappeared.

Critique

Ethical questions regarding the use, misuse and limits of management approaches are of utmost importance to the practice of classroom management. Schools are ethical communities in a pervasive and overarching way. As ethical communities, schools manifest implicit and explicit norms of conduct, standards of jurisprudence and ethical obligations. Every management technique, every classroom rule and every teacher action, as viewed within the ethical constraints imposed by schools, communities and society, reflects an ethical dimension.

Perhaps more than any other model of classroom management, behavior modification has given rise to ethical unease in the minds of some educators. The phrase "behavior modification" conveys to many teachers a meaning synonymous with manipulation. Further, the extensive use of rewards engenders among some educators fear that excessive inducement is being offered, and in the extreme, that students are being bribed. If the charge of manipulation is taken to mean that proponents of behavior modification attempt to change behavior, then behavior modification is most certainly a set of manipulative techniques. All approaches to classroom management are concerned with student change and its promotion. If manipulation is taken to mean that teachers use behavior modification to change students in insidious ways and toward self-serving ends, then it is the teacher who is manipulative, not the technique. In other words, it is the intentions and goals of the users of behavioral techniques that render such techniques manipulative. Behavior modification is simply a collection of teaching strategies and techniques based on research findings in the general area of operant learning. As such, it can, like any other approach, be used ethically or unethically, humanely or inhumanely, autocratically or democratically.

The extensive use of rewards in behavior modification perhaps invites the accusation that it is a form of bribery; yet again it must be noted that this concern may confuse subtle but critical distinctions. Bribery means to induce others, by means of reward, to behave unethically. Thus, we say quite legitimately that a judge who accepts a reward to dismiss a legal case against a patently guilty man is taking a bribe. The judge has been rewarded for an unethical act. In sharp contrast, behaviorists do not advocate that teachers use rewards to promote unethical behavior in students. That some teachers of very dubious character might do so is clearly a function of the nature of the teacher, not the nature of behavioral techniques. The determining factor in the ethical use of these techniques rests with the teacher, not with the technique.

Teachers sometimes feel uncomfortable with behavioral techniques in that they may appear unfair. For example, rewarding one student for completing homework may be seen as unfair to those who receive no such reward. Several points deserve consideration in this regard. First, most individually-based classroom management techniques prescribe the differential treatment of students. Indeed, the very heart of individual approaches both to management and instruction rests with meeting the needs of individuals. Accepting this, it is certainly permissible that teachers treat students differently in accordance with their needs.

More to the point, however, fairness must be seen as something more than equity in all things. In a larger sense, fairness means providing opportunities for all students to benefit from classroom instruction. In order to provide equal opportunity for learning, teachers must meet the individual needs of students. In so doing, extra time and extra inducement for some students would seem warranted. If teachers were to do otherwise, they would be diminishing opportunities for some students and this would certainly be unjust.

Nonetheless, there are valid questions to be raised regarding the relationship between the nature of behavior modification and particular educational aims. That behavior learning theory is concerned with overtly expressed behavior to the exclusion of distinctive cognitive and affective processes provides for its greatest strength but perhaps also for its greatest weakness. A focus on overt behavior furnishes clear and concise criteria for implementing and evaluating behavior modification programs. On the other hand, concern with the most obvious or accessible indicators of learning may not be the best way of meeting the educational aims we hold. Many of the things we wish learners to acquire, such as the ability to apply critical reason, and develop one's own understandings, attitudes and values, cannot always be reduced to observable behaviors, and more importantly, may actually precede and determine students' actions. To be a self-directed learner means to be cognitively proactive, rather than behaviorally reactive; to be able to engage reason, distinguish the subtleties of novel situations, consider alternatives, weigh consequences and then act in accordance with one's knowledge.

In light of educational aims of promoting reason, knowledge, and understanding, behavioral change is not enough. We want learners to become "response-able," able to respond to the previously unencountered as well as the familiar by behaving on the basis of rational reflection, not by simply reacting or performing according to past reinforcement contingencies. Thus, it would seem desirable that classroom contexts not only provide, but maximize individuals' opportunities to come to and construct understandings and beliefs about their behaviors and relevant subject matters. In so doing, emphases must be placed appropriately on cognitive and affective factors and their interrelationship with behaviors.

In the final analysis, operant learning theory may not be the best choice for dealing with the totality of classroom concerns. Nonetheless, behavior modification techniques can be effective for changing specific behaviors and as such, should be retained as an option in many teachers' repertoires of classroom management strategies. Further, there is nothing more or less intrinsically immoral or unethical about behavior modification than there is about any human interaction system. The responsibility is ultimately upon individual practitioners to ensure reasonable and ethical use.

References

Abramowitz, A.J., O'Leary, S.G. & Futtersak, M.W. (1988). The relative impact of long and short reprimands on children's off-task behavior in the classroom. *Behavior Therapy, 18,* 243-247.

Anderson, L., Evertson, C. & Brophy, J. (1979). An experimental study of effective teaching in first-grade reading groups. *Elementary School Journal, 79*(4), 193-223.

Alberto, P. & Troutman, A.C. (1990). *Applied behavior analysis for teachers (3rd. ed.)*. Columbus, OH: Merrill Publishing.

Baer, R.A., Blount, R.L., Detrich, R. & Stokes, T. (1987). Using intermittent reinforcement to program maintenance of verbal/nonverbal correspondence. *Journal of Applied Behavior Analysis, 20*(2), 179-184.

Bandura, A. (1978). The self system in reciprocal determinism. *American Psychologist, 33,* 344-358.

Bates, J.A. (1979). Extrinsic reward and intrinsic motivation: A review with implications for the classroom. *Review of Educational Research, 49,* 557-576.

Brophy, J. (1979). Teacher praise: A functional analysis. Review of *Educational Research, 51*(1), 5-32.

Becker, W.C. (1986). *Applied psychology for teachers: A behavioral cognitive approach.* Chicago: Science Research Associates.

Becker, W.C., Englemann, S. & Thomas, D.F. (1971). *Teaching: A course in applied psychology.* Chicago: Science Research Associates.

Cipani, E. (1998). *Classroom management for all teachers: 11 effective plans.* Upper Saddle River, NJ: Merrill.

Creel, R. (1980). Radical epiphenomenalism: B.F. Skinner's account of private events. *Behaviorism, 8,* 31-54.

Good, T. & Brophy, J. (1997). *Looking in classrooms (7th ed.).* New York: Harper and Row.

Homme, L. (1972). *How to use contingency contracting in the classroom.* Champaign, IL: Research Press.

Jones, V.F. (1980). *Adolescents with behavior problems: Strategies for teaching, counseling, and parent involvement.* Boston: Allyn and Bacon.

Jones, F.H. (1987). *Positive classroom discipline.* New York: McGraw-Hill.

Jones, V.F. & Jones, L.S. (1998). *Comprehensive classroom management: Motivating and managing students (5th ed.).* Boston: Allyn and Bacon.

Kazdin, A.E. (1972). Response cost: The removal of conditioned reinforcers for therapeutic change. *Behavior Therapy, 3,* 533-546.

Kazdin, A.E. (1977). *The token economy: A review and evaluation.* New York: Plenum.

Kazdin, A.E. (1989). *Behavior modification in applied settings (4th ed.).* Pacific Groves, CA: Brooks Cole Publishing.

MacDonough, T.S. & Forehand, R. (1973). Response-contingent time-out: Important parameters in behavior modification with children. *Journal of Behavior Therapy and Experimental Psychiatry, 4,* 231-236.

Maher, C.A & Forman, S.G. (1987). *A behavioral approach to education of children and youth.* Hillsdale, NJ: Erlbaum.

O'Leary, K.D. & O'Leary, S.G. (1977). *Classroom management: The successful use of behavior modification.* New York: Pergamon.

Premack, D. (1965). Reinforcement theory. In D. Levine (Ed.), *Nebraska symposium on motivation* (pp. 123-180). Lincoln: University of Nebraska Press.

Schonewille, J., Martin, J. & Winne, P.H. (1978). A comparison of punishment and positive reinforcement group contingencies in the modification of inappropriate classroom behavior. *Canadian Journal of Education, 3,* 21-26.

Smith, C.J. & Laslett, R. (1993). *Effective classroom management: A teacher's guide. (2nd ed.).* Routledge: New York.

Smith, M.A. & Misra, A. (1992). A comprehensive management system for students in regular classrooms. *The Elementary School Journal, 92*(3), 353-371.

Stone, L. (1990). *Managing difficult children in school.* Oxford: Blackwell.

Thomas, J.D. (1980). Agency and achievement: Self-management and self-regard. *Review of Educational Research, 50,* 213-240.

Thoresen, C.E. (Ed.). (1973). *Behavior modification in education.* N.S.S.E. Yearbook (Part I).

Walker, H.M. (1979). *The acting-out child: Coping with classroom disruption.* Boston: Allyn and Bacon.

Wielkiewicz, R.M. (1986). *Behavior management in schools: Principles and procedures.* New York: Pergamon Press.

Woolfgang, C.H. (1995). *Solving Discipline Problems: Methods and models for today's teachers. (3rd ed.).* Needham Heights, MA: Simon & Schuster.

Woolfolk, A.E. & Nicolich, L.M. (1980). *Educational psychology for teachers.* Englewood Cliffs, NJ: Prentice-Hall.

Wyatt, W.J. & Hawkins, R.P. (1987). Rates of teachers' verbal approval and disapproval: Relationship to grade level, classroom activity, student behavior, and teacher characteristics. *Behavior Modification, 11,* 27-51.

Chapter Six
Social Learning and
Cognitive Approaches

Overview and Rationale

In the previous chapter we explored one perspective on the nature of learning and extended its application to issues of classroom management. Concerned primarily with overt behaviors, operant learning theory explains learning as behavioral change. In this chapter you will be introduced to a different perspective, one that places considerable importance on covert cognitive events presumed to occur inside the minds of learners. In both social learning theory and cognitive learning theories, the emphasis is not on behavioral change per se but on those cognitive and motivational events that mediate and precipitate behavioral change.

In operant learning theory, learning is said to result from the reinforcing or punishing consequences of the behavior. But how can reinforcement or punishment cause learning if they only have effect *after* the behavior has taken place? In other words, in order for a behavior to be reinforced or punished, the behavior must be performed; and in order for it to be performed, the behavior must already have been learned. Clearly, behavioral contingencies like reinforcement and punishment can affect the future frequency with which behaviors will occur. However, what determines the actual type and form of behavior in the first place? As reinforcement and punishment only occur after a behavior has been learned, they can not be seen to account for learning itself (see Bruner, 1985). This brings us once again to the puzzle of how learning occurs.

In attempting to provide a solution to this puzzle, social learning and cognitive learning theories share a common focus on the ways that learners construct their own conceptions of things. According to these theories, learning springs from our capacity to use language and other symbolic systems to construe events. The understandings that are formed from such "construals" allow us to anticipate and evaluate the consequences of behaviors, prior to our acting (Bandura, 1986). Thus, in social and cognitive learning theories, behavior is viewed as a function of cognition.

The implication of this shift in emphasis from behavior to cognition is that teachers should be more concerned with influencing the conceptions and thinking strategies that learners use to guide their behaviors, than with influencing learners' behaviors directly. This perspective recommends instructional methods that help learners develop general learning strategies that hopefully then may be applied to a wide range of school and extracurricular topics, issues and problems. The instructional techniques used to teach students these general learning strategies are intended to help learners become their own teachers – to solve their own problems and to control their own social and academic behaviors in a responsible fashion (see Meichenbaum, 1985a; Zimmerman & Schunk,1989).

Chapter 6 begins by describing the essential principles of social learning theory. The chapter then moves to a consideration of a few fundamental principles of cognitive learning, and a discussion of ways that cognitive factors can serve to inform classroom practices. Next, some specific techniques for teaching general cognitive strategies will be described, with suggestions to assist teachers in developing these strategies in students, thus assisting learners to control their own classroom behaviors in a responsible manner.

Principles

Social learning theory

Social learning theory (see Bandura, 1969, 1977, 1986; Bandura and Walters, 1963; Rosenthal & Zimmerman, 1978) is based on the notion that much learning is accomplished by observing and imitating the behavior of others. Social learning theory presents a two-stage model of *observational* learning. In the first stage of the learning process, the *acquisition* phase, a learner acquires the actions of a *model* (i.e., another person) by observing the model. It is assumed that while observing, the *observer* (i.e., learner) commits images and verbal representations of the model's behaviors to memory. In the second stage of the learning process, the *performance* phase, the learner actually performs the modeled behavior. The distinction between acquisition and performance is very important. It is often the case that an action acquired through observation is never actually performed by the observer (Rosenthal & Zimmerman, 1978). For example, a student watching a video on constructing log cabins may cognitively learn the steps entailed (acquisition phase), even though he or she has yet to take axe in hand and actually perform the behaviors involved.

According to social learning theory, the learning of actual performances results from the sort of operant principles discussed in the previous chapter. Direct reinforcement and punishment moderate the strengthening or weakening of the performance of behaviors. However, during the acquisition phase of observational learning, a different type of reinforcement is at play.

Vicarious reinforcement

During the acquisition stage, vicarious reinforcement operates in much the same way as direct reinforcement operates during the performance stage. Vicarious reinforcement may be defined as the strengthening of a behavior resulting from observing a model being directly reinforced for that behavior. Vicarious reinforcement is derived from observing others and construing their experience as being reinforcing. For example, let's say Joe observes the teacher reinforcing Richard when Richard "tidies" his desk before leaving the classroom. By attending to the events and forming a cognitive representation of them (Richard's desk "tidying" and his being reinforced for it by the teacher), Joe becomes vicariously motivated to perform this same behavior at some future date because he has vicariously experienced reinforcing consequences for this behavior.

Just as direct consequences can strengthen or weaken behavioral performances, vicarious consequences can strengthen or weaken cognitive acquisition and subsequent likelihood of performance. If a model's actions are directly reinforced, the observer's cognitive acquisition will be strengthened. If a model's actions are directly punished or extinguished, the observer's cognitive acquisition will be weakened. To illustrate this latter point, a learner acquires much more information about, and motivation to perform the behavior of, "cheating on classroom assignments' if he or she observes classmates cheating and obtaining high marks, than if classmates are observed cheating, getting caught and losing marks. It should be noted that it is possible to speak about vicarious punishment and vicarious extinction as well as vicarious reinforcement (Bandura, 1977).

In fact, vicarious learning principles can in many respects be seen as parallel to direct operant learning principles. The important distinction is that vicarious learning principles operate during the acquisition stage to strengthen or weaken cognitive acquisition of modeled behaviors and their future likelihood of being performed. In contrast, direct operant principles operate during the performance phase to strengthen or weaken actual performance of modeled behaviors.

Vicarious reinforcement, through modeling, has two major learning effects. It *provides* cognitive *information* about specific modeled behaviors, and it *motivates* the observer to attempt to perform the modeled behaviors (Rosenthal & Zimmerman, 1978). The motivational effect of modeling is just as important as the informational effect. We not only learn what to do (and how to do it) from observing the actions of others, but we also may learn about the goals we want to accomplish. A good teacher must attend to both functions. The basketball coach who models a cross-over dribble and demonstrates how this behavior (in particular situations) can result in open shots and team points, helps players to understand and to work hard to develop this important basketball skill.

Vicarious reinforcement is also a source of information on which students might base their efficacy beliefs (Reeve, 1996). Efficacy beliefs may be defined as self-judgments of how well or poorly one will perform a task given the skills one possesses and the circumstances one faces (Bandura, 1993). When observers watch a model perform a behavior, they frequently imagine the effectiveness of their own performance on the same task. As a result, when the model fails at a task, the observer's personal efficacy expectations may decrease, and when the model succeeds, the observer's personal efficacy expectations may increase. These possible effects of vicarious reinforcement are especially likely when the observer has little experience with the task against which to balance vicarious judgments of personal task-specific efficacy (Schunk, 1989).

While modeling is an extremely powerful instructional approach, vicarious reinforcement, by itself, has one major limitation. It does not directly strengthen the actual performance of modeled behavior. It is exceedingly important to remember that while learners may be informed about and motivated to perform specific behaviors through modeling, direct operant reinforcement of the learners' actual performances is necessary if such performances are to be maintained and strengthened. Remember that social learning is a two-stage process.

There are four important elements in modeling (Woolfolk, 1995). First, the observer must give proper *attention* to the modeled behavior. Therefore, the instructor should ensure that the critical elements of the modeled behavior are salient to the observer. Presentation of the behavior must be clear and such important elements should be highlighted. Second, the observer must *retain* the required elements of the modeled behavior. The behavior is usually retained in a verbal or visual mental representation. Retention can be improved by the instructional arrangement of opportunities for mental rehearsal or explicit practice. Third, even if the relevant information is retained it is not necessarily performed efficiently. *Production* of the behavior may be dependent upon practice, feedback and coaching. Self-efficacy is important at this phase because it increases the motivation of a student to perform the behavior. Fourth, *motivation and reinforcement* increase the likelihood that a desired behavior will be used when the student encounters a novel situation. Students are more likely to be motivated and persist with new behaviors if they are positively reinforced (Ollendick, Dailey & Shapiro, 1983).

Research on modeling indicates that certain model characteristics are essential for strong observational learning (acquisition) effects. Some of the more important model characteristics that have been identified are (Kanfer & Goldstein, 1991; Kauffman, Mostert, Trent & Hallahan, 1998; Reeve, 1996):

1. Models who are competent and possess prestige in the eyes of the observer are more likely to facilitate positive acquisition effects.

2. Models who are viewed as being similar in important ways to the observer (e.g., same sex or ability level) are more likely to have an influential effect. Watching someone, who you believe shares your concerns or anxiety, successfully complete a task makes you believe that you can do the same.

3. Models who are regarded by the observer as warm and nurturing are more likely to produce positive acquisition effects.

4. A model who is too dissimilar to the observer, or whose behavior is far superior (or more sophisticated) than that presently possible for the observer will generally produce poor acquisition effects. In other words, models should be competent, but at a performance level not too far removed from that of the observer. Modeling instruction, like most other kinds of teaching, advocates increasing competency step-by-step. A "*slider*" model (i.e., one which presents progressively more difficult stages of performance) is strongly advocated.

5. *Multiple models* (using a number of different models with slightly different characteristics) are very effective in promoting acquisition learning. Where possible, a variety of "live" models is generally superior to a variety of "symbolic" models (e.g., videotaped models). However, symbolic models are very useful for self-study and for the acquisition of extremely complex behaviors, because they can be directly controlled by the learner (stopping and starting, replaying, etc.). Also, reliance on one model or small group of models may result in the class believing that the teacher has favorites who are the only ones who can fulfill the teacher's expectations. This possibility, if it occurs, can destroy the effectiveness of the models.

6. Efficacy beliefs may be strengthened more when observers watch models who struggle and cope to overcome task difficulties, than when observers watch expert models who perform perfectly.

In observational learning, learning by modeling requires forming verbal or imaginal (visual) cognitive representations that preserve information about events (Bandura, 1977, 1986). It is through such cognitive representations that behaviors can be organized, rehearsed and then performed. People's capacity to construct cognitive representations is a central tenet of social learning theory. As such, social learning theory can be considered a kind of cognitive theory.

Cognitive learning theory

Cognitivist theories of learning attempt to describe those changes or alterations in the elaboration or structure of information inside our heads that are believed to be prerequisites to any overt behavioral changes. Cognitive learning theory begins with the notion that learners construct meaning, thereby creating their own understandings of events. In cognitive terms, learning is an internally mediated process; not an externally mediated process in which individuals respond automatically to the sensory qualities of their environments. When confronted with an environmental stimulus (object, event, instruction, etc.), the learner *constructs meaning* for this stimulus by cognitively relating (with the assistance of personalized cognitive rules) the new information conveyed by the stimulus, to abstract and distinct memories and knowledge (verbal or imaginal) stored inside the learner's head (Ausubel, 1968). The task of learning is one of comprehending instructional events by actively relating them to existing cognitive structures often referred to as *prior knowledge*. The task of teaching is one of assisting the learner to perform these mental elaborations and revisions (i.e., the extensions to cognitive structures brought about by the assimilation of new information into existing structures, and the accommodation of cognitive structures to the inclusion of new information).

These processes of learning and teaching can be illustrated vividly by the case of a new resident trying to find her way about a downtown area entirely new to her. Over time, as a result of many cumulating experiences, she develops a conceptualization of the downtown area based upon her memories and partial memories of her experiences. In other words, she comes to possess a cognitive structure or "cognitive map" of the downtown center. At first, this structure is very sketchy, containing only images or verbal cues for a few main streets, signposts and landmarks, with little information relating them to one another, or to other, as yet undiscovered, routes, buildings and intersections. Nonetheless, each time she acquires a new set of experiences, our new resident actively relates these to her existing cognitive map, and each time she does this, her cognitive map (structure) is extended and fleshed-out (elaborated). Such changes and elaborations in her cognitive structure constitute her learning about the downtown area.

Of course, this natural learning process could be augmented by the instructional efforts of a long-time city resident who might volunteer to teach our newcomer. This "teacher" could assist the learning process of the new resident in many ways – by drawing maps, by driving her around and pointing out connections between different areas and alternate routes to the same destinations, by questioning her about her current understandings, by asking her how to get from A to B and then providing her with informational feedback about her answer, by providing her with simple mnemonics (memory aids) for street names, by telling her historical stories and anecdotes about particular sites and buildings that will cue their accurate recall and so forth. All of these teaching techniques help the learner to admit new information that expands her existing cognitive structure of the downtown city center.

In cognitive terms, *learning* may be defined as a *change in cognitive structure. Teaching* is the stimulation of relations between new information and existing cognitive structures through *the inducement of verbal or imaginal elaborations* (Smith, 1975). In other words, teaching is an activity that assists a learner to alter his or her cognitive structures.

A major implication of cognitive learning theory, is that each learner perceives and understands classroom occurrences in terms of their existing cognitive structures. Since cognitive structures are, in a sense, the sum total of each learner's previous experience (cognitively represented), it follows that different students will perceive and understand classroom events in different ways. Indeed, we should not be too surprised to discover that some students understand, and thus respond to, classroom instructions, rules and activities in ways that the teacher (operating from the framework of his or her own cognitive structures) did not intend. Such individual differences seem the very essence of learning and teaching. The teacher's task is to expand the cognitive structure of learners so that they can perceive and understand information in ways appropriate to specific situations and interactions (Smith, 1975). Unfortunately, this is not always an easy process, and if a student's understanding and interpretation of classroom information is too divorced from that of his or her teacher and peers, problems can be expected to occur. Such problems are usually manifested in classroom behaviors. For example, a student who is asked a difficult probing question by a teacher (who asks the question in an honest effort to help broaden the student's understanding) may perceive the teacher as "picking on me," and subsequently withdraw and pout (or alternately, "act-out") for the rest of the day.

Cognitive learning theory alerts teachers to problems of this kind and carries a strong admonition to teachers to tell students exactly what they are doing as teachers, why they are doing it and how what they are doing is intended to help students learn. Providing learners with such information (either through verbal explanations, modeling demonstrations or various forms of curricula) can help ensure that classroom information is not comprehended by learners in unintended manners.

Cognitive strategies

Living would be difficult, to say the least, if every situation required taking immediate action and personally suffering the consequences of those actions. If such were the case, it would be surprising if human beings could survive childhood. Fortunately, we are spared much trial and error learning by our capacity to invoke *cognitive strategies* to think through situations and plan prior to taking action. Learning to apply cognitive strategies is of tremendous adaptive significance.

Cognitive strategies can be thought of as collections of cognitive operations that individual learners can undertake themselves to facilitate purposeful matching of new information to existing cognitive structures, and to generate appropriate solutions to problems. The purpose in teaching cognitive strategies to learners is to provide them with thinking skills applicable (generalizable) to a range of specific situations, content domains and learning tasks. It is held that such strategies, if acquired, can move students toward the overall goal of self-directed learning (see Driscoll, 1994; Garcia & Pintrich, 1994; Meichenbaum, 1985a; Jones, Palincsar, Ogle & Carr, 1987; Mayer, 1987).

Specific cognitive strategies have been studied that assist learners in solving problems, coping with stressful situations and motivating their own learning. More will be said about such strategies in a subsequent section of this chapter.

Techniques and Applications

Modeling

An important practical advantage of modeling techniques over regular operant techniques is that the former can teach entirely novel behaviors, whereas the latter only can shape and strengthen behaviors already present. If a teacher wants to instruct a child in the use of a pencil sharpener, it would be silly to employ pure operant techniques. This would require that the teacher wait patiently until the child, through extensive trial and error, accidentally puts a pencil in the correct hole and simultaneously moves the sharpener's handle, at which time the teacher would reinforce this approximation of the desired pencil sharpening response. Obviously, use of shaping and direct positive reinforcement alone would require a great many learning trials and a great deal of time and effort. This is so because purely operant methods require a learner to emit some approximation of a desired on-task behavior before instruction can occur through the purposeful arrangement of consequences.

Modeling methods, on the other hand, are perfectly suited to the teaching of novel on-task responses. Using modeling techniques, a teacher can demonstrate the desired "pencil-sharpening" behavior, and then can cue the learner to attempt an imitation of the teacher's performance. Modeling methods, unlike operant methods, do not require excessive time and effort because they do not need to wait upon novel voluntary actions on the part of the learner before they can be implemented. Models influence individuals to change the ways they attend to, represent and organize information (Bandura, 1986). Because acquisitional learning does not require performance, skills can be acquired more quickly.

Modeling has been employed widely as an instructional tool for promoting cognitive and behavioral change (see Rosenthal & Steffek, 1991). There are many ways a classroom teacher can employ modeling and vicarious reinforcement to provide information about, and to motivate, desired on-task student behaviors.

1. Instructional *videos and peer modeling* in classroom group sessions can be used to stimulate a wide variety of academic, social and interpersonal behaviors. Students can be taught appropriate academic and classroom behaviors by viewing, and subsequently attempting to imitate, other students' (either live or symbolic) performances of these actions (see Donahue & Bryan, 1983, and Gredler, 1992, for an example of using videotape models to teach appropriate conversational practices). During such sessions, teachers can cue and actively coach (provide specific feedback to) the learning performances of observing students (see Hazel, Schumaker, Sherman & Sheldon, 1982, for an example of combining modeling and coaching techniques for teaching social skills).

2. Some classroom games, *peer tutoring* systems and cooperative learning programs make extensive use of natural modeling and imitation to teach on-task classroom behaviors. Much of what we vaguely refer to as "positive group influence" can be understood in terms of social learning principles. Classroom games, peer tutoring systems and cooperative learning programs provide learners with many opportunities to observe effective models (their own peers possess most of the characteristics of effective models specified in a previous section of this chapter) engaging in a variety of on-task academic and social behaviors, and being positively reinforced for doing so. Any imitation of such models is also shaped and reinforced by the peer group itself. Thus, both vicarious reinforcement through observation (acquisition) and direct operant reinforcement for actual performances are readily available. Extensive information about on-task

behaviors and motivation to perform them are also present. In a recent review of research on peer tutoring, Schunk (1987) asserts that peer tutoring has been found to promote the development of social skills, build self-efficacy and remedy skill deficiencies.

3. Csapo (1972) provides a vivid illustration of positive classroom modeling effects through the use of a kind of *"buddy system'* approach. Csapo paired emotionally disturbed students with successful classroom learners (peer models). The task of the peer model was to sit together with the emotionally disturbed peer, in adjoining desks, and to show him or her (the emotionally disturbed peer) appropriate kinds of behavior required in various classroom situations. The emotionally disturbed children were told that some behaviors interfered with their chances to learn and get along well in school, and that in order to learn better ways to act in the classroom, their peers had offered to help them. They were told to look carefully at what the peer models did, and to try to do what they were doing. There are, of course, many possible variations on such "buddy systems," all of which can make extensive use of ongoing peer modeling influences (e.g., Fox, 1989; Strain & Odom, 1986).

4. Many teachers find it very useful to employ modeling when initially demonstrating the kinds of on-task behaviors required by classroom rules and/or limits. Telling children (and for that matter, even older adolescents) exactly what to do and what not to do, is generally more difficult and less effective than demonstrating (or having a peer demonstrate) the "talked-about" actions. This is so because oral language often does not provide enough information to convey the nuances of behavior basic to any rule or limit.

5. Modeling can be used to teach social as well as academic skills (Kauffman, Mostert, Trent & Hallahan, 1998). Appropriate social skills are often unfamiliar to younger students. Paying attention, sharing, waiting your turn and so forth are types of behavior that some students may not understand. For these students, modeling of such behavior, coupled with positive feedback on their subsequent performance of the behaviors, can be a powerful social learning experience.

6. Modeling and vicarious reinforcement can be used in conjunction with the basic attention-ignorance behavior modifi-

cation strategy described in chapter 5. When deliberately ignoring disruptive off-task behaviors (e.g., out of seat, talking to a neighbor), locate another student who is currently engaged in the opposite on-task behavior (e.g., in seat, quietly attending to the lesson), and reinforce the on-task student with descriptive praise. This simple strategy gives the teacher something active to do when having difficulty in completely ignoring off-task behavior. Further, it provides a solid model of, and vicarious reinforcement for, appropriate on-task classroom conduct.

As should be readily apparent, modeling is an extremely flexible and efficient generic teaching strategy. While there are a great many specific modeling-related instructional techniques, one must not lose sight of the more general application of modeling theory to school classrooms. Recognition of the general and pervasive influence of modeling on learners in classrooms begins with the realization that the classroom teacher, simply by virtue of his or her very presence and every action, is a continuous model of social values, interpersonal behaviors and attitudes toward learning and life in general. Teachers do not behave in vacuums. Their actions are continuously observed and recorded by learners. They are, in this sense, extremely powerful models of how members of the school community, and the larger society, might interact. Therefore it is highly desirable that teachers, in their relationships with students, colleagues and parents, demonstrate appropriate, reasonable and effective conduct (Gathercole, 1993). Educators should always act in the best interests of their students. In light of this reality, teachers cannot afford, any more so than can parents, to fall back upon the deceptive adage, "Do as I say, not as I do." The effective teacher must learn to accept the role of an ongoing model of social behaviors and attitudes, and to become aware of the resultant impact of his or her own attitudes and values upon the behaviors and values of learners. The teacher who models authoritarian, punitive interactions with students directly imparts these same modes of behavior to students. The teacher who models enthusiasm for learning and effective methods of acquiring knowledge tends to pass along these attitudes and skills to learners. The *teacher "as model"* is a difficult and complex topic, but it is one that every instructor must analyze and examine in relation to his or her own instructional styles and efforts. There are no easy answers to the host of ethical and social issues and questions that arise from such careful, painstaking reflection. In the final analysis, teachers must be guided by their own values and the values and expectations of the general society and specific social context within which they teach.

Although modeling is a useful tool in the classroom, it may not be appropriate for all individuals under all circumstances. In a relatively recent review of relevant research, Hallenbeck and Kauffman (1995) describe how students with emotional or behavioral difficulties may not fare well in vicarious learning environments. These researchers found that students with behavioral and emotional difficulties displayed deteriorating behavior when they were placed in settings where their peers were being rewarded for desirable behavior, while they received little direct reinforcement for appropriate conduct. Unfortunately, observing peers being rewarded for appropriate behavior may serve as implicit or tacit punishment for these students.

Cognitive approaches

In this section we will be discussing specific applications of cognitive theory to issues of classroom management. The application of cognitive theory to classroom contexts involves externalizing various aspects of cognitive strategies and cognitive experience (e.g., beliefs, expectations, images, problem-solving cognitions and coping self-statements) and making them apparent to learners. Teaching cognitive strategies involves providing *metacognitive* information to learners. Metacognitive information refers to the knowledge one has about one's own thinking processes and about how to regulate them (see Woolfolk, 1995). Metacognitive information is information about thinking and includes such things as planning what one is going to do, monitoring what one is presently doing and checking what one has done. Metacognitive information is not to be considered specific to any one task. Rather, it is to be seen as the basis for broadly applicable, generic strategies.

Self-control strategies (Coates & Thoresen, 1980; Thoresen & Mahoney, 1974) are among the most well-known and widely-studied generic cognitive learning strategies. Self-control strategies are intended to instruct learners in how to use and take advantage of metacognitive information (see Brown, Campione & Day, 1981; Wong, 1991). Three of these strategies, *self-reinforcement, self-instruction* and *self-regulation*, have become particularly popular among educational and psychological researchers and practitioners. Self-reinforcement is a cognitive-behavioral strategy composed of both covert and overt learner actions that assist learners to plan, execute and motivate their own learning. Self-instruction is a cognitive strategy that consists of a brief series of internalized control behaviors that help learners comprehend and cope with stress and other cognitive and affective factors that undermine learners' efforts in instructional settings.

Self-reinforcement

Self-reinforcement parallels and elaborates upon the now familiar process of external operant reinforcement. The essential difference between self and external reinforcement systems is that many important instructional actions in self-reinforcement are initiated and implemented by learners themselves. A series of classroom experiments conducted in the early 1970s (see Felixbrod & O'Leary, 1973; Glynn, Thomas & Shee, 1973; Kaufman & O'Leary, 1972; O'Leary, Drabman & Kass, 1973; Santogiossi, O'Leary, Romanczyk & Kaufman, 1973) vividly illustrates the differences between teacher-controlled, external reinforcement systems and learner-controlled, self-reinforcement strategies. These experiments typically began with the implementation of teacher-controlled, token reinforcement group modification programs. The teachers in these studies set classroom behavior rules and standards, monitored (observed) students' classroom actions and evaluated these in terms of the rules for on- and off-task behavior by administering the tokens to on-task students. Students were kept well-informed about the rules, standards and contingency arrangements, and were further informed about the rationale for, and nature of, the teacher's classroom management procedures. After the teacher-controlled token reinforcement system had been in operation for a stable period of time (usually around a month), students in the experimental classrooms were asked to take over the teacher's role as behavior manager, and to set standards for, monitor, evaluate and reinforce their own classroom behaviors. In most cases, students' cognitive-behavioral, self-reinforcement strategies maintained on-task student behaviors about as well as did the previously-present teacher-controlled strategies. The advantage of the self-reinforcement strategies however, lay in the fact that the students in the studies were learning to control and motivate their own learning behaviors, and were thus better able to make effective use of their potential as learners with, and without, the direct physical presence of a "teacher." By developing their own self-reinforcement strategies, students in these experiments were becoming their own teachers, at least with respect to managing their own classroom behaviors.

The cognitive strategy of self-reinforcement can be seen to consist of at least four distinct, but related, actions (Bandura, 1976; Gredler, 1992; Martin, 1979, 1980): (a) *self-prescription* of performance standards, (b) *self-monitoring* of performances, (c) *self-evaluation* of observed performances in light of the performance standards and (d) *self-reward* contingent upon performances that meet or exceed the standards. In general, students who establish performance standards for themselves tend to respond in self-rewarding ways if their performance matches such standards. Conversely, they tend to respond in self-criticizing ways if their performance fails to meet these standards. Once learners can be helped to understand and perform these actions, they can employ self-reinforcement strategies for a variety of purposes. In addition to controlling classroom behaviors, students can use self-reinforcement systems to plan and motivate effective studying behaviors, successful project or assignment completion, successful acquisition of new academic skills and so forth.

To assist learners in developing self-reinforcement strategies, teachers, like the experimental teachers in the studies described above, should model, describe and discuss the four self-reinforcement steps in their own classroom interactions. Demonstrating the practical advantages of setting specific goals and standards for behavior, and systematically monitoring, evaluating and rewarding targeted actions should be an ongoing part of a teacher's classroom repertoire. It is largely through the observation and imitation of such procedures on the part of a teacher that learners are helped to develop the cognitive structures and rules for generic self-reinforcement strategies. Good initial teacher structuring is always necessary for the successful teaching of self-reinforcement strategies (Jones & Evans, 1980).

Self-instruction

Like self-reinforcement, self-instruction is a strategy that assists learners to teach themselves (see Meichenbaum, 1977, 1986). The specific objective of self-instruction, however, is to provide means to learners for dealing effectively with the stress and anxiety that is often experienced in response to instructional situations. Learners are helped to become aware of their difficulties, to question their beliefs about themselves in relation to stressful situations, to conduct "personal experiments" to test the validity of these beliefs, and to develop new skills that allow them to regulate their thoughts, feelings and actions. Self-instructional training focuses primarily on *self-statements*, the things we believe and say to ourselves during stressful situations.

The technique of self-instruction can be illustrated by recounting one of the first experiments in this area (Meichenbaum & Goodman, 1971). This study was concerned with helping impulsive, primary grade children talk to themselves (instruct themselves) in ways that would promote a more considered and reflective response to standard academic problems and tasks (e.g., copying line patterns, coloring figures within boundaries). The instructional program employed in the study was conducted on a one-to-one basis, and consisted of several phases. Initially, an adult male model (teacher) performed a task while talking to himself out loud in ways that helped him (the model) define the problem ("What is it I have to do?"), focus attention and guide his response ("Carefully now, draw the line down."), reward and motivate his efforts ("Good, I'm doing fine."), and evaluate his performance and cope with the process of error-correction ("That's okay – Even if I make an error I can go on slowly"). Next, the child (learner) performed the same task under the direction of the model's instructions. Gradually over time, the instructional process moved to the child performing the task while self-instructing out loud; to the child performing the task while whispering; and finally, to the child performing the task while guiding performance via private covert speech. In other words, the self-instructional training in the Meichenbaum and Goodman study consisted of gradually moving the process of teaching from an external agent (a teacher) to learners themselves. As a result of using their newly discovered self-instructional strategies, children in this study significantly improved their performance on standardized tests that require similar controlled, reflective responses to those that they had been practising (e.g., performance IQ on the WISC; increased cognitive reflectivity on the Matching Familiar Figures test, etc.).

Self-instructional training can be applied to social and academic concerns. It is comprised of three essential phases: (a) education, (b) rehearsal and (c) application. The educational phase of self-instruction consists of increasing the learner's awareness of his or her learning problem, particularly in terms of the self-defeating things that learners often say to themselves (e.g., a student who acts out during math classes may discover, with the teacher's assistance, that he is actively telling himself that "I'm no good at this and never will be, so I may as well have some fun" or "I'm stupid so I'll act that way.") By gradually becoming more aware of their own maladaptive self-statements, learners are helped to understand their difficulties. It is also the task of the teacher, at this stage, to emphasize that since the way that the learner is currently talking to himself or herself is causing problems, it is possible to solve these problems by changing the manner and type of self-talk.

During the *rehearsal* phase of self-instruction, the learner is taught to counter his or her negative self-statements by positive coping self-statements. Every time the problem situation (math class) occurs and the negative statements begin, the learner is taught to self instruct (just like the students in the Meichenbaum & Goodman study) with more productive statements (e.g., "O.K. that's enough of that. I'm not stupid and I can learn, but as long as I believe I can't, I won't. So forget about this 'stupid' business and find out exactly what the question is – O.K., that's better. At least I'm not panicking. If I can control my own overblown reactions, I may get the hang of this after all."). Teachers can use a combination of modeling, simulations, role-playing and overt dialogue to help a learner acquire such positive coping self-instructions.

Finally, the *application* phase of self-instruction involves applying the newly acquired self-instruction strategy in the actual problem situations without the direct external prompting and assistance of the teacher. At this stage, the student hopefully has learned to prepare for, confront and cope with "problem-related" classroom stimuli in new ways. In cognitive terms, the elaboration of the cognitive structures of the learner through the acquisition of the self-instruction strategy now permits a more viable and controlled perception of, and reaction to, the same classroom situations that were distorted by the old cognitive structures in ways that occasioned self-defeating, stressful learner reactions.

Self-instruction training has been applied to a broad range of classroom management and discipline problems (see Meyers & Craighead, 1984; Snyder & White, 1979). When using such approaches, a teacher must, however, keep in mind the usual one-to-one nature of such training and its resultant time-demands, as well as the requirement of verbal sophistication on the part of the learner. While group applications and methods of self-instruction that are less verbal can be employed in some situations, it is generally the case that self-instruction training is best employed with older, more verbally-sophisticated students outside of regular classroom hours and settings (especially for the education and rehearsal phases – the application phase of self-instruction does, of course, occur in the regular classroom context).

The experiences of Nan, a shy, retiring grade 12 student, illustrate the practical benefits that can accrue to students who learn basic self-instructional strategies. For as long as she could remember, Nan had never spoken out during classroom discussions. It was not that she didn't wish to speak, but somehow she could never bring herself actually to express an opinion or make a comment to the rest of the class. Oftentimes, just as she really felt she had something to say and was about to say it, she would suddenly become very tense and confused. The result of the tension and confusion was invariably the same – she would momentarily "go blank," and would remain quiet. When Ms. Boisvert had suggested that they might work together to help her learn to speak out in class, Nan had been initially excited about the possibility, but was also pessimistic about any chances for success. Nonetheless, Ms. Boisvert had been so kind about it that Nan had agreed to meet with her each day after school (one-half hour a day) for an entire school week.

At their first meeting, Ms. Boisvert had explained how we all say things to ourselves about what we are doing or are about to do, and that the things that we say to ourselves can sometimes affect the ways in which we act. Ms. Boisvert had then given Nan a number of examples about the way that she (Ms. Boisvert) often said things to herself in different situations. She indicated how some of the things she would say to herself were more effective than other things in terms of helping her actually do the things she wanted to do. At that first meeting, Ms. Boisvert asked Nan to try to notice (and to write down) some of the things she thought or said to herself during classroom discussions. At this stage, Nan could remember not really knowing what all this stuff was about, but she was interested enough to do what Ms. Boisvert had suggested.

When she met Ms. Boisvert the following afternoon, she had written down a few of the things she had found herself thinking during the day's classes. By the end of their second meeting, Ms. Boisvert had helped Nan to extend her list by asking her to imagine classroom discussion periods and to say out loud some of the thoughts that occurred to her as she imagined herself in these situations. When she looked at this extended list, Nan was somewhat surprised by the kinds of things she seemed to be telling herself during discussion periods. Again and again, she came across statements such as: "Gee, maybe this is a kind of dumb thing to say. What if they all laugh? What are they talking about now? I don't even know what's going on here, good thing I kept my mouth shut. Oh, why am I so stupid? Jeez, I almost feel sick. O.K., just sit back, who cares about this dumb class anyway."

By the end of their third meeting, Ms. Boisvert had helped Nan to construct a different kind of list from the one based on her current "self-statements" (a word that Ms. Boisvert used). Nan could still remember that new list and how she had worked so hard to practice saying it to herself – first with Ms. Boisvert, and then in actual class discussion periods the following day. The new list went like this:

"O.K., here's another discussion period."

"Don't worry about saying anything, just listen carefully to what other people are saying."

"Try hard to look at each speaker and to understand the point being made."

"Good, I can do this, let's keep it up."

"Remember that if I don't understand, I can say that I don't and ask to have it explained more fully."

"There's nothing wrong with my intelligence. If a point is well made, I will understand it."

"Great, this is easy."

"I'm really enjoying this discussion."

"Do I agree with that point or not?"

"Just stay relaxed now, no one is forcing me to say or do anything I don't want to do."

"I think I can add something to that."

"When I think like this, all I need to do is gently raise my hand and say what I think."

"I'm an intelligent, thoughtful person."

Nan laughed when she thought about how the next day she'd been so busy saying the new list to herself that she couldn't even attend to what was being said in class. But with another practice session with Ms. Boisvert, reciting the new list (or at least some of the ideas in it) had become almost automatic. On the last school day of that week, Nan had really enjoyed the discussion period. She hadn't yet said anything, but she had been able to follow everything that was being said, and had not felt confused or tense. She was now looking forward to next Monday, pretty sure that she would have at least one thing to say during an upcoming discussion on the novel that she was now reading as part of her grade 12 Literature course.

Self regulation

Self regulation refers to the process whereby students activate and sustain cognitions, behaviors and emotions that are systematically oriented toward the attainment of goals (Schunk, 1994; Schunk & Zimmerman, 1994). The social learning described in this chapter assumes that behaviors are contingent upon a chain of responses that have been built up over time, such that a particular response is automatically (unconsciously) cued by the completion of the immediately preceding response. In other words, the execution of a response becomes "automatic" as it is practiced and performed over a period of time. However, in novel situations, such automatic responses may not be available, or previously learned responses may no longer be effective or appropriate. These situations may result in achievement of a student's goals being blocked. When this occurs, the self-regulatory system is activated. Self-regulatory strategies may assist students to reach a "blocked" goal or in learning in a new task environment. Self-regulatory strategies may include attending to and concentrating on instructions, organizing and sequencing information, self-evaluating, rehearsing and memorizing, goal-setting and planning, or simply seeking assistance. Self-regulation assumes that students are active participants in their own learning, and have a large degree of control over the attainment of their goals (Schunk & Zimmerman, 1994).

Self-regulatory strategies can be learned in two ways. First, students can develop these strategies through trial and error. By focusing on what learning strategies improve performance and what strategies do not improve performance, a student can develop a repertoire of effective self-regulatory strategies. Second, self-regulatory strategies can be developed through teacher-student interactions. Graham and Harris (1994) describe how teachers can be effective facilitators of self-regulation in a writing lesson. Teachers begin by helping students develop writing pre-skills such as planning, organizing and goal-setting. The teacher and students then discuss the strategies that will be needed to accomplish the writing assignment. The teacher models a proven strategy, and explains its purpose, as well as how and when to use it (conditional knowledge). The final step involves a further collaborative discussion about how the strategy can be refined so that it will be effective for individual students. By modeling and supporting students' efforts to learn self-regulatory strategies, teachers empower students with the resources needed to become active participants in their own learning.

Stress inoculation training

A variation of self-instructional training that also targets maladaptive beliefs is stress inoculation training (see Meichenbaum, 1985b). Stress inoculation training is designed to help individuals overcome their anxieties to specific stress-provoking stimuli or situations. Similar to self-instructional training, students learn to produce positive coping statements in the face of stressful situations. However, in stress inoculation, an extended practice phase is added in which students take part in situations that are graded from evoking little stress (e.g., imagining taking a quiz) to being highly stressful (e.g., actually taking a final exam). By gradually being exposed to situations with increasing levels of stress, students experience concomitantly increasing levels of efficacy and confidence in being able to overcome their anxiety. This helps to ensure success with and continued use of the self-instruction strategy.

Problem-solving training

Another useful and widely advocated cognitive approach is cognitive problem-solving training (see D'Zurilla, 1986; D'Zurilla & Goldfried, 1971; Haaga & Davison, 1991). Problem-solving training is concerned with teaching skills to learners that enable them to distinguish the particularities of problems, assess and evaluate them, generate an array of alternative solutions, and choose from among alternatives. The purpose of teaching problem-solving to students is to enable them to acquire a variety of potentially effective response alternatives for dealing with a problem, and to increase the probability that they will select an effective response.

Problem-solving training is firmly based in the empirical literature on problem-solving and the characteristics of good and poor problem-solvers. While there are many ways to solve problems successfully, it appears that people who are poor problem-solvers, are so for one of two basic reasons (Bloom & Broder, 1950).

1. They are typically unable to generate alternative courses of action in the face of problem situations.

2. When, and if, alternatives for action are generated, poor problem-solvers are typically incapable of deciding upon and implementing one particular alternative.

In light of such information, D'Zurilla and Goldfried (1971) developed a cognitive problem-solving strategy that (a) makes available a variety of potentially effective response alternatives for dealing with a problem situation, and (b) increases the probability of selecting the most effective response from among these various alternatives. The general goal in problem-solving training is not to provide students with specific solutions to specific problem situations; but rather, to provide a general coping strategy enabling them to deal more effectively with a wide variety of problem situations.

There are five steps in the D'Zurilla and Goldfried problem-solving strategy. Teachers can work through these steps (modeling and informing students about them through discussion, demonstration, rehearsals, role-plays, examples, etc.) with their students, until individual students are able to "internalize" the strategy. At this stage, learners are equipped with cognitive coping skills that they know how to apply to a variety of problematic situations. Strengths and weaknesses of individual students at each step in the process can be measured with the *Social Problem-Solving Inventory* (D'Zurilla & Nezu, 1993). The five steps in the problem-solving strategy are:

1. *General orientation* – The first step in problem-solving is to recognize that when we feel "upset about something," we must refocus our attention from our emotional states to the situations creating the upsets. Step 1 teaches the learner to recognize problem situations when they occur, to recognize that such situations are a normal aspect of living and can be dealt with by making active attempts to cope with them, and that it is important to stop and think through a solution before acting. This step is mainly motivational, whereas the remaining five steps describe specific skills necessary for problem-solving (D'Zurilla, 1990).

2. *Problem definition and formulation* – Once a problem situation has been recognized, it must be analyzed and specified so that the problem-solver becomes aware of the true nature of the problem and his or her present reactions to it. When and where the problem situation arises, how the learner reacts to it, what he or she thinks and feels, and how others react are all aspects that must be examined at this stage.

3. *Generation of alternatives* – During this third step, the problem-solver generates (first with the teacher's assistance and then by him or herself) a variety of alternative responses to the problem situation. This is done through an active "brainstorming" technique, during which the problem-solver generates a host of alternatives by temporarily withholding any evaluation of the quality of solutions. The more alternatives produced, the greater the likelihood that "good" ones will be included in the list.

4. *Decision-making* – Now that a range of alternatives has been generated, each one must be placed against the situational information developed in step 2 to determine which alternatives are most promising. A process of "reality testing" is begun during which the problem-solver considers the likely personal, social, short-term and long-term consequences of engaging in each alternative. Once a decision has been made upon a specific course of action, attention is directed toward the formulation of a viable plan to implement the proposed problem solution. In working through step 3, the teacher must keep in mind that there are some problem situations (e.g., severe illness, death of a family member) for which there are no really good solutions, and that in such situations, the task is to look for alternatives that are best fitted to help the student cope with situations, as opposed to completely mastering or resolving them.

5. *Verification* – The final step in the problem-solving strategy consists of implementing the problem solution decided upon in steps 1-4. The consequences of this implementation should be monitored carefully. If the solution chosen produces unsatisfactory consequences, the problem-solving procedure is resumed and other alternative solutions are adjudicated and tested through implementation.

The general problem-solving strategy is adaptable to a wide variety of school situations and problems (see Spivack, Platt & Shure, 1976; Weissberg & Allen, 1986, for examples). Teachers can find the five steps detailed above to be valuable guides in structuring and conducting one-to-one interviews and trouble-shooting sessions with students who are consistently disrupting classroom routines, who are damaging school property, who are "bullying" (or "being bullied by") other students both inside and outside the classroom, who are trying to cope with the immediate and pervasive impacts of familial disruptions, who are abusing alcohol or drugs, or who are experiencing difficulty with sexual behavior.

Critique

The modeling and cognitive learning strategies discussed in this chapter can be extremely versatile and valuable in promoting the goals of self-directed learning and problem-solving. There is much research to support the general view that teachers can play an active role in assisting learners to acquire such cognitive strategies. It is, however, extremely important that each teacher recognize his or her own limitations and level of expertise in dealing with student concerns (such as several of those discussed above) that go beyond the immediate classroom and school context. Teachers should always respect the rights of parents and other prominent social agents, and should avoid unilateral actions that override "significant others" in students' lives. Where teachers are not properly equipped to deal competently with students' problems and difficulties, they should consult agencies and professionals who are. Every teacher should take the time to become familiar with the various social and medical referral services in the immediate community within which a school is located, and with school and legal policies governing referrals.

There are at least two frequently voiced criticisms of the strategy of teaching generic cognitive strategies to students as means of fostering desired forms of classroom behavior and academic accomplishment. One criticism concerns the extent to which such generic strategies can be effective across different content and contexts. Another concerns the possibility that in adopting such methods, teachers may be forcing individual solutions to classroom problems that might more properly be understood as arising from a variety of social and contextual factors.

Several philosophers of education (e.g., McPeck, 1990; Schrag, 1988) have criticized the idea that any problem-solving or thinking strategy can be applied to a wide variety of contexts without a rather thorough knowledge of those contexts and important differences across them. They argue that strategies such as the problem-solving method discussed in this chapter depend heavily on a problem solver's knowledge of the domain and context in which a problem is embedded. Thus, no amount of sophistication in generating alternatives, making decisions, verifying results, or any other problem-solving steps or skills is likely to promote successful problem solutions if individual problem solvers do not possess relevant knowledge and abilities. For example, one might attempt to use a general problem-solving strategy to reduce the stresses of daily living, only to discover that much of the stress experienced is financially motivated, and in the absence of specific knowledge of budgeting and the mathematics involved, little in the way of effective problem resolution can be achieved. The essential point of such criticisms is that cognitive strategies need to be accompanied by adequate, relevant knowledge in areas of potential application if they are truly to be effective. The central implication for teachers who might wish to use such strategies is to provide opportunities for students to acquire knowledge relevant to the problems and difficulties they may be experiencing at the same time that they are learning strategies for coping, problem solving and so forth.

As stated previously, another criticism of social learning and cognitive approaches to classroom management and teaching focuses on the possible mismatch that might result if individualized solutions are proposed for what really are not individual problems.

The aim of teaching students self-directedness, strongly advocated by social learning and cognitive approaches, makes certain presuppositions. Within social learning and cognitive theories is the central assumption of an autonomous, "individual knower." Excepting those instances where there is some neurological deficiency, learners are presumed to have the cognitive resources and skills that enable them to construct knowledge, to determine appropriate courses of action, and to adapt effectively to the demands of classroom life. If a learner is unable to meet these demands, it is thought that there is something wrong with his or her cognitive functioning. In other words, learners are seen either to adapt or to malfunction in classrooms. If a learner is assessed as "malfunctioning," it is believed that there is a deficit in the learner to be ameliorated. This promotes a "fix the learner," or deficit model of classroom management in which the task of the teacher is seen as remedying the social or academic deficiencies in the learner that prohibit reaching the ideal of the autonomous, responsible, individual knower. Modeling and cognitive strategies as conceived within social learning and cognitive theories (such as those presented in this chapter) can be seen to fit this sort of general deficit model.

Is a deficit model an adequate and useful characterization of learner performance? If all behaviors result from cognitive strategies, then maladaptive behaviors are also learned and represented in the cognitive structures of students. Learned behaviors and ways of thinking, considered problematic in the classroom, may be viable, effective, adaptive and highly reinforcing in certain environments outside the classroom. If this was not the case it is unlikely that such behaviors and cognitive strategies would have been learned in the first place or persist strongly in the face of non-reinforcing circumstances provided by teachers attempting to curb them. For example, the student who assertively interrupts others in class may find such behavior productive in getting care and attention at home, in competition with a large number of siblings. Thus, what might be a deficit in one context may be an asset in another. The outcome of applying a cognitive strategy, and whether or not an outcome is seen as reflecting an asset or a deficit, would seem to be highly dependent upon the particular context in which the strategy is applied and the particular norms and values that attend that specific context.

Thoughts, feelings and behaviors are socially located and transmitted. They are defined by and are meaningful only within the particular social and cultural contexts in which they occur. Whether a raised fist is an act of aggression or a symbol of solidarity depends upon the social norms and values that provide the context of meaning in which the act occurs. Likewise, what it means to be defiant, to be supportive, to be creative or to be deficient is contingent upon the particular values and norms held by others who comprise the immediate and overarching social-cultural context in which an act takes place. Such values and norms are deeply embedded in what is considered viable or nonviable, functional or dysfunctional, appropriate or inappropriate. Values and norms provide the glue for social relationships and the meaning ascribed to any individual's action.

That family, school, community and societal influences (values and norms) are strongly impressed upon learners' lives brings to light the question of whether behaviors or cognitions viewed as maladaptive in the classroom (or elsewhere for that matter) can be seen as deficits residing solely within the individual learner. It would seem that individual deficits cannot easily be separated from the specific interpersonal and communal, relational contexts and situations in which they occur, or from which they were learned. To impute deficits solely to the learner may be useful in perpetuating beliefs in the ideals of autonomy and individual responsibility. However, it may fail to acknowledge sufficiently the role of family, school, community and society in the acquisition and maintenance of so-called deficits. To the extent that the values and beliefs of others create, define and maintain the viability of learners' thoughts and actions, they can be seen to have some ownership in "deficits," and in turn, issues of classroom management. The school-wide approaches to classroom management discussed in the next chapter are, in part, a response to this important insight.

References

Ausubel, D.P. (1968). *Educational psychology: a cognitive view*. New York: Holt, Rinehart & Winston.

Bandura, A. (1969). *Principles of behavior modification*. New York: Holt, Rinehart & Winston.

Bandura, A. (1976). Self-reinforcement: Theoretical and methodological considerations. *Behaviorism, 4*, 135-155.

Bandura, A. (1977). *Social learning theory*. Englewood Cliffs, NJ: Prentice-Hall.

Bandura, A. (1986). *Social foundations of thought and action: A social cognitive theory*. Englewood Cliffs, NJ: Prenctice-Hall.

Bandura, A. (1993). Perceived self-efficacy in cognitive development and functioning. *Educational Psychologist, 28*, 117-148.

Bandura, A. & Walters, R.G. (1963). *Social learning and personality development*. New York: Holt, Rinehart & Winston.

Bloom, B.S. & Broder, L.J. (1950). *Problem-solving processes of college students*. Chicago: University of Chicago Press.

Brown, A.L., Campione, J. & Day, J.D. (1981). Learning to learn: On training students to learn from texts. *Educational Researcher, 10* (2), 14-21.

Bruner, J.S. (1985). Models of the learner. *Educational Researcher, 14*, 5-8.

Coates, T.J. & Thoresen, C.E. (1980). Behavioral self-control and educational practice or, Do we really need self-control? *Review of Research in Education, 7*, 3-45.

Csapo, M. (1972). Peer models reverse the "one bad apple spoils the barrel" theory. *Teaching Exceptional Children, 4*, 20-24.

Donahue, M. & Bryan, T. (1983). Conversational skills and modeling in learning disabled boys. *Applied Psycholinguistics, 4*, 251-278.

Driscoll, M.P. (1994). *Psychology of learning for instruction*. Boston, MA: Allyn and Bacon.

D'Zurilla, T.J. (1986). *Problem-solving therapy: A social competence approach to clinical intervention*. New York: Springer.

D'Zurilla, T.J. (1990). Problem-solving training for effective stress management and prevention. *Journal of Cognitive Psychotherapy: An International Quarterly, 4*, 327-354.

D'Zurilla, T.J. & Goldfried, M.R. (1971). Problem-solving and behavior modification. *Journal of Abnormal Psychology, 78,* 107-126.

D'Zurilla, T.J. & Nezu, A. (1990). Development and preliminary evaluation of the *Social Problem-Solving Inventory (SPSI)*. *Psychological Assessment: A Journal of Consulting and Clinical Psychology, 2,* 156-163.

Felixbrod, J.J. & O'Leary, K.D. (1973). Effects of reinforcement of children's academic behavior as a function of self-determined and externally imposed contingencies. *Journal of Applied Behavior Analysis, 6,* 241-250.

Fox, C. (1989). Peer acceptance of learning disable children in the regular classroom. *Exceptional Children, 56*(1), 50-57.

Garcia, T. & Pintrich, P.R. (1994). Regulating motivation and cognition in the classroom: The role of self-schemas and self-regulatory strategies. In D.H. Schunk & B.J. Zimmerman (Eds.), *Self-regulation of learning and performance: Issues and educational applications* (pp. 127-153). Hillsdale, NJ: Lawrence Erlbaum.

Gathercole, F. (1993). *Judicious discipline (3rd ed.)*. San Francisco, CA: Caddo Gap Press.

Glynn, E.L., Thomas, J.D. & Shee, S.M. (1973). Behavioral self-control of on-task behavior in an elementary classroom. *Journal of Applied Behavior Analysis, 6,* 105-113.

Graham, S. & Harris, K.R. (1994). The role and development of self-regulation in the writing process. In D.H. Schunk & B.J. Zimmerman (Eds.), *Self-regulation of learning and performance: Issues and educational applications* (pp. 203-228). Hillsdale, NJ: Lawrence Erlbaum.

Gredler, M.E. (1992). *Learning and instruction: Theory into practice.* New York, NY: Macmillan Publishing Co.

Haaga, D.A.F. & Davison, G.C. (1991). Cognitive change models. In F.G. Kanfer, & A.P. Goldstein (Eds.). *Helping people change: A textbook of methods (2nd ed.).* Elmsford, NY: Pergamon.

Hallenbeck, B.T. & Kauffman, J.M. (1995). How does observational learning affect the behavior of students with emotional or behavioral disorders? A review of research. *The Journal of Special Education, 29,* 45-71.

Hazel, J.S., Schumaker, J.B., Sherman, J.A. & Sheldon, J. (1982). Application of a group training program in social skills and problem solving to learning disabled and nondisabled youth. *Learning Disability Quarterly, 5,* 398-408.

Jones, R.T. & Evans, H. (1980). Self-reinforcement: A continuum of external cues. *Journal of Educational Psychology, 72,* 625-635.

Jones, B.F., Palincsar, A.S., Ogle, D.S. & Carr, E.G. (Eds.). (1987). *Strategic teaching and learning: Cognitive instruction in the content areas.* Alexandria, VA: Assoc. for Supervision and Curriculum Development.

Kanfer, F.G. & Goldstein, A.P. (1991). *Helping people change: A textbook of methods (2nd ed.)*. Elmsford, NY: Pergamon.

Kauffman, J.M., Mostert, M.P., Stanley, C.T. & Hallahan, D.P. (1998). *Managing classroom behavior: A reflective case-based approach (2nd ed.)*. Needham Heights, MA: Allyn and Bacon.

Kaufman, K.F. & O'Leary, K.D. (1972). Reward cost and self-evaluation procedures for disruptive adolescents in a psychiatric hospital school. *Journal of Applied Behavior Analysis, 5*, 293-309.

Martin, J. (1979). Laboratory studies of self-reinforcement phenomena. *Journal of General Psychology, 98*, 103-149.

Martin, J. (1980). External versus self-reinforcement: A review of methodological and theoretical issues. *Canadian Journal of Behavioral Science, 12*, 111-125.

Mayer, R.E. (1987). *Educational psychology: A cognitive approach*. Boston: Little, Brown & Co.

McPeck, J.E. (1990). *Teaching critical thinking*. New York: Routledge.

Meichenbaum, D. (1977). *Cognitive behavior modification: An integrated approach*. New York: Plenum.

Meichenbaum, D. (1985a). Teaching thinking: A cognitive-behavioral perspective. In S.F. Chipman, J.W. Segal & R. Glaser (Eds.), *Thinking and learning skills volume 2: Research and open questions* (pp. 407-426). Hillsdale, NJ: Erlbaum.

Meichenbaum, D. (1985b). *Stress inoculation training*. Elmsford, NY: Pergamon.

Meichenbaum, D. (1986). Cognitive-behavior modification. In F.H. Kanfer & A.P. Goldstein (Eds.), *Helping people change: A textbook of methods* (3rd ed., pp. 346-380). Elmsford, NY: Pergamon.

Meichenbaum, D. & Goodman, J. (1971). Training impulsive children to talk to themselves: A means of developing self-control. *Journal of Abnormal Psychology, 77*, 115-126.

Meyers, A. W. & Craighead, W.E. (1984). *Cognitive behavior therapy with children*. New York: Plenum.

O'Leary, K.D., Drabman, R.S. & Kass, R.E. (1973). Maintenance of appropriate behavior in a token program. *Journal of Abnormal Child Psychology, 1*, 127-138.

Ollendick, T.H., Dailey, D. & Shapiro, E.S. (1983). Vicarious reinforcement: Expected and unexpected effects. *Journal of Applied Behavior Analysis, 16*, 485-491.

Reeve, J. (1996). *Motivating others, nurturing inner motivational resources*. Needham Heights, MA: Allyn & Bacon.

Rosenthal, T.L. & Steffek, B.D. (1991). Modeling methods. In F.G. Kanfer & A.P. Goldstein (Eds.), *Helping people change: A textbook of methods* (4th ed., pp. 70-121). New York: Pergamon.

Rosenthal, T.L. & Zimmerman, B.J. (1978). *Social learning and cognition.* New York: Academic Press.

Santogiossi, D.A., O'Leary, K.D., Romanczyk, R.G. & Kaufman, K.F. (1973). Self-evaluation by adolescents in a psychiatric school token program. *Journal of Applied Behavior Analysis, 6,* 277-287.

Schunk, D.H. (1987). Peer models and children's behavioral change. *Review of Educational Research, 57*(2), 149-174.

Schunk, D.H. (1989). Self-efficacy and cognitive development: Implications for students with learning problems. *Journal of Learning Disabilities, 22,* 14-22.

Schunk, D.H. (1994). Self-regulation of self-efficacy and attributions in academic settings. In D.H. Schunk & B.J. Zimmerman (Eds.), *Self-regulation of learning and performance: Issues and educational applications* (pp. 75-99). Hillsdale, NJ: Lawrence Erlbaum.

Schunk, D.H. & Zimmerman, B.J. (1994). *Self-regulation of learning and performance: Issues and educational applications.* Hillsdale, NJ: Lawrence Erlbaum.

Schrag, F. (1988). *Thinking in school and society.* New York: Routledge.

Smith, F. (1975). *Comprehension and learning: A conceptual framework for teachers.* New York: Holt, Rinehart & Winston.

Snyder, J.J. & White, M.J. (1979). The use of cognitive self-instruction in the treatment of behaviorally disturbed adolescents. *Behavior Therapy, 10,* 227-235.

Spivack, G., Platt, J.J. & Shure, M.B. (1976). *The problem-solving approach to adjustment.* San Francisco: Jossey-Bass.

Strain, P.S. & Odom, S.L., (1986). Peer social initiations: Effective intervention for social skills development of exceptional children. *Exceptional Children, 52*(6), 543-551.

Thoresen, C.E. & Mahoney, M.J. (1974). *Behavioral self-control.* New York: Holt, Rinehart, & Winston.

Weissberg, R.P. & Allen, J.P. (1986). Promoting children's social skills and adaptive interpersonal behavior. In B. Edelstein & L. Michelson (Eds.), *Handbook of prevention* (pp. 153-175). New York: Plenum Press.

Wong, B.Y. (1991). The relevance of metacognition to learning disabilities. In B.Y. Wong (Ed.), *Learning about learning disabilities* (pp. 231-258). San Diego: Academic Press.

Woolfolk, A. (1995). *Educational Psychology (6th Ed.).* Needham Heights, MA: Simon & Schuster Co.

Zimmerman, B.J. & Schunk, D.H. (Eds.). (1989). *Self-regulated learning and academic achievement: Theory, research, and practice.* New York: Springer-Verlag.

Chapter Seven
School-Wide Approaches

Overview and Rationale

William Glasser's ideas about interpersonal involvement and the promotion of realistic and responsible social behaviors were initially developed while working with delinquent adolescent girls and U.S. war veterans (Glasser, 1965). Since then, Glasser has extended and adapted *Control Theory* and the methods of *Reality Therapy* to educational settings (see Glasser, 1969, 1972, 1978, 1986, 1990). In 1996, Glasser changed the name of the theory he has been developing since 1965 from "control theory" to "choice theory." Basic to this approach is the notion that all of us (and particularly learners in classrooms) must be truly involved with other people if we are to fulfill our basic needs in socially responsible and realistic manners. In his advocacy of classroom meetings and responsible teacher-student interactions, Glasser continually stresses the importance of developing warm, supportive human relationships within the classroom (Glasser, 1998).

Assertive Discipline, developed by Lee and Marlene Canter (see Canter, 1978, 1989; Canter & Canter, 1976, 1992), is a method of classroom management based on techniques of assertiveness training (Assertion Training) made popular in the 1970s (see Alberti & Eamons, 1975; Smith, 1975). The central premise of Assertion Training is that in building and maintaining self esteem it is essential that individuals come to possess skills that permit them to communicate their needs and feelings (assert themselves) in social relations with others. Assertive Discipline is concerned with helping teachers develop assertive communication skills that enable them to uphold certain fundamental rights of teachers and students.

The third model discussed in this chapter is Daniel Duke's *Systematic Management Plan for School Discipline* (see Duke, 1980; Duke & Meckel, 1984). In advocating a school-wide program for problem management, Duke's approach is predicated on organizing the individual efforts of teachers and administrators to deal with problems in a collaborative and systematic fashion. The function of Duke's program is to reorganize a school such that procedures are put into place for formulating rules on a collaborative basis, implementing team approaches to monitoring problems and ensuring that consequences for rule violations are applied consistently.

Principles

Choice Theory and Reality Therapy

According to Glasser, all human behavior is directed towards meeting four basic psychological needs: the need to belong, the need for power, the need for freedom and the need for fun (see Glasser, 1981, 1986, 1989, 1998). These needs, encoded as part of our genetic structure and built into our nervous system, cause pain and suffering if not satisfied. Contrary to the view that all human needs issue from a basic survival instinct, Glasser argues that needs such as belonging, power, freedom and fun are fundamental and independent from the need for survival. Acts of suicide, risk taking and self-sacrifice may reveal needs for belonging, power, freedom and fun that can supersede the need for survival. Further, such acts demonstrate that people exercise an inherent capacity for choice and that their behavior is a function of internal needs, not primarily a response to external stimuli. In fact, external stimuli are simply sources of information that, by themselves, don't make us do anything. We choose how and if we react to stimuli (Glasser, 1997).

Choice Theory puts forth the basic proposition that all human behavior results from choice. We choose actions we believe will control and affect the world in ways that will secure basic needs. When there is a difference between what we want and what we have, we choose to act in ways we think (and have learned) will transform the present such that our needs are fulfilled. Choice Theory holds that although we have choice among actions and that all our actions are the result of our own choices, we always must choose to do something to satisfy basic needs. This aspect of our existence, that we are compelled to act in meeting basic needs, is the source of all human accomplishments and difficulties.

Choice Theory attributes all human problems to an individual's inability to fulfill basic needs within environmental limits. Disruptive and inappropriate behaviors arise within this context and actually are chosen as means of meeting unfulfilled needs. When students act disruptively, it is because they choose to do so. If teachers react angrily to a disruption, it is because anger is the way they have chosen to deal with their frustration. In both cases, the student and the teacher are attempting to satisfy their needs by manipulating others who participate in the social context of the classroom. The social context of the classroom forms environmental limits, constraining the conditions under which needs must be met. In order to have needs met, it is important to develop behaviors that are both effective and appropriate, given the constraints imposed by the particular social context. Behaviors may be effective in meeting needs. However, they are inappropriate if they attempt to deprive others of the ability to fulfill their needs. According to Choice Theory, inappropriate behaviors are seldom properly attuned to the reality of the world around us.

Reality Therapy (see Glasser, 1965, 1989), consistent with the tenets of Choice Theory, is concerned with helping individuals give up denying the world and to recognize (1) that reality exists and (2) that they must fulfill their needs within its framework. While insight into reality is important to Reality Therapy, it is assumed that such insight must (if it is to be useful) always be accompanied by the learning of responsible behaviors that provide better choices for fulfilling basic needs in the real world.

The two basic psychological needs with which Reality Therapy is most concerned are (1) the need *to love and be loved*, and (2) the need *to feel worthwhile* to ourselves and others. These two basic needs are thought to be essentially unchanging from birth to death. Unfortunately, while we are naturally endowed with these needs, we are not naturally endowed with the abilities required to fulfill them.

Love, in many respects, is synonymous with *involvement.* In the context of school, love can best be thought of as social responsibility and a sense of belonging (Brophy & Putnam, 1979). The extent to which we become involved with others determines the extent that our basic need to love and be loved is fulfilled. Feeling worthwhile is tied to a sense of power and control. In order to feel worthwhile, one must perceive oneself as having a meaningful influence on the world. However, in gaining some influence over things, events or others, one must maintain a satisfactory standard of behavior. All actions taken to secure basic needs are imbued with certain morals, standards and values of right and wrong. Only when actions measure up, and tasks are performed that respect the needs of others as well as our own, is the feeling of self-worth realized.

Although conditions for love and self-worth are separate, it is generally the case that a person who loves and is loved will feel worthwhile. In fact, while it is possible to consider love and worth separately, they become so intertwined within the contexts of social existence, that they may be more properly understood in terms of the overarching concept of *identity*. Identity, the conception we have of ourselves, is closely linked to the actions we choose in attempting to meet our basic needs.

Glasser (1972) contends that the single basic need possessed by people in our society is the requirement for an identity. There are two types of life styles that develop as a result of the identity that we choose – one is based on a *success identity*; the other is based on a *failure identity*. If individuals choose to behave in a socially responsible (and realistic) manner and become involved with others, it is probable that they will develop a success identity. If they choose to act irresponsibly (and unrealistically) and do not become involved with others, they will invariably develop a failure identity.

A success identity is characterized by a positive appraisal of oneself. When problems are encountered, people with success identities have confidence in their ability to choose behaviors that will not only resolve difficulties, but do so in a manner deemed responsible by appropriate social standards and values. Such individuals know that they must accept the consequences of their actions, so irresponsible actions are ruled out. People with success identities have a sense of belonging and are closely involved with others in their families, communities and peer groups.

In contrast, a failure identity is characterized by loneliness, negative self-appraisal, suffering and pain. People with failure identities feel that everything is wrong but that they can't do anything about it. Such individuals withdraw from others, social realities and from conceptions of responsible social behaviors. Convinced that no one who is worthwhile cares for them, they suffer the pain of uninvolvement while attempting ineffectively to deny the reality of their loneliness. In attempting to reduce the pain of uninvolvement, people with failure identities resort to unrealistic and irresponsible modes of action. They may display depression, engage in anti-social or acting out behaviors, entertain delusions or obsessive concerns, or demonstrate nondescript, vague symptoms of physical sickness (Kaltenbach & Glasser, 1982).

Glasser's (1969, 1978) earlier work regarding the application of Reality Therapy to classroom contexts, focuses on fostering learners' success identities and eliminating conditions likely to evoke failure experiences (e.g., grading). The aim of Reality Therapy is to resolve problems stemming from unrealistic, irresponsible modes of action and failure identities, by teaching learners how to succeed in meeting their basic needs within the context of social reality imposed by schools. However, do the structures and conditions of contemporary classrooms and schools allow learners to meet their needs in socially responsible ways?

Glasser (1969) alleges that many long-standing, traditional and widely-accepted conventions for structuring schools, classrooms and curricula are unsuitable to learners' needs, and that they perpetuate failure experiences for learners. Consequently, Glasser's more recent efforts have centered on school reform (see Glasser, 1986, 1990). Glasser claims that many learners simply cannot meet their needs within the constraints and limitations imposed by present school environments and curricula. Basic needs are biologically determined and cannot be changed. Thus, Glasser argues, learning environments, curricula, and norms and rules for behavior, must be constructed such that they are more amenable to basic needs such as involvement, worth and others to be considered below.

Glasser (1986, 1990) contends that difficulties presently facing schools (attrition, widespread inattention and apathy, low achievement, drug and alcohol abuse, and violence) can be understood given the tenets of Control Theory. These problems arise because students find such behaviors more satisfying than the kinds of curricular activities presently available in many contemporary school settings. Glasser alleges that four basic needs are strikingly neglected by the present structure imposed by schools: (1) *belonging* – a sense of acceptance by others, (2) *power* – a sense of control over one's life, (3) *freedom* – the sense that one is directing and responsible for one's own life and (4) *fun* – enjoyment and pleasurable experience.

Glasser (1986, 1990) advocates restructuring schools to better promote learners' fulfillment of their basic needs. To such an end, Glasser endorses cooperative learning programs that place students in small *learning teams* consisting of two to five students. According to Glasser, implementing cooperative learning programs and small learning teams would provide greater opportunities for students to develop a sense of belonging. Also, students' needs for power could be fulfilled in a more positive fashion through their providing of assistance to other group members.

Glasser proposes a changing role for teachers and administrators in which they are less authoritarian, conceding more responsibility to students. By displacing some of the authority of teachers to students (a natural consequence of cooperative learning), there is increased opportunity for students to experience a sense of personal freedom and responsibility. Glasser suggests that students' needs for power and freedom might be fulfilled by involving students in setting school and classroom rules. Additionally, Glasser advocates that time be allotted for groups of teachers to meet and discuss their concerns about any students who currently are experiencing problems. Such consultations assist in the development of optimal solutions and their consistent implementation.

In advocating such reforms, Glasser's recent efforts (1986, 1990, 1998) show a movement away from the deficit model reflected in his earlier work (1969, 1978). Rather than attributing inattention and misbehavior exclusively to students' inappropriate choices and failure identities, an increased responsibility for students' behavioral difficulties is placed on those who administer the social contexts provided in schools.

Assertive Discipline

Assertive Discipline (see Canter, 1978, 1989; Canter & Canter, 1976, 1992) is a model of classroom management designed to help teachers gain greater control in dealing with students' disruptive behaviors in classrooms. Assertive Discipline was conceived, in large part, as a response to the powerlessness experienced by many teachers in dealing with students' misbehavior. Like Reality Therapy, Assertive Discipline is concerned largely with the ways in which individuals go about fulfilling their needs. The Assertive Discipline model holds that the needs of both teachers and students follow from certain fundamental rights that properly govern the nature of social relations in classrooms. According to the Canters (1992), teacher rights include:

1. The right and duty to establish conditions in the classroom that provide for an optimal learning environment, given the teacher's own strengths and weaknesses.

2. The right to establish order and prevent disruptions by being assertive in word and manner.

3. The right to set expectations as to what constitutes appropriate student behavior, with respect to promoting positive social and educational development.

4. The right to apply consequences for serious or repeated offenses.

5. The right to request help from parents, administrators and others who might serve as resources, whenever assistance with a learner is required.

Teachers attempt to establish warm relationships with students. Students are given positive recognition and incentives in an effort to increase classroom cooperation, and create a positive learning environment.

Student rights include:

1. The right to have a teacher who will help the learner to curb inappropriate, unproductive or self-damaging behavior.

2. The right to have a teacher who will provide positive support for appropriate and productive behavior.

3. The right to choose how to behave and be informed of the consequences that will follow from behaviors.

The Canters (1976) contend that when these rights are enforced and abided, disruptive classroom behaviors are prevented. In ensuring these rights and in dealing with violations, the Canters propose the following set of five competencies that incorporate Assertive Discipline into teaching practice.

1. *Recognizing and eliminating roadblocks to achieving Assertive Discipline.* When teachers have negative expectations of students, such expectations are likely to produce *roadblocks* to teacher assertiveness. By accepting that students have particular negative attributes (arising from their health, personality or home environment) that prevent them from behaving acceptably, teachers undermine their own efforts to be assertive. Such negative expectations of students need to be supplanted by positive expectations. Teachers must acknowledge that they have the ability to influence students' behavior in a positive fashion despite such apparent detriments. Further, as teachers, they have the right to set limits and to request and receive the assistance of other school staff, parents and community resources in enforcing limits. Students respect teachers who hold high expectations rather

than those who take laissez-faire approaches to teaching (Canter & Canter, 1992).

2. *Practicing the use of an assertive response style.* The Canters discern three distinct styles that characterize teachers' responses to conflict. It is held that these response styles are central to understanding the teacher's role in management problems. Response styles help define the atmosphere of the classroom and can have a direct impact on students' self esteem. In *non-assertive responding*, there is an inability to communicate openly and straightforwardly. Non-assertive responses are characterized by passivity and generally involve compliance (given begrudgingly) for fear of rejection or of committing a mistake. Teachers with a non-assertive response style fail to establish and/or enforce clear standards for the behavior of students. Teachers using this response style often ask students to "try to behave," or "try to keep on task."

Hostile responding is characterized by aggressive threats or sarcasm. The teacher with a hostile response style attempts to control students by deprecating them in a hurtful fashion or provoking fear through intimidation. Teachers who use hostile responses may enforce standards, but do so in a manner that disregards the rightful needs and feelings of learners. This response style is often used when teachers are struggling to maintain control of the classroom.

In *assertive responding*, the teacher communicates needs and feelings directly and is prepared to take firm, positive action. However, in assertive responding, actions are chosen that do not violate the rights of others. Teachers with an assertive response style clearly express their expectations and are prepared to stand resolutely behind them. When students misbehave, assertive teachers inform students why such behavior is inappropriate and follow through with fitting consequences (Canter, 1978). In assuming an assertive posture, teachers attempt to gain students' cooperation, but do so in a manner that preserves everyone's self-respect.

In cultivating assertive responding, teachers must restrict their non-assertive and hostile responding. In voicing their disapproval of inappropriate student behaviors, teachers should not threaten, coerce or berate students; nor should teachers plead or whine. If threats are made but not carried out, they are quickly perceived as hollow. On the other hand, when teachers follow through with threats, it leads to an atmosphere of distrust and revenge. Rather, when faced with inappropriate student behavior, teachers should state their disapproval clearly and, in a businesslike way, point out what is wrong, specify precisely what the student is supposed to do, and insist that the student conform accordingly.

3. *Learning to set limits.* Teachers need to determine and be able to recognize what constitutes acceptable classroom behavior (e.g., not interrupting, staying at their work locations and so forth). Teachers need to set rewards for compliance as well as establish steps to be taken in dealing with noncompliance. Most importantly, teachers must instruct students about the limits and conditions that they have set.

The limits and rules as well as the consequences of classroom behaviors must be clear (Canter & Canter, 1992). Rules must state exactly how students are to behave. The number of rules should be limited to a few, and must be used every day, all day.

4. *Following through on limits.* Teachers make commitments (not threats) to follow through with consequences for misbehavior. In following through, it is necessary that consequences for misbehavior are specified in advance. Consequences for misbehavior may include warnings, loss of privileges, detentions, being sent to the principal, notification of parents, or suspension. In determining consequences it is important that the consequences be acceptable to the teacher and unpleasant, but not damaging to the learner.

5. *Implementing a system of positive assertions.* While there would appear to be much emphasis on dealing with misbehavior, Assertive Discipline places greater importance on positive reinforcement (Canter & Canter, 1992). It is essential that students who display proper classroom behaviors are praised and rewarded. This demonstrates to students who misbehave persistently the kinds of appropriate behaviors that are effective in getting needs fulfilled in the classroom setting.

Consistency is seen as a cornerstone of Assertive Discipline. A teacher's disciplinary actions may be weakened substantially, if not undermined totally, by administrators and parents who allow students to circumvent or ignore teachers' disciplinary actions. The Canters affirm the right of the teacher to enlist the help of school administrators, other school personnel and parents in dealing with students' behavioral difficulties. In many cases, student behavioral change may depend upon the consistent enforcement of consequences by all those in a position to do so. Thus, when necessary, teachers are encouraged to apply their assertive skills in seeking cooperation from parents, other teachers and administrators. The Canters (1976, 1989) believe that there is no reason why teachers should have to "go it alone."

Duke's systematic management plan for school discipline

Findings from comparative research suggest that schools vary in the overall effects they have on the behavior patterns of their student populations (see Duke, 1990; Duke & Seidman, 1982; Watkins & Wagner, 1987). Such research can be interpreted to support the view that a school's staff, policies and environment align as organizational factors to influence the overall nature of interpersonal social relations in the school, and consequently, the classroom behavior patterns of students. The Systematic Management Plan for School Discipline (SMPSD) (see Duke, 1980; Duke & Meckel, 1984) is based on the notion that students' classroom behavior is greatly affected by school organization. In recognizing the importance of organizational factors, the SMPSD is directed at transforming school structures and policies to maximize the organizational resources available in a school to deal with problems.

The SMPSD is a response to key issues that would seem to call for a school-wide approach (see Duke, 1980; Duke & Meckel, 1984). Akin to Glasser's (1986, 1990) more recent ideas, Duke alleges that widespread or persistent student misbehavior may be more indicative of a school organization that does not permit students to meet their needs, than of a high ratio of "problem" students. The rationale behind modifying school structures rather than learners is that the purpose of schools is to serve the needs of students, not vice versa. A second issue pertains to the ideal of eliminating all misbehavior. Duke contends that student behavior problems are inevitable despite even the best efforts at prevention. Thus, a more realistic and practical goal is to furnish schools adequately with problem-management strategies so that problems are kept manageable and not allowed to get out of hand. A third issue raised by Duke regards consistency. Duke advocates the necessity of having rules that are common across classrooms, consistently enforced throughout the school and supported by parents. As discussed in the section on Assertive Discipline, the best efforts of individual teachers can be sabotaged when rules and consequences are not upheld by significant others. A fourth issue pertains to the protection of students' and teachers' rights. In the current climate of court reviews and litigation, it is advantageous to both students and teachers for schools to initiate explicit school-wide disciplinary policies.

The SMPSD is a collaborative program. It requires that a school's teachers and administrators work jointly in providing a unified and comprehensive response to student behavior problems. However, the SMPSD is not solely the responsibility of school employees. Students and parents also have important roles. The SMPSD incorporates seven essential components (Duke, 1980):

1. *Understanding that schools are rule-governed organizations.* Students, school personnel and parents, must be made aware of the importance of rules for the functioning of the school. In achieving this goal, students, teachers, administrators and parents should participate in the setting of rules and consequences. As well, instruction should be provided to students regarding rules and the consequences for violating them. Rules should be regularly publicized throughout the school, and students' knowledge of rules should be tested periodically. It is suggested that the number of rules be kept to a minimum. Fewer rules are remembered and enforced more easily.

2. *Data collection procedures for implementing disciplinary measures.* Effective management decisions depend on complete and accurate information about problems. To ensure that such information is available, standardized reporting and record-keeping procedures need to be implemented. Report forms can be developed to assist in collecting information about problems and specific school personnel can be delegated responsibility for data management. Data describing trends in student behavior should be utilized in devising rules and objectives. Such composite data should be made available not only to teachers and administrators, but also reported annually to the general public.

3. *Means and procedures for conflict resolution.* In expediting the resolution of conflicts, specific situations should be dealt with as soon after they occur as possible. Teachers and students should first attempt to resolve conflicts themselves. However, if a dispute cannot be resolved, there should be a trained resource person available who could assist in negotiations. It is important that such resource persons are not involved in enforcing rules or dispensing punishment.

Rather, their role is specifically to listen to grievances and negotiate solutions. The importance of students' participation in resolving their conflicts with others is emphasized.

4. *Staff-team troubleshooting.* Grade-level teams of teachers should be assembled to deal with particular students' instructional and disciplinary needs. Team meetings should be scheduled for the purposes of troubleshooting potential as well as current problems. Discussion should be focused, addressing specific concerns. Clear plans, outlining particular actions, should be set, with responsibilities delegated to specific people. Meetings should be documented and kept confidential. However, there needs to be provision for administrators, special resource persons, parents and students to attend meetings when their participation would facilitate solutions to problems.

5. *Parental involvement.* Parents need to be included in the setting, reviewing and revision of rules, and the resolution of major behavior problems involving their children. Parents should be notified about problems and absences immediately, and kept up to date on school disciplinary policies. Further, the school should provide resources (e.g., workshops, seminars) for helping parents acquire new parenting skills, particularly in dealing with children's behavior problems.

6. *Providing reinforcing learning environments.* Emphasis should be placed on developing rewards for positive behavior, not on increasing punishments for misbehavior. Special privileges should be accorded students who abide by school rules, but withheld from students who persistently violate rules. Specialized learning environments should be constructed to deal with students requiring more individualized attention. Administrators and teachers should assist in developing student peer groups and other programs that support positive student behavior.

7. *Providing for staff professional development.* Inservice activities for providing new knowledge and skills about particular problems should be developed in collaboration with all school personnel. Inservice training for dealing with student behavior problems should be provided not only for teachers but also for non-teaching staff.

Duke and Meckel (1984) suggest that teachers or administrators interested in the SMPSD should begin by examining the relationships between student behavior problems and the nature of their school's organization. Duke and Meckel present the following four questions should be considered as a first step:

1. How frequent is the problem?

2. If the problem is chronic, under what circumstances does it occur?

3. What rules, consequences or characteristics of the organization of the school might be contributing to the persistence of the problem?

4. In what ways can the problem be addressed in a comprehensive, school-wide fashion, and what roles might teachers, administrators, other school personnel, students and parents play in providing a solution?

Implementing the SMPSD takes part in three phases: an assessment of school needs and resources, the development and institution of plans, and an ongoing process of review and revision. We refer readers to *Managing Behavior Problems* by Duke (1980) for a more in depth discussion of these implementation procedures.

The SMPSD cannot be used by a single teacher acting alone. In dealing with students' behavior problems the SMPSD does not provide prescribed interventions for individual teachers to manage particular classrooms. Rather, the SMPSD puts forth a method for a school-wide system of response. The SMPSD is not a set of distinctive techniques, but the design for a collaborative, systematic framework in which techniques are administered. Duke and Meckel (1984) advocate that teachers adopt an eclecticism in their approach to managing their individual classrooms, encouraging teachers to exploit techniques from a variety of models depending on the particular context. Thus, we will not be considering the SMPSD in the subsequent section reserved for discussion of specific techniques and applications. We now turn, however, to some of the specific techniques and applications of Reality Therapy and Assertive Discipline. More will be said about assisting classroom teachers to develop their own eclectic approaches to classroom management in the final chapter of this book.

Techniques and Applications

Reality Therapy

As discussed previously, establishing responsible interactions between teachers and students is at the heart of building a well-managed classroom. Reality Therapy seeks to enhance and develop positive social relations in classrooms. The application of Reality Therapy to these purposes may be described as a series of seven phases.

1. *Involvement* – The most essential phase of Reality Therapy in classrooms is establishing a warm emotional involvement between learners and teacher. The ability of a teacher to get involved is a major skill required for Reality Therapy. However it is difficult to describe precisely how to do this (Kaltenbach & Glasser, 1982). It is not enough simply to establish an initial rapport with students, and then remain aloof or impersonal. The teacher must extend involvement in a warm, friendly manner, showing an openness and willingness to become involved with each learner. If teachers engage students in warm relationships that accept students' rights to have their needs satisfied, students will be motivated to learn (Porter, 1996).

Glasser is very careful to emphasize that teachers' involvement must be reasonable and realistic. While he encourages teachers to challenge learners with values and opinions, he discourages attempts to develop involvement by focusing on learners' problems or miseries. Overemphasizing a learner's problems gives credence and value to a preoccupation with self and failure. Teachers should listen actively to students who behave inappropriately. However, they should not perpetuate student problems by prolonged, overly sympathetic interactions that serve only to keep problems "alive" (Glasser, 1994). Involvement thus means concern, challenge and confrontation as well as warmth and patience. Like the good parent, the involved teacher must care enough to set limits and to teach values of right and wrong. Involvement is not synonymous with unconditional acceptance of everything a learner does.

Porter (1996) describes how classroom rules and limits must be *reasonable*. Reasonable rules and limits must have salient and rational relationships to student behaviors. If students understand these relationships, they will be more likely to abide by the rules or limits and also feel like the school is a good place to be. By providing students with the tools to understand behavior and its consequences, teachers help students to feel resp(nsible for their own behavior.

Another important aspect of involvement is that teachers must never promise more than they can give. It is better to be dependable within limits than it is to attempt excessive involvement with every student. The latter strategy is bound to fail and prevents teachers from leading a responsible life of their own.

Specific methods for becoming involved are numerous and differ from one person to another. However, some of the suggestions in a subsequent section of this chapter, particularly those with respect to classroom meetings, should help to make the concept of involvement much more concrete.

2. *Focus on Current Behavior* – In all interactions between learners and teachers concerning classroom problems, Glasser emphasizes the importance of focusing attention on present behavior. Talking, at length, about the past history of a student does not help the student change and may even be detrimental, as it may reinforce a belief in the importance of past events in terms of present predicaments. The danger here is that learners may come to see their problems as inevitable and refuse to take any responsibility for their present situations.

For similar reasons, a teacher should focus on behavior, not feelings. To focus on feelings rather than behavior offers the student an easy way to avoid facing and taking responsibility for his or her present behavior. Feelings are important in any relationship. However, the crucial factor in relationships is how we behave toward other people.

Teachers can help learners solve their problems (many of which are manifest in disruptive, irresponsible classroom behavior) by continuously focusing on current behavior and its ramifications or consequences. Feelings should be accepted, but it must be pointed out to the learner that these are not as important as the way the learner behaves. A good example might be, "I believe you, you have convinced me that you are very upset (or depressed or whatever); but what are you doing about it right now?" Such statements direct learners' attention to the fact that they are responsible for their own behavior. Questions that ask "What are you doing?" are much superior to questions that ask "Why are you doing that?" "What" questions create a focus on current behavior and help teach responsibility and realistic awareness of behavior and its consequences. "Why" questions often cloud the issue by providing escape options for irresponsible conduct and preventing awareness of current behaviors. "What are you doing?", "What did you do then?", "What did you do just now?", provide the impetus for becoming aware of behavior and provide the opportunity to choose or consider new behavior that has a better chance of leading to success and involvement with others (Kaltenbach & Glasser, 1982).

3. *Evaluating Behavior* – Once learners have been assisted in becoming aware of inappropriate behaviors, they must be assisted in examining and evaluating those behaviors to see if they are beneficial in helping meet the learners' needs. To do this, Glasser advocates a system of reality-testing similar to that detailed in D'Zurilla and Goldried's problem-solving strategy discussed in chapter 6. The teacher helps the learner examine his or her current behavior and a series of alternate behaviors, in terms of the consequences or outcomes likely to be associated with each action. Through this process, the teacher gradually assists the learner in deciding upon, and choosing to implement, a more responsible and realistic form of behavior than that which is currently getting the learner into difficulty.

4. *Planning Responsible Behavior* – Learning to plan for responsible behavior is a very important aspect of Reality Therapy in classrooms. At this phase, relearning begins. The learner has now examined the irresponsible behavior and has decided on a more responsible alternative. The learner must now develop a realistic plan for changing from the irresponsible to the responsible behavior. Plans for implementing change may vary greatly in form, but they should be very specific, should be organized in small manageable steps, and the immediate goals contained in such plans should be well within the grasp of the learner's current behavioral repertoire, so as to encourage success experiences. *Behavioral contracts* (such as those described in chapter 5) can be written that detail the specifics of such plans.

5. *Commitment* – Plans, however reasonable and feasible, will not succeed without a strong commitment on the part of the learner to carry them out. Such commitment reflects social as well as selfish interests. Commitment is social responsibility that grows out of involvement. It says "I'll do it for you as

well as for me." It is at the same time motivating and binding. Written commitments in the form of behavioral contacts are stronger, more binding and clearer than verbal commitments. A written contract that specifies the change plan should be signed by both teacher and learner. Two copies are made so that both teacher and learner can refer readily to the contract (Kaltenbach & Glasser, 1982).

6. *Accept No Excuses* – If change plans should fail, the teacher must make it clear that no excuses are acceptable. This is so, because no matter how valid the excuse, it still represents failure. The teacher must never appear to the learner to say "OK, that's fine. It's about all I could have expected from a miserable failure." If the teacher is concerned and involved, he or she will hold the learner to the commitment. A commitment made is a commitment important enough to be worth keeping. When a contract fails, the alternative course of action contained in the change plan should be reevaluated. Slight adjustments may be made to the contract if necessary to ensure that the expected behavior changes are not unreasonable. If the change plan is still valid, it should be reaffirmed. The teacher does not emphasize the failure. After a reexamination of the contract (and some minor modification if necessary), the teacher asks "When are you going to do it?" This question continues to be put in various ways until a new commitment to the plan on the part of the learner is generated. The teacher never gives up on the learner.

7. *No Punishment* – Glasser (1965) defines punishment as any treatment of a person that is intended to cause him or her pain. Punishment is to be distinguished from the natural consequences of irresponsible behavior. Glasser (1992) discusses how punishment is often not appropriate for students whose offenses do not hurt anyone but themselves. In such cases, punishment does not teach students a lesson, rather it detracts from their quality of life and decreases their motivation to learn. When contracts are broken, teachers should avoid punishment. Students with failure identities do not fear punishment, they identify with it. Praise given when learners succeed provides much more effective motivation than punishment for failure. When inappropriate behavior is exhibited, students' privileges or freedoms can be removed

temporarily. Students then have control over when their freedom or privileges are reinstated.

Classroom meetings

One of the most powerful ways a teacher can become involved with students is through the vehicle of the classroom meeting. Glasser has found that such meetings improve the general educational environment in classrooms and stimulate learning (Glasser, 1969).

Three types of classroom meetings are advocated:

1. *Social Problem-Solving Meetings* attempt to solve individual and group problems. Such meetings are basic task-orientated, problem-solving meetings that can be used to generate and reality-test alternative courses of action, develop change plans and commitments, and involve learners with their fellow students. These types of meetings should focus on finding a solution rather than finding fault with individuals.

2. *Open-Ended Meetings* allow discussion of any area related to the lives of individual learners. The intent here is to stimulate thinking about social and behavioral concerns. Students are encouraged to express their feelings, opinions or anything that will stimulate a thoughtful conversation regarding their own lives.

3. *Educational-Diagnostic Meetings* are concerned with evaluating what learners know about the school curriculum; but may be extended to evaluate the strategies that learners are using to learn and the strategies that the teacher is using to teach. The aim of these meetings should be to evaluate whether the teaching strategies used in the classroom are effective in producing a working understanding of the concepts being taught.

Frequent use of classroom meetings helps ensure the kind of responsible teacher-student social interactions that lead to the type of social involvement necessary for a well-managed classroom. The following suggestions are given to help teachers conduct such group meetings.

1. Arrange students in a circle.

2. The teacher acts as leader and sits in a different place in the circle each time.

3. Facilitate the meeting by the use of specific seating arrangements – separate two talking students, sit beside a disruptive student and assert control by your physical proximity.

4. Don't direct specific questions to individual members of the group unless they have indicated their willingness to respond by raising their hands.

5. Use open-ended meetings at first. Choose questions for which you have no preconceived answers.

6. The teacher should proceed in a non-judgmental manner.

7. Conduct meetings every day, or at least every two days, from five to 30 minutes. Keep them short at first. Try to end the meeting on a high note.

8. Make use of supportive comments. "That's an interesting way of looking at it," "I can tell you have been listening." Avoid comments like, "That's a good idea."

9. If a student talks at length, try to direct the discussion back to the group, without discouraging the enthusiastic member. "Thank you for your ideas. We'll come back to you. What do some others think?"

10. Initially paraphrase students' comments. This gives you time to think, as well as refreshing the topic for the students. Be careful, however, not to overdo this.

11. Give no assignment, but use the information gained to build a relevant curriculum for students.

12. Encourage students to challenge each other's ideas once respect is established.

Reality Therapy for excessive disruption

In addition to the seven major phases of Reality Therapy discussed earlier, Glasser (1977) describes *ten progressive steps* that teachers can take in dealing with students who are being excessively disruptive.

In many respects, these ten steps are more specific than the general phases described earlier, but it should be obvious that they are predicated on precisely the same notions of involvement, responsibility, commitment, planning and evaluation.

The ten steps are arranged in a sequence that moves from the least severe to the most severe form of management intervention.

Hopefully, most behavior problems can be dealt with without resorting to the latter steps in the sequence. The sequence itself is intended to be useful in dealing with a wide range of classroom problems – students who are behind in their work, disruptive, inattentive, tardy, aggressive and so forth.

1. *List Your No-No's* – Make a careful list of all the things you (the teacher) are presently doing in response to Billy's (the student) disruptive behavior. Be as honest as you can in stating your own reactions. Now make a pact with yourself not to respond to Billy in any of these conventional ways for the next four weeks. The point is that what you are currently doing is not working (even though it may work very well with other students). By stopping what is ineffective you may find that the problem disappears.

2. *Start Fresh* – Promise yourself that tomorrow no matter how disruptive Billy is, you will attempt to respond to him as if this was the first time such behavior had occurred. Give Billy no indication that his behavior is repetitive (e.g., Don't say "Look, you're doing it again," or "This time I've had enough of that"). Most importantly, don't let your negative feelings for Billy's disruptive behavior prevent you from giving him positive verbal and non-verbal attention and recognition for good, responsible forms of behavior.

3. *A Better Day Tomorrow* – Plan to do something special for Billy each day for the next four weeks. Think in terms of things that will help him have better days. You might, for example, greet him warmly with a "Good to see you this morning Billy," or give him special little errands to do such as, "Billy, would you do me a favor and take this notice across the hall to Mr. Stevens and come right back?" Do these things calmly and matter-of-factly. Try to show Billy that he is of value in the classroom.

(Note: the first three steps suggest changing your attitude toward Billy and resolving to start fresh. The next set of steps suggest non-punitive, but socially-accountable responses to Billy when he breaks classroom rules.)

4. *Quiet Correction* – When a rule is broken, keep your tone cool and crisp until Billy gives some recognition of the rules and makes some effort to comply. Try to establish that, while Billy must take responsibility for doing something wrong, you are willing to correct him, and that if he accepts the cor-

rection, that ends it. Be calm and give Billy the impression that you knew he could do it. The following scenario gives an example of how you might behave when Billy disrupts a classroom norm (say that this time Billy has jumped out of his seat and punched another student during a seatwork period).

You: "O.K. Billy, to your desk."

(Billy returns to his seat, and you follow him.)

"What did you do, Billy?"

Billy: "Nothing."

You: "Billy, I just asked you what you did. Tell me, please."

Billy: "Well, he was bugging me."

You: "What did you do, Billy?"

Billy: "He was a jerk, so I hit him."

You: "Can you work quietly at your seat now?"

Billy: "What are you going to do?"

You: "I just asked if you could work quietly now. We'd all like to get our work done without any distractions."

Billy: "O.K., I'll try."

5. *Make a Plan* – Unfortunately, a situation may inevitably arise in which step four doesn't work. For example, if Billy balks and digs his heels in at step four (perhaps running away, sitting down and having a tantrum, or playing "deaf and dumb"), get the rest of your class taken care of (ask another teacher or teacher aid, or appoint a student monitor), and continue calmly, but insistently, to make Billy aware of the classroom rules and his responsibility in relation to them.

You: "What did you do Billy?"

Billy: (Nothing)

You: "What's the rule about hitting other people, Billy?"

Billy: "I didn't hurt him."

You: "Did you break the hitting rule, Billy?" (Keep plugging away until you cut through all Billy's evasions and get him to acknowledge in some way that he knows the rule and that he broke it.)

Billy: "Well O.K., but so what?"

You: "Well, Billy, can you make a plan to follow the rules?"

Billy: "What do you mean?"

You: "Can you promise to avoid hitting anyone for the next four days?"

Billy: "What if I don't?"

You: "I just asked if you think you can keep from hitting anyone for the next four days."

Billy: "Ah, I don't know." (If Billy agrees to a plan at this stage, stop here. If not, go on to step 6.)

6. *Conference Time* – Persist with Billy until he agrees to sit down with you and talk matters over. Explain to Billy that he won't be punished and that you'd simply like to help him work things out. Listen to Billy's complaints, talk, joke a little, get to know him better and gradually work out a plan that will help him follow the rules. You may consider using a behavioral contract at this stage if it seems necessary. Keep stressing to Billy that he has the power to make a good plan.

(If all the above steps fail, you probably need to move on to a graduated series of progressively more severe "benching" techniques. These last four steps should only be considered when Billy becomes so disruptive that he must be "taken out of the game to cool off.")

7. *Off to the Castle* – Arrange a place in your classroom where Billy can sit apart from the rest of the class, but still can observe what's going on. Make this an enrichment spot with books, coloring materials, puzzles and quiet games.

When Billy disrupts, tell him to sit in the Castle. Don't do or say anything else. Send him there firmly with no discussion. Casually observe him, but pay no obvious attention to him. The partial isolation of the Castle (don't worry if Billy sends several hours or most of the day there), has a way of making the normal classroom routine look very attractive. It also helps Billy learn that he can be non-disruptive.

When you believe Billy has settled down and is anxious to return to the rest of the class, ask him to do so. If he does, in your next break, go over the class rules with him, and ask him to make a brief plan (commitment) to follow them. This may be as simple as "O.K., I'll try," or "O.K., I'm ready to work quietly and not disturb anyone else." However simple, some kind of plan must be agreed upon.

8. *Off to the Office* – If Billy still disrupts, he must be removed from the class. You've bent over backwards, and at this stage,

the limit for your tolerance has been reached. Calmly tell Billy to go down to the office and take a rest. The principal's or counselor's office may be used for this procedure.

To work effectively, step eight requires some earlier planning with the principal or counselor. The office rest place should again be made comfortable – an atmosphere that shows that you care and that you don't want to hurt Billy. The principal or counselor works with the student in the same manner as you did in steps four, five and six. He or she makes it clear to Billy that he must return to the classroom, but that he must first develop a plan to help himself follow the classroom rules.

9. *A Tolerance Day* – If Billy becomes totally out of control and can't be contained in the office rest spot, his parents will have to be contacted to take him home. If this occurs, the next school day is a tolerance day in which Billy is brought to school in the morning and asked to make a plan and commit himself to the classroom rules. If he does this, you may return to using steps one to three. If not, he is asked to remain at step eight until he can do so.

10. *Where There's Life There's Hope* – If all else fails, and regular school can't contain a student, the student must stay home or be placed in some special agency in the community. While this may sound harsh, it too is sometimes a reality. Even at this stage, the occasional tolerance day can be attempted during which the student is returned to school for further trials.

Assertive Discipline techniques

Like Reality Therapy, Assertive Discipline offers particular techniques that can be applied by individual teachers. The Canters (see Canter, 1978, 1989; Canter & Canter, 1976, 1992) offer the following suggestions for applying Assertive Discipline:

1. Set a maximum of five classroom rules that clearly describe expectations for students. Canter and Canter (1992) suggest appropriate rules for grades K-6 might include: follow directions, keep hands, feet and objects to yourself, do not leave your seats, raise your hand, do not interrupt others who are working, stay in seats, and don't leave the room without permission. Rules for grades 7-12 might include: follow direc-

tions, no swearing or teasing, and be in your seat when the bell rings.

2. There are four ways of setting limits verbally: *hints* ("Everyone should be working."); *questions* ("Would you please begin your reading?"); *I-messages* ("I want you to open your books and get to work"); and *demands* ("Get to work now."). Canter (1978) is quick to caution that in making a demand, a teacher must be prepared to follow through with consequences that demands imply. Don't make demands when you are not prepared to follow through.

3. Use a one-to-one problem-solving conference. This is a meeting between the teacher and the student where a specific inappropriate behavior is discussed. This meeting should be used to gain insight into the student's behavior without making the behavior public. During this meeting, Canter and Canter (1992) suggest that the teacher show empathy to the student in order to find out why the behavior occurred. This is followed by a discussion about what the teacher can do to help the student's behavior improve. The teacher and student then draw up a joint action plan that is based on this "common ground."

4. When communicating a directive to a particular student, use the student's name. Using the student's name enhances the forcefulness of the communication and makes clear to whom the message is intended. In delivering directives, non-verbal communication is also important. Use a serious tone of voice, have direct eye contact with the student, and use appropriate hand gestures and facial expressions to accentuate the message.

5. The *broken-record technique* is a method that redirects a message to a student who persistently attempts to deflect it. The broken-record technique involves insistent repetition of the message. Below is an illustration of how you (the teacher) might use the broken-record technique with Roger (a student) when he interrupts another student who is speaking:

You: "Roger, I want you to raise your hand and wait until you are called upon before you speak out."

Roger: "But what Ray said is wrong."

You: "That's not the point. I want you to raise your hand."

Roger: "You don't see me when I put my hand up."

You: "I understand, I'll watch more closely but, I want you to raise your hand."

As can be seen from the example, in repeating the message preface it with "That's not the point, . . ." or "I understand but, ..." It is suggested that the message not be repeated more than three times. Also, teachers should be prepared to follow through with an appropriate consequence if the student fails to accept the rule.

6) Develop beforehand a plan outlining the consequences for breaking rules. Unless teachers have thought about what actions they are going to take, they are left to improvise consequences on a moment to moment basis. This prevents a consistent application of consequences, and may lead to students feeling that they are being treated unfairly. Suggested consequences include: time-out (as described in chapter 5), loss of privileges, detention, referral to the principal and being sent home from school. A system can be set up that designates increasingly severe consequences each time the same rule violation occurs. For example:

first violation – warning and name on board

second violation – check beside name and 10 minute time-out

third violation – second check beside name and 30 minute detention

fourth violation – referral to principal

fifth violation – parents are notified

sixth violation – suspension from school.

A systematic plan should be explained to students at the beginning of the school year. The plan should not only make clear the consequences for misbehavior, but of equal importance, the kinds of appropriate behavior expected of students. Plans should be appropriate to the needs of the teacher, while at the same time protecting the best interests of the students.

7. Positive consequences should also be forthcoming to students who comply appropriately with expectations. Use positive assertions to commend students displaying desirable behaviors (e.g., "Jo-Anne, I like the way you are working"). Teachers must show students that they not only care about their positive behaviors, but that they sincerely care for them as individuals. Also, implementing rewards such as those

discussed in chapter 5 can be valuable in positively reinforc-ing students' respect of classroom rules.

A token reward system popularized by the Canters (1976) is *mar-bles in a jar*. When the class is exhibiting appropriate behavior the teacher drops a marble into a jar. The sound of the marble hitting the jar signals to students that they are acting appropriately and that the teacher recognizes their efforts. Each marble is allocated some unit of value. When so many marbles accumulate, a class reward is given (e.g., party, trip).

Critique

The values, rights, rules and responsibilities resident in interper-sonal relations are interlocked in what could be termed a *moral order* (see Harré, 1984). A moral order is comprised of the roles or posi-tions attributed to individuals by themselves and by others. The moral order of a classroom arises from the beliefs held by those who influence classroom activities (e.g., students, teachers, other school personnel and parents) concerning their role-related rights and responsibilities, and the beliefs they hold about the rights and responsibilities of others. It is through such beliefs that learners and teachers are "positioned" in the moral order of a classroom. These beliefs provide a framework (moral order) for social relations and steer the kinds of interpersonal interactions that occur. To illustrate, if a learner believes that she is a worthwhile person and that her con-tributions to classroom activities are valued, and others (e.g., the teacher, classmates, parent/s) demonstrate their belief in her effica-cy, then she is likely to adopt particular kinds of behaviors – behav-iors that position her in her interpersonal relations so that she is per-ceived by herself and by others to be worthwhile and efficacious. In other words, her behaviors will perpetuate her particular role in the moral order.

The three models discussed in this chapter are attempts to struc-ture the moral order of classrooms and schools, by positioning stu-dents, teachers, school personnel and parents in particular ways. A major question to be asked in appraising the programs of manage-ment emerging from these models is, are the kinds of values, rights, rules and responsibilities countenanced and administered through these models consistent with our educational aims? Are the moral orders that these programs of management attempt to sustain con-sistent with our educational goals?

The expressed *purposes* of the three models or the kinds of moral orders they propose to create, do not appear to be at odds with an educational aim of developing responsible, independent learners able to manage their own behavior. However, are the *means* employed by these programs of management also consonant with achieving this aim? Being responsible and independent requires skill at negotiating when in conflict with others. It demands being able to articulate one's reasons, to understand the reasons of others and to choose responsible actions. Assertive Discipline seems to provide little in the way of opportunities for learners to develop such skill. In Assertive Discipline, students are seen to rely on the teacher who is made responsible to intervene and exercise authority in dealing with disruptions and conflicts. Although Assertive Discipline acknowledges that learners have rights that need to be protected, teachers and students are not encouraged to explore the causes of misbehavior or reasons why violations of rights might occur. The possibility that problems may arise from legitimate concerns or unfulfilled needs seems to be ignored. The practice of Assertive Discipline seeks to eliminate problems without first gaining an understanding of them. Is this is an approach to resolving difficulties we wish to convey to learners?

Further, Assertive Discipline makes no special provision for assisting learners to acquire a sense of what it means to work cooperatively, to appreciate the notion of democracy or to develop regard for their membership in a community. If these are also our educational aims then it would seem desirable to have a style of classroom management that imparts (models) these values and helps to build a moral order in which they figure.

With an emphasis on classroom meetings during which students attempt collaboratively to understand problems, explore solutions and set rules, Reality Therapy would seem to convey cooperative, democratic and communitarian values. Through the vehicle of classroom meetings, Reality Therapy also would seem to provide more opportunity for learners to grasp skills necessary for thoughtful and responsible actions in resolving interpersonal problems. Thus, it would appear that Reality Therapy eclipses Assertive Discipline in being able to meet the particular educational aims alluded to above.

However, another aspect of becoming responsible and independent is learning how to cope effectively with failure. The experience of failure and being able to learn from it would seem fundamental to learners' social and academic development. With its emphasis on avoiding failure, Reality Therapy appears to ignore a valuable piece of the reality of learning. In focusing on averting failure in trying to ensure the meeting of needs, Glasser equivocates about when students should be permitted to fail. Certainly, we would not want to mandate failure as a compulsory component in achieving educational aims. However, it would seem that the ideal of eliminating all circumstances where students are likely to fail is not only unrealistic, but also may deny learners experiences necessary to the development of skills and dispositions that enable them to learn from failing.

Similar to Reality Therapy, the SMPSD promotes the understanding of problems and the development of solutions, an approach to problem-solving in line with our educational goals. Also, in advocating students' participation in determining rules and setting consequences, the SMPSD embodies cooperative, democratic and communitarian values. Such participation provides opportunities for learners to develop a sense of responsibility by having some say in determining rules and the consequences for their own actions.

In addition to whether or not these programs of management are conducive to our educational aims, there is the issue of practicality. The techniques of Assertive Discipline and Reality Therapy can be implemented by a teacher working independently in his or her classroom. However, in order to be a school-wide program that utilizes the potential support of other institutional and community resources, relative consensus and cooperation from other teachers, administrators, school support personnel and parents are required. Duke and Meckel (1984) concede that such consensus may be difficult to achieve. As well, implementing Assertive Discipline, Reality Therapy and the SMPSD on a school-wide basis requires substantial amounts of time. Given the consequences of budgetary restraints (e.g., increased class sizes, fewer school personnel), finding time to implement and sustain such school-wide programs may be difficult.

The strength of school-wide models is in a more efficient approach to problems ameliorated by consistency in responses among those who are in a position to help. By mobilizing resources both inside and outside the classroom to help deal with problems of student conduct, school-wide approaches can provide a supportive and empowering context for teachers. Distributing the disciplinary load lessens the burden on teachers and allows them to devote more of their time and effort to more positive instructional activities.

References

Alberti, R.E. & Emmons, M.L. (1975). *Stand up, speak out, talk back*. New York: Pocket Books.

Brophy, J.E. & Putnam, J.G. (1979). Classroom management in the elementary grades. In D.L. Duke (Ed.), *Classroom management: The seventy-eighth yearbook of the National Society for the Study of Education, Part II* (pp. 182-216). Chicago: The University of Chicago Press.

Canter, L. (1978). Be an assertive teacher. *Instructor, 88*, 60.

Canter, L. (1989). Assertive discipline: More than names on the board and marbles in the jar. *Phi Delta Kappan, 71*(1), 57-61.

Canter, L. & Canter, M. (1976). *Assertive discipline: A take-charge approach for today's educator*. Seal Beach, CA: Canter and Associates.

Canter, L. & Canter, M. (1992). *Assertive discipline: Positive behavior management for today's classrooms (2nd ed.)*. Santa Monica, CA: Lee Canter & Associates.

Duke, D.L. (1980). *Managing student behavior problems*. New York: Teachers College Press.

Duke, D.L. (1990). School organization, leadership, and student behavior. In O. C. Moles (Ed.), *Student discipline strategies: Research and practice* (pp. 19-46). Albany, NY: State University of New York Press.

Duke, D.L. & Meckel, A.M. (1984). *Teacher's guide to classroom management*. New York: Random House.

Duke, D.L. & Seidman, W. (1982). Are public schools organized to minimize behavior problems? In D.L. Duke (Ed.), *Helping teachers manage classrooms* (pp. 140-162). Alexandria, VA: Association for Supervision and Curriculum Development

Glasser, W. (1965). *Reality therapy*. New York: Harper & Row.

Glasser, W. (1969). *Schools without failure*. New York: Harper & Row.

Glasser, W. (1972). *The identity society*. New York: Harper & Row.

Glasser, W. (1977). Ten steps to good discipline. *Today's Education, 66*, 61-63.

Glasser, W. (1978). Disorder in our schools: Causes and remedies. *Phi Delta Kappan, 59*, 322-325.

Glasser, W. (1981). *Stations of the mind*. New York: Harper & Row.

Glasser, W. (1986). *Control theory in the classroom*. New York: Perennial Library.

Glasser, W. (1989). Control theory. In W. Glasser (Ed.), *Control theory in the practice of reality therapy: Case studies* (pp. 1-15). New York: Harper & Row.

Glasser, W. (1990). *The quality school*. New York: Harper & Row.

Glasser, W. (1994). *The quality school teacher*. New York: Harper Collins.

Glasser, W. (1997). A new look at school failure and school success. *Phi Delta Kappan, 78,* 596-602.

Glasser, W. (1998). *Choice theory in the classroom.* New York : Harper Perennial.

Harré, R. (1984). *Personal being: A theory for individual psychology.* Cambridge: Harvard University Press.

Kaltenbach, R.F. & Glasser, W. (1982). Reality therapy in groups. In G.M. Gazda (Ed.), *Basic approaches to group psychotherapy and group counseling* (pp. 276-318). Springfield, IL: Charles C. Thomas.

Porter, L. (1996). *Student behaviour: Theory and practice for teachers.* New South Wales, AU: Allyn & Unwin Pty Ltd.

Smith, M.J. (1975). *When I say no, I feel guilty: How to cope – using the skills of systematic assertive therapy.* New York: Dial Press.

Watkins, C. & Wagner, P. (1987). *School discipline: A whole-school approach.* Oxford: Basil Blackwell.

Chapter Eight
Socio-cultural Approaches

Overview and Rationale

Socio-cultural approaches to classroom management consider the broader social and moral contexts in which classrooms and schools are embedded. These perspectives look beyond the confines of the mind of an individual student in proposing an explanation for his or her thoughts and actions. They paint a portrait of individual thoughts and actions as manifestations or expressions of social and cultural (socio-cultural) practices. In this chapter, we examine these approaches to classroom management.

Socio-cultural perspectives on education have proliferated in recent years and occupy an important place in current educational theory. Consequently, we believe it is instructive to consider a brief overview of the socio-cultural position before turning more directly to its implications for classroom management. Socio-cultural perspectives share an emphasis on human relationships. More specifically, they pay attention to the means and practices we have of relating to one another; the most conspicuous being conversation.

According to socio-culturalists, long established psychological explanations of thought and behavior mistakenly focus on individuals acting in isolation. This narrow focus on the individual has neglected the historical, social and cultural contexts in which all human thoughts and actions take place. These are contexts of relationship, composed of the means and practices with which human beings relate to one another. We enter societies and cultures at birth, and they provide the medium for learning and psychological development. Socio-culturalists argue that thoughts and actions take shape within complex traditions of belief, ways of learning and understanding, and means of expression that have been bequeathed as products of human history. In this light, the richness of mental life, as shown in our ability to reflect on our thoughts and ourselves, is an effect of participating in historical traditions of socio-cultural practice.

It may be relatively unproblematic to accept the claim that the beliefs and actions of individuals are influenced by the societies and cultures in which they live. However, socio-culturalists make a stronger claim. They assert that the very nature of human individual psychological processes and functions can be explained in terms of socio-cultural practices. As discussed in the subsequent chapter, Vygotsky's (1978, 1986) theory of development charts the way in which we are taught to direct our thoughts and behavior through increasingly sophisticated forms of linguistic control. Vygotsky describes the link between thought and language, and how, through our relations with others, thought takes its form largely as a kind of conversation. The course of psychological development consists in learning to think by adopting social, collective conventions for conversation as forms for private, individual thought.

Some socio-culturalists have drawn attention to the storied nature of our memories and experiences (Bruner, 1987; Egan, 1997; Howard, 1989; McAdams, 1988; Polkinghorne, 1988). Memories and experiences consist not only in thoughts, feelings and actions, but also, in narrative elements such as plots, characters and scenes. The events and phenomena in our memories and experiences derive meaning from their place in narratives (forms of storytelling). These narratives lend frameworks of causality, coherence and temporality to human experience. A number of researchers have attempted to detail the characteristics of conversations by which adults impart to children narrative forms for elaborating past events, and the ways in which children increasingly conform to narrative structures when recounting their experiences (e.g., Eisenberg, 1985; Fivush, 1994; Fivush & Reese, 1992; Hudson, 1990). This work indicates how such seemingly individual psychological processes and functions as memory depend on exposure to socio-cultural practices such as narrative.

A complementary view is offered by Bakhtin (1986), who explains the conversational nature of thought as a reflection of the relationship between speaker and listener in public dialogue. When we think, it is as if we are having a conversation with another person. We perform the roles of both speaker and listener. We ask ourselves questions, we make demands of ourselves, we point things out to ourselves, we offer alternatives, we debate, we agree or disagree, and so forth. We learn to treat and relate to ourselves as if we were another person. George Herbert Mead (1934) described this intrinsically relational feature of the self in terms of learning to take the role of the other. As Mead states, a person "becomes a self insofar as he can take [the] attitude of another and act towards himself as others act" (p. 171). Without immersion and participation in socio-cultural practices, human beings would not have access to the tools for reflective thought. Consequently, without participating in our cultures and societies, we could not learn in the ways we do, nor could we develop the particular kind of psychology we have.

Socio-cultural perspectives focus on the situated character of all human learning (Solomon & Perkins, 1998). Most simply, theories of situated learning emphasize context by claiming, "that much of what is learned is specific to the situation in which it is learned" (Anderson, Reder & Simon, 1996, p. 5.). For example, Lave and Wenger (Lave, 1988; Lave & Wenger, 1991) suggest that the kinds of mathematical calculation students learn in school won't necessarily help them balance a checkbook. Situated learning means that what and how something is learned is tied to the context in which that learning takes place. So, learning to make mathematical calculations in school often is learned to be applicable in school, but not at the grocery store.

Lave and Wenger (1991) construe learning, knowledge and understanding as distributed within communities of practice. They argue that learners do not acquire discrete skills in isolation. Rather, learning occurs in the context of a community that sustains various kinds of practices. These practices include ways of acting and inter-acting, remembering, imagining, knowing and understanding. A community of practice could be practitioners of a spiritual faith. It could be physicians or mathematicians. Teachers and students in a classroom could be described as a community of practitioners. From this perspective, learning means becoming able to participate appro-priately in the practices of a community. Lave and Wenger use the concept of "legitimate peripheral participation" to draw attention to the gradual process of development in which learners progress toward increasing competence. Learners initially enter into a com-munity of practice, and through gradually increasing participation and learning, eventually become full-fledged community members. In turn, as full community members, they inevitably perpetuate the community by teaching its practices to new members.

Socio-cultural practices also include negotiation, persuasion, power and authority (e.g., Gergen & Gergen, 1991; McNamee & Gergen, 1992). A major contributor to this line of thought, Michel Foucault (1967, 1979, 1981), argued that all human knowledge and activity is enacted through practices of power. Foucault's writings are concerned largely with how, throughout history, certain minority groups have used power to impose notions of what is right and wrong, true and false, normal and abnormal on the majority. Foucault's historical analyses illustrate how power is used to uphold conventions of normality and, in turn, to sustain the institutions and conventions of modern society. The issue of power is relevant to classroom management. As we elaborate in this chapter, some theorists believe that classroom management depends fundamentally on the different ways in which teachers draw on their sources of power and authority, thereby creating different kinds of social orders in classrooms.

Principles

Five kinds of power

Forty years ago, French and Raven (1960) described five different bases of social power. Tauber (1995) recently has extended French and Raven's analysis to the context of classrooms. According to Tauber, teachers may not adequately understand the nature of power and its effects in the classroom. Consequently, he argues, teachers may unwittingly be utilizing power bases that create negative feelings, non-compliance, and a lack of commitment among students toward teachers and schools. At the same time, however, Tauber suggests that teachers can cultivate those power bases conducive to positive and productive classroom relations between teachers and students.

French and Raven's (1960) taxonomy of power includes the following forms and functions:

1. *Coercive power* stems from the perception that an individual has control over administering punishment. In the context of the classroom, coercive power operates when students allow teachers to dictate their behavior because students believe that teachers are in a position to impose sanctions or punishment.

2. *Reward power* is derived from the belief that an individual is in control of dispensing rewards. Reward power is at play in the classroom when students perceive the teacher as being in a position of making available desired rewards such as praise and grades.

3. *Legitimate power* stems from the belief that certain individuals in society have the right to prescribe the behavior of others. The source of legitimate power is found in people's acceptance of social institutions, and their belief that the control regulated by a hierarchical structure is necessary for social institutions to fulfill their designated functions. Churches, the military, the legal system, government and schools all depend on legitimate power in order to perform the various duties and responsibilities with which they are charged. Legitimate power brings about compliance insofar as individuals recognize the authority of the institution. The structure of educational institutions gives teachers legitimate power. Teachers are hired by school boards, and delegated the responsibility to ensure that students learn and that classrooms are safe environments. Legitimate power operates in classrooms when students perceive that teachers have the right and duty to assert themselves regarding what is appropriate and inappropriate, and to direct students' conduct accordingly.

4. *Referent power* occurs as a result of the respect or admiration people hold for the attributes and actions of an individual. The referent power of an individual stems from his or her charisma or appeal. Teachers to whom students are attracted, and with whom students identify positively, possess referent power. A teacher with referent power gains students' loyalty, and students act in ways that merit the teacher's respect and approval.

5. *Expert power* results when an individual is perceived to have particular knowledge and expertise that is valued or desired. Teachers hold expert power by virtue of the subject matter knowledge they are expected and required to possess. When students believe that teachers have knowledge of a subject matter of value, students are more likely not only to be cooperative, but to take an interest in learning.

Power takes a variety of forms, and the foregoing analysis provides a source of ideas for considering the use of power in classrooms. As Tauber (1995) points out, coercive power and reward power function primarily by exploiting the desires and fears of students. However, coercive and reward powers can easily be undermined. For the student who no longer finds detentions adverse, or praise rewarding, the power of the teacher is diminished. An exclusive use of coercive power and reward power shares much in common with the application of behavioral theory, and much of the criticism leveled at behaviorism similarly applies.

Tauber (1995) terms coercive power, reward power and legitimate power *position* powers. These forms of power rely at root on the official professional status of the teacher. Students listen to, and comply with, teachers' demands because teachers can reward, they can punish or simply because they are teachers. The advantage of position powers is that they demand less of the teacher, and can quickly precipitate responses. A sharp reprimand or prospect of a good grade often can achieve immediate results. However, the disadvantage of position powers is that the most they can accomplish is compliance.

By contrast, Tauber (1995) terms referent power and expert power *personal* powers insofar as they are the result of personality characteristics, knowledge, skills and abilities. With respect to personal powers, Tauber claims that students respond to the teacher in ways that reflect students' respect for, and commitment to, the teacher as a person.

The basis of authority

While the concept of authority bears a close relationship with the concept of power, some theorists argue that there is an important distinction to be drawn between these two concepts (e.g., Leriche, 1992; Mitchell & Spady, 1983). As Leriche explains, power connotes force, and implies that the will of a person in power can be imposed on others without their consent. By contrast, authority works more indirectly. Authority implies influence that has been earned. People with authority command the respect and confidence of others, thus gaining their voluntary cooperation.

An extensive and thoughtful analysis of teachers' authority in schools and classrooms is presented by Clifton and Roberts (1993). You will notice in our discussion of their work some overlap between concepts used by Clifton and Roberts to elucidate the nature of authority and those used by Tauber (1995) to explain power. Clifton and Roberts examine the socio-cultural practices and conditions that support the authority of teachers in fulfilling their responsibilities. Clifton and Roberts' starting point is the socio-cultural position that societies and cultures furnish conceptual tools, theories and beliefs with which human beings interpret the world.

These concepts, theories and beliefs contribute to a shared under-standing among members of a social group which, in turn, provides individuals with social identities. Sharing perspectives and goals, and defining oneself and others in terms of the social identities accepted and sustained by the group, promotes cohesion and col-laboration among group members. This cohesion and collaboration furnishes the resources needed to build socio-cultural structures and institutions.

Social structures are constructed by assigning statuses to group members. A *status* is a socially defined position in a social system. Administrator, staff, teacher and student are statuses in the social structure of school. Typically, social groups are structured with sta-tuses arranged hierarchically. This is the case not only with highly formal structures like the legal system or the military, but also with more informal groups such as gangs. This hierarchical arrangement defines social statuses within the group, and contributes to individ-uals' identity and sense of belonging. The hierarchy of statuses also circumscribes roles. *Roles* are patterns of behavior judged appropri-ate to particular social statuses. Not only do shared perspectives and beliefs function to maintain the social structure, but conversely, the social structure serves to maintain the shared perspectives and beliefs of the group. Social and cultural institutions preserve and often enforce certain beliefs. For instance, the public's belief in a need for safety and security supports the existence of social institu-tions of law enforcement. In turn, the existence of these institutions and the various functions they perform lead us to define certain activities as crimes, and further perpetuate belief in the need for institutions designed to ensure our collective safety and security.

Clifton and Roberts (1993) assert that teaching is essentially a social process conducted between people who are ascribed the social statuses of teacher and student. "Teacher" is both a status and a role that encompasses certain rights and responsibilities. These rights and responsibilities issue from the institutional attributes of schools and classrooms, as well as the individual attributes of teachers. The central claim undergirding the approach to classroom management provided by Clifton and Roberts is that in order to fulfill their responsibilities to provide safe and productive learning environ-ments, teachers require authority to manage their classrooms effec-tively. This authority stems both from the organizational structure of educational institutions (i.e., institutional authority) and from their competencies as teachers (i.e., individual authority).

It is important to note that while Clifton and Roberts (1993) recognize various criticisms leveled at the educational system as it currently exists, including the possibility that more humanistic approaches to education are needed, they argue that radical transformations of the present system are unlikely. Hence, their approach is aimed at enhancing teachers' authority within the existing school structure.

A framework for understanding classroom interactions

Clifton and Roberts (1993) point out that the difficulty teachers have in maintaining order in the classroom can be traced to the problem of conflict between statuses. The status of teacher conflicts with the status of student. In order to explain this conflict, Clifton and Roberts apply the concepts of integration and adaptation. Teachers are charged with the responsibility of socializing and enculturating students into the knowledge, practices, norms, conventions and values of communities. From the perspective of teachers, a primary classroom consideration is integration. *Integration* refers to the task of organizing and coordinating the activities of different actors. "Applied to classrooms, the integration task for teachers is to coordinate the conduct of students so they can master the prescribed curriculum" (p. 44). Integration requires teachers to focus on collective considerations. In contrast, students are concerned with adaptation. For students, *adaptation* "involves getting whatever is possible from the classroom to serve their particular interests" (p. 45). In other words, while teachers see their responsibilities in terms of the classroom as a whole, students view what goes on in the classroom in terms of their own individual needs and considerations.

Clifton and Roberts (1993) claim that the divergent perspectives spawned by the goals of integration and adaptation create discord between teachers and students. However, the social structure of schools tips the balance of authority in favor of teachers. In order for teachers to achieve the task of integration, the social structure of schools invests more of its resources in the status of teacher than in the status of student. As Clifton and Roberts make plain, schools are social institutions that have the intended purpose of changing students. Changing students involves imposing constraints upon them, and the social structure of schools gives teachers the authority to impose constraints. However, students frequently perceive the imposition of constraints as a threat to their individual autonomy. Consequently, they respond with resistance. A fundamental conflict ensues between teachers and students regarding whose perspectives and interests should dictate classroom conduct. Clifton and Roberts contend that the divergent statuses of teachers and students, and the perspectives they maintain as a result of the goals of integration and adaptation, form a contentious framework for classroom interactions.

Structural tightness and looseness

Order is the imposition of structure for the purpose of achieving integration. We impose order to align and coordinate the activities of individuals. Clifton and Roberts (1993) propose that strategies teachers use for maintaining order in their classrooms can be conceptualized along a continuum from structural tightness to structural looseness. *Structural tightness* and *structural looseness* refer to the degree to which the classroom order constrains students' autonomy. In structurally tight classrooms, teachers enforce their perspective in ways that highly constrain the individual autonomy of students. Students are required to succumb to the order, and teachers employ coercion or reward to force students to refrain from the pursuit of needs that interfere with teachers' conceptions of the task of integration and goals of teaching and learning.

Clifton and Roberts (1993) argue that although teachers may have resources at their disposal to impose tight orders and create conditions that enable them unilaterally to dictate students' conduct, it is not advisable to do so. There is considerable risk of detrimental consequences for students. Clifton and Roberts caution that severe frustration of students' needs may foster feelings of resentment, demoralization and alienation. Structurally tight classrooms are likely to provoke disengagement from classroom learning, manifested as boredom, apathy, rebellion or hyperactivity. From this perspective, structurally-tight orders are inappropriate if we wish to promote values such as openness, discussion and freedom to voice critique, and if we wish learners to cultivate an enjoyment of learning and school.

At the other end of the continuum from structural tightness is structural looseness. In a structurally-loose classroom order, the teacher's perspective and preferences are not forced upon students, but rather, are proposed to students. Students do not submit unquestioningly to the teacher's directives. Instead, they are given the latitude to agree or disagree with the teacher's proposal, and to participate in negotiations concerned with setting the bounds of acceptable conduct. In characterizing the structurally loose approach, Clifton and Roberts (1993) cite the words of A. S. Neill (1960) with reference to the philosophy of education at the groundbreaking Summerhill school: "to make the school fit the child – instead of making the child fit the school" (p. 4). Summerhill was designed to encourage autonomy and maximize opportunities for the pursuit of individual expression. With these humanistic aims in place, conditions were created that enabled students to articulate their individual needs and receive conditional support in meeting them.

Clifton and Roberts (1993) argue that structurally loose classrooms are not devoid of order, but they are devoid of coercion. Order emerges out of the socio-cultural practices of persuasion and negotiation. In structurally loose classrooms, teachers and students collaborate in conversation, employing the socio-cultural practices of persuasion and negotiation, with the aim of accommodating their differing objectives. The successful outcome is a working consensus. The key for teachers wishing to retain the capacity to moderate classroom order is that they must successfully convince students of the merits of their proposals.

Clifton and Roberts (1993) also are critical of structurally loose classroom orders. Teachers must have the ability to articulate themselves persuasively and to negotiate effectively. However, this is not sufficient to ensure that classrooms will function productively. A structure that is founded on persuasion and negotiation can lead to the malaise of overly participatory democracies: endless arbitration over an interminable array of points of disagreement. It is not difficult to imagine the difficulties that would arise in the classroom if a teacher believed it necessary to hold negotiations with every student over his or her every activity.

Clifton and Roberts (1993) believe that the problem with structurally loose classrooms is fueled by two factors. One pertains to the uncertain and controversial nature of the objectives of schools. To illustrate, historically, most educators have focused on the goals of achievement and self-esteem. But what we mean when we use these terms has changed with the times. As McCaslin and Good (1992) describe,

> *Achievement can refer to mastery of a curriculum that is currently undergoing change or to performance on standardized tests that are themselves in the midst of criticism, self-scrutiny, and planned revision (e.g., SAT). Conceptions of self-esteem have shifted. In the popu-*

lar culture, self-esteem is presently defined less as an emergent con-
ception of the self-as-competent and more as a "feel-good" trait. (p. 10)

Even fundamental educational aims, such as the cultivation of the intellect and socialization, can be shown to be at cross purposes and not easily reconciled (Egan, 1997).

A second, related factor that Clifton and Roberts (1993) believe creates problems with structurally loose classrooms, is that students' participation in schools is mandated. However, students are not necessarily committed to the objectives advocated by schools and the broader communities in which schools are situated. In sum, it is not difficult to comprehend how a climate of ambiguous and unsupported objectives can easily breed protracted debates that elude constructive resolution.

The authoritative approach

Clifton and Roberts (1993) attempt to steer a middle course that avoids pitfalls at the extremes of structural tightness and looseness. They term their proposal for a middle position *the authoritative approach*. Clifton and Roberts explain the difference between authoritative and tight/loose classroom orders in terms of distinctions between rights and claims, and whether rights and claims are perceived as legitimate and binding. Individuals make assertions about how people should behave towards one another. These assertions about acceptable standards of conduct are adjudicated as being either rights or claims.

The difference Clifton and Roberts (1993) draw between a right and a claim concerns how each answers the question, "Does it legitimately achieve the objectives of the institution?" *Rights* are seen as legitimate ways of achieving objectives, *claims* are not. For example, a student might assert that she should be able to talk to her classmates while the teacher is giving a lesson. According to Clifton and Roberts, the student's assertion is a right or a claim depending on whether the teacher interprets the assertion as being legitimate with respect to meeting the objectives of the institution. On one hand, if the teacher deems it to be a right, there is a binding moral obligation for the teacher to accept and uphold the assertion. The teacher must at least permit the student to talk to her classmates, if not encourage her to do so. On the other hand, the assertion is a claim if the teacher judges it to be simply an expression of a student's personal preference that would prevent or hinder achieving institutional objectives.

In the case of a claim, there is no binding obligation, and thus the teacher does not feel any moral misgivings about denying its validity.

Clifton and Roberts (1993) believe that the difference between rights and claims explains how structurally tight classrooms work by attempting to enforce demands that are perceived by students as binding, but not legitimate. Students in structurally tight classrooms see teachers' assertions as illegitimate claims because students do not experience any moral obligation to institutional objectives. Students' objectives are individual preferences. However, students experience teachers' claims as binding because in structurally tight classrooms, teachers enforce their claims by means of coercion and reward. A similar problem occurs with structurally loose classrooms. However, in this case, teachers' assertions are considered as legitimate claims, but students similarly do not feel any binding moral obligation to them, particularly when they run counter to individual objectives.

Clifton and Roberts (1993) argue that structurally tight and loose orders require coercion or negotiation because they both are organized around the weaknesses of claims. In contrast, an authoritative order plays to the legitimacy and binding features of rights. There is authority when individuals are committed to accepting the rights and responsibilities which they are accorded in the service of meeting shared objectives. In an authoritative classroom, there is voluntary compliance because teachers and students mutually accept the legitimacy and binding obligations of their respective statuses in the social structure.

> *The key to understanding authoritative relationships is the appreciation that both superordinates and subordinates acknowledge the right of the former to make demands and the duty of the latter to obey. In this sense, superordinates can lead subordinates only if a mutual relationship of trust exists between people who hold the two statuses. In this respect, both teachers and students need to identify with each other and accept their respective statuses and obligations as being legitimate. (p. 55)*

An authoritative classroom order, in which students accept the directives of the teacher, is grounded in students' acceptance of institutional objectives, and in the trust that teachers are acting in students' best interests.

Institutional and individual authority

Authoritative orders are supported by two kinds of authority. *Institutional authority* is the authority vested in the various statuses comprising the structure of a social institution. It is authority derived from holding a particular position. Clifton and Roberts (1993) illustrate the nature of institutional authority with the example of principals. In the hierarchical structure of schools, the status of principal encompasses more rights and responsibilities than the statuses of teacher, staff member or student. However, these rights and responsibilities are attached to the status of principal, not to the individual holding the office. As Clifton and Roberts elaborate, if a principal resigns her position, she loses the status accorded to the office of principal. She does not take the rights and responsibilities of principal with her, just as the individual who replaces her cannot refuse to assume those rights and responsibilities with her new status. Institutional authority bears a close similarity with the concept of legitimate power previously described. They both focus on a certain group of socio-cultural practices in providing an account of what can be expected of people on the basis of their statuses or positions in a social structure.

In contrast to institutional authority, which is derived from the positioning of statuses within the social structure, *individual authority* is derived from attributes of the individual. Individual authority comes with being a professional who possesses expertise and is accorded authority as a consequence. It also can emerge from the charisma and appeal of the individual. These two dimensions of individual authority are similar to what were described earlier as expert and referent powers.

Clifton and Roberts (1993) argue that institutional and individual authority can reinforce each other when all participants appreciate that the structure of schools is directed at meeting the educational needs of students. The authoritative approach advocates capitalizing on these two sources of authority so that teachers can manage their classrooms effectively, and do so in a way that avoids the difficulties of imposed and negotiated classroom orders.

Methods and Applications

Tauber (1995) recommends that teachers cultivate their sources of referent and expert powers. Clearly, a preferred classroom climate is one in which students willingly follow the teacher's directions out of genuine respect for the teacher both as a professional and as a person, rather than in anticipation of coercion or reward. This kind of power is earned by judgments rendered by students regarding the merits of the teacher's actions. The following recommendations made by Tauber are specific actions teachers can take to promote their expert and referent powers.

Enhancing expert power.

1. *Use self-disclosure.* Relating the concepts and principles you teach to your own life assists students to see the relevance of what you are teaching, and helps students to relate this knowledge to their lives. According to Tauber (1995), self-disclosure helps to forge a sense of common identity, so long as it stops short of self-absorption.

2. *Build associations with students.* Tauber (1995) recommends that teachers participate with students in activities outside of regular classroom teaching. However, Tauber is quick to point out that these activities should be undertaken with an attitude of professionalism, and he cautions against trying to be a peer. Coaching, advising a students' club, participating in charity events and so forth, are appropriate avenues for building positive associations. Tauber contends that the associations built through such activities also help teachers to relate better with students.

3. *Distribute your attention fairly.* Tauber (1995) advises teachers to be aware of which students are attended to most often, and whether others have equal access to attention. If teachers allow certain students to monopolize their attention at the expense of attending to others, they will be perceived as unfair.

4. *Be accepting, but not patronizing.* Show an appreciation of students' interests, but don't allow class discussions to stray off topic too frequently.

5. *Discipline with dignity.* Tauber (1995) asserts that many students tend to comprehend criticism of their behaviors as criticism of them as people. Discipline in a manner that allows students to preserve their self-respect.

6. *Monitor biases and expectations.* It would be difficult for people to exist without having expectations. However, Tauber (1995) cautions that teachers sometimes can form expecta-

tions of students that are not accurate reflections of students' abilities and circumstances. When teachers operate on incorrect assumptions, their conduct toward students can be inappropriate. Making assumptions about students on the basis of such factors as socio-economic status, race, gender, ethnicity or what their older brothers or sisters are like can lead to difficulties.

7. *Learn and use communication skills.* Tauber (1995) extols the merits of developing the kinds of communication skills taught through Gordon's (1974) *Teacher Effectiveness Training* (see Chapter 2).

8. *Be a good role model.* Behave in the manner in which you would like your students to behave.

Enhancing referent power.

1. *Prepare.* Experts prepare. It is unreasonable to expect to know everything about your subject matter. Moreover, preparation not only increases what you know, but also alerts you to what you don't know.

2. *Practice what you preach.* Continue your own education in your subject areas and teaching practices, and keep current with educational trends and issues. Tauber (1995) admonishes that if you want your students to have an appreciation of their education as a life-long process, then, as a teacher, you need to act with that same appreciation.

3. *Foster students' intellectual independence.* Allow students the opportunity to discover knowledge for themselves. Excessive "spoon feeding" encourages dependence.

4. *Acknowledge your own accomplishments.* Tauber (1995) claims that teachers may be too humble with respect to their own accomplishments. He recommends that teachers find tactful ways of making their achievements known to students and to the broader community. Tauber suggests that this helps to create positive expectations about teachers' expertise.

5. *Acknowledge students' expertise and incorporate it in classroom activities.* Providing students with classroom opportunities to demonstrate their particular areas of expertise helps teachers to know students better. Tauber (1995) contends that part of being an expert includes recognizing and capitalizing on the expertise of others.

Enhancing institutional authority

When students begin a new school year, entering their new classrooms for the first time, they encounter teachers with whom they usually are unacquainted. Although teachers' individual authority can develop as students become increasingly familiar with the personal and professional attributes of their teachers, at least initially, teachers must rely on institutional sources of authority to maintain classroom order. While teachers gradually build their individual authority with students, they depend on institutional authority for support. However, even after individual authority begins to take hold, institutional authority persists in helping to sustain an authoritative classroom order. Clifton and Roberts (1993) make four recommendations for enhancing institutional authority:

1. *Establish a restricted set of clearly articulated objectives.* Objectives that are controversial, ambiguous and not clearly stated undermine institutional authority. According to Clifton and Roberts (1993), the specific content of institutional objectives may be of less importance in advancing institutional authority than the requirements that objectives be focused, stated clearly and supported by the community. Clifton and Roberts argue that schools cannot respond effectively to the educational needs of students while attempting to appease the diverse and often contradictory agendas of various interest groups. Priorities need to be set.

2. *Decentralize schools.* We already have discussed the problem that occurs when students are not committed to the institutional objectives of schools. This problem is amplified when teachers and parents equally are not invested in school objectives. Students, teachers and parents are likely to be less committed to objectives imposed by external sources than to objectives they have had a hand in establishing. Clifton and Roberts (1993) argue that the decentralization of schools would diminish this undesirable effect of bureaucratic administration. One means of attempting to promote commitment to objectives is for students, teachers and parents to participate actively in constituting them. For this to be accomplished, however, schools need to be decentralized with greater control given to the members of the community served by a particular school.

3. *Stipulate and publicize the rights and obligations of all statuses in the school.* Clifton and Roberts (1993) contend that reaching

consensus on institutional objectives would constitute a significant accomplishment. However, it is equally important that the institution provides a structure that supports the pursuit of those objectives that have been established. Clifton and Roberts recommend that the positions, rights, obligations and responsibilities of all statuses comprising the school be stipulated clearly and publicized. This helps to ensure that administrators, staff, teachers and students know what they can expect of others, what others can expect of them and what each individual contributes in meeting collectively shared objectives. Clifton and Roberts suggest that increasing awareness of various statuses and roles in the social structure of the school can serve to strengthen this structure. Such increased awareness serves to give individuals an appreciation of the collective good, lends credibility to the organization and ultimately enhances institutional authority.

4. *Establish systematic methods of evaluation.* Clifton and Roberts (1993) characterize the three preceding policy recommendations as perhaps idealistic. Numerous factors can interfere with individuals' commitments and responsibilities despite a well-structured and -supported set of objectives. Students' intentions can be diverted by peer pressures, and teachers may be distracted by personal obligations. Thus, Clifton and Roberts advise that a system of monitoring objectives, as well as the means used to achieve them, needs to be established and implemented. Evaluations of efficiency and effectiveness are necessary to determine whether and how objectives are being met. In addition, evaluation in the service of accountability demonstrates to the community that the institution takes its mandate seriously. This, in turn, enhances institutional authority.

Enhancing individual authority

As mentioned, individual authority is the second form of authority teachers employ in an authoritative approach. Clifton and Roberts (1993) provide the four following recommendations directed at teachers as ways of enhancing their individual authority.

1. *Become members of society's intellectual elite.* This recommendation pertains to teachers not only developing expertise in their particular subject areas, but further, acquiring knowl-

edge more broadly, and persistently pursuing their own education. This is necessary if teachers wish to ensure their intellectual competence, and secure legitimacy and respect within their communities as well as their classrooms. Clifton and Roberts (1993) imply that teachers need to perceive themselves as important members of society who serve as guardians of our socio-cultural traditions of knowledge and ways of knowing. If the status of teacher is to be respected in the eyes of the broader community, then teachers must work both individually and collectively to earn this respect.

2. *Develop pedagogical expertise.* While subject matter expertise is necessary, it is not sufficient. Teachers not only need to be well versed in the subjects they teach, but also, they need to be adept at teaching the subject matter in ways that facilitate students' learning and understanding. Knowledge of the diverse aptitudes, abilities and psychological needs of students also is requisite to good pedagogy. Clifton and Roberts (1993) advocate that teachers become knowledgeable in relevant psychological topics, such as cognitive, affective and moral development; learning theories; and measurement techniques.

3. *Become knowledgeable about the social organization of classrooms and schools.* This recommendation assumes the importance of having a socio-cultural as well as a psychological perspective. Teaching and learning take place in the socio-cultural contexts of schools and classrooms. Clifton and Roberts (1993) argue that unless teachers have a firm understanding of the socio-cultural aspects of educational institutions (such as those described in this chapter), teachers will have a thin appreciation of the nature of the activities taking place in their classrooms.

4. *Develop empathy toward students.* Clifton and Roberts (1993) argue that self-respect is a fundamental human need. Students, like everyone else, need to preserve their self-respect. As mentioned, education is about changing students. But change is difficult. If teachers expect students to change in ways that are positive, then they need to attend to students' concerns in ways that are sensitive and respectful. Teachers need to understand the identifications that students make as a consequence of their experiences of success and failure in classrooms. Clifton and Roberts recommend that

teachers actively pursue the development of empathy and the kinds of communication skills that convey their understanding of students' experiences (such as those described in Chapter 2).

Empirical illustrations

One way of illustrating the relevance and utility of concepts and theories is through the kinds of scenarios that have appeared in previous chapters. The foregoing recommendations for enhancing referent and expert powers, and individual authority, such as developing good communication skills and empathy, already have been exemplified in this fashion in Chapter 2. Another way of illustrating the relevance and usefulness of concepts and theories is by means of research. At this juncture, we turn to a discussion of research that appears to lend credibility to an authoritative approach, and to the recommendation that teachers cultivate sources of expert and referent powers, and individual authority.

Clearly, there are differences between the kind of relationship parents have with their children and the relationship teachers have with their students. Parents and teachers have different obligations and responsibilities. However, if we accept that good parenting and effective teaching consist in holding some similar attitudes and values about how adults should relate to children, perhaps some useful parallels can be drawn. In studying different parenting practices, Baumrind (1967, 1971, 1972) differentiated among what she observed to be three distinct parenting styles; namely, authoritative, authoritarian and permissive. *Authoritative* parenting is similar to the authoritative approach described by Clifton and Roberts (1993). Authoritative parents are described as showing high levels of warmth and love, while at the same time providing guidance by setting clear rules and encouraging high expectations of their children. The authoritative parent attempts to steer his or her child's activities in a rational, issue-oriented manner, being firm but fair, and avoiding coercive means of discipline. By contrast, *authoritarian* parents demonstrate little warmth or love, set strict rules and enforce rules rigidly. The authoritarian parent demands obedience and is prepared to resort to highly punitive measures in attempting to bridle the child's will. *Permissive* parents demonstrate high levels of warmth and love, but do little in the way of setting rules and providing guidance. The permissive parent makes few demands and places few restrictions on the child's conduct. Authoritarian and permissive parenting styles resemble respectively the imposed and negotiated orders described by Clifton and Roberts.

Baumrind (1972) observed that preschool-aged children of authoritative parents display greater self-esteem, self-reliance and interest in achievement compared with children of authoritarian or permissive parents. This pattern of differences also seems to hold as children progress to adolescence. Steinberg, Lamborn, Dornbusch and Darling (1992) conducted an extensive study of approximately 6400 students of varied family backgrounds and from ages 14 to 18. Steinberg et al. (1992) found higher levels of school engagement (effort and concentration in the classroom) and school performance among students from authoritative home environments compared to students whose parents tended to employ other parenting styles. Students of authoritative parents demonstrated higher grade-point averages, devoted more time to homework, aspired to higher levels of post-secondary education and maintained more positive academic self-conceptions. They showed a stronger orientation toward school, better relations with teachers and lower levels of misconduct (e.g., cheating on exams, copying homework, and tardiness or absence from class). Subsequent analyses of the data showed the results to be independent of socio-economic status, ethnicity and whether students were from duo- or single-parent families (Steinberg, Mounts, Lamborn & Dornbusch, 1991).

Studies such as these help to illustrate the claim that the nature of our relationships with children mediates the beliefs they develop about themselves and the kind of people they want to be. The authoritative approach in relationships with children seems to help children feel better about themselves and develop a sense of independence. Further, children from authoritative home environments appear to have an interest in doing well in school, are motivated by their own aspirations and by classroom activities, and tend to get along with others. It seems reasonable to suggest that if teachers adopt the practices and characteristics of authoritative parents, both they and their students will benefit.

Consider the alternatives. We find disconcerting historical accounts of early 20th century classrooms in which students sit in chairs bolted to the floor, facing the teacher's raised platform (Getzels, 1978). Even more troubling are images of oppressive disciplinarians meting out harsh corporal punishments with birch rods, canes, or taws [leather whips split at the end into several strips] (Tavares, 1996). Corporal punishment, as a coercive technique, has been applied consistently throughout the history of North American schools (Ryan, 1994). The authoritarian approach to classroom management is rooted in this history of coercion and fear. Today, this form of dictatorial and oppressive social control offends our moral sensibilities. We see it as an insidious abuse of power and authority. Yet, the use of corporal punishment in attempts to coerce students' behavior is still widespread despite research findings that indicate its ineffectiveness in deterring students from further misconduct. For example, McFadden, Marsh, Price and Hwang (1992) report that students who are punished are more likely to be referred for discipline problems, and often are repeat offenders.

At the same time, however, teachers who adopt a permissive approach and fail to set necessary boundaries are seen by their students as weak and ineffectual, and these teachers more frequently encounter student misconduct (Gnagey, 1981; Grossman, 1995). Burgess (1986) provides a compelling example of the kinds of problems that ensue when teachers adopt a permissive approach. In this example, the teacher had negotiated an arrangement with students in which students would be permitted to make themselves a cup of coffee in the classroom upon completion of their work. However, the students successfully manipulated the arrangement such that they only would agree to do their work on the condition that they be allowed to make cups of coffee. As Burgess describes, inevitably, classes degenerated into "extended coffee making sessions" (p. 196).

A classic experimental study by Lewin, Lippitt and White in 1939 and 1940 (cited in Lippitt & White, 1958/1963) frequently is cited in support of an authoritative approach to parenting and teaching. The experiment attempted to demonstrate the differential effects of three distinct leadership styles: authoritarian, democratic and laissez-faire. [Laissez-faire, literally translated from French is, "let do." It means letting people act without interference or direction.] Group leaders were provided with a script of actions appropriate to each of the following three leadership styles.

Plan for authoritarian leadership role. Practically all policies as regards club activities and procedures should be determined by the leader. The techniques and activity steps should be communicated by the authority, one unit at a time, so that future steps are in the dark to a large degree. . . . The dominator should keep his standards of praise and criticism to himself in evaluating individual and group activities.

Plan for democratic leadership role. Wherever possible, policies should be a matter of group decision and discussion with active encourage-

ment and assistance by the adult leader. The leader should attempt to see that an activity perspective emerges during the discussion period with the general steps to the group goal becoming clarified. . . . The leader should attempt to communicate in an objective, fact-minded way the bases for his praise and criticism of individual and group activities.

Plan for laissez faire leadership role. In this situation, the adult should play a rather passive role in social participation and leave complete freedom for group or individual decisions in relation to activity and group procedure. The leader should make clear the various materials which are available and be sure it is understood that he will supply information and help when asked. . . . He should make no attempt to evaluate negatively or positively the behavior or productions of the individuals or the group as a group, although he should be friendly rather than "stand-offish" at all times. (p. 143)

Leaders were taught their roles using the foregoing scripts, and subsequently placed in charge of groups of 11-year-old males described as (extracurricular) activity clubs. Lewin et al. observed the groups, noting the kinds and frequencies of behaviors, writing descriptions of activities and events, and conducting interviews. Observations showed that the leaders were quite successful in creating the three leadership styles. For example, 60% of the behavior of authoritarian leaders was classified as "orders," "disrupting commands" and "nonconstructive criticism" compared with only 5% of behaviors of democratic and laissez-faire leaders. Comparisons among the groups revealed that the authoritarian and laissez-faire groups displayed more expressions of irritability and aggressiveness toward the leader and other group members than the democratic groups. As reported by Lippitt and White (1958/1963), incidents observed in the authoritarian groups included "an aggressive outburst against a sheet of three-ply wood with hammer and chisels" (p. 148) and a "sit down strike "(p. 151). The outcome of one laissez-faire group was described as "complete disintegration" (p. 151). The democratic groups displayed more enjoyment and less hostility toward the leader and group members, and they managed to maintain their higher levels of productivity and morale even in the absence of the leader.

It often is argued that Lewin et al.'s three descriptions correspond, respectively, to authoritarian, authoritative, and permissive approaches as described in this chapter. One might claim that there are differences between what Lewin et al. refer to as "democratic" and others refer to as "authoritative." However, McCaslin and Good

(1992) argue that before fair comparisons can be made, it is important to note that in most families and classrooms, decisions are not made by majority vote. In other words, in family and school environments, democratic leadership isn't really democratic. Parents and teachers are charged socially with the responsibility of control. Considered in this light, democratic and authoritative arrangements seem to have much in common.

As mentioned, Lewin et al.'s research often is cited as support for an authoritative approach to building classroom structure. However, it is important to point out that in the 1940s and 1950s a rash of studies followed Lewin et al.'s original experiment, and gave rise to a contradictory and inconclusive pattern of findings (Anderson, 1959/1963). Amongst the criticism that ensued was the charge of widespread bias toward a learner-centered view of education that was gaining popularity at the time. Anderson argued that researchers often used unreasonably extreme definitions to conceptualize the differing leadership styles.

It serves no practical or scientific objective to prove that unreasonably extreme leadership types are ineffective; yet, there is reason to feel that a number of researchers have been led to this specious demonstration by the moralist inherent in the authoritarian-democratic conceptualizations. The greatest number of studies in which the "bad" leadership type is overdrawn have a democratic bias. (p. 159)

Nonetheless, Lewin et al.'s study is an intriguing look into the history of educational research. The outcomes of productivity and morale, studied more than 50 years ago, reflect current concerns with achievement and self-esteem. The experimental manipulations, and expressions such as "proper indoctrination" (Lippitt & White, 1958/1963, p. 143) to describe training of the leaders, would be considered highly controversial if used today. Nonetheless, the combination of observational, descriptive and interview data collection is impressive from a methodological standpoint, particularly given the relatively recent resurgence of interest in descriptive analyses and other "qualitative" approaches to educational research.

Critique

The foregoing examination of power and authority shows the inadequacy of overly "psychologized" perspectives that neglect important socio-cultural practices that form the contexts of classrooms. Moreover, paying heed to these contexts allows us to question the structure of our educational institutions and the kinds of relationships on which they are modeled. We need to attend particularly to the kinds of powers and authorities that enable teachers to fulfill their responsibilities as teachers. But are power, authority and control the primary considerations in managing a classroom? As Clifton and Roberts (1993) state, teachers are charged with the responsibility of changing students. A fundamental question with respect to classroom management is thus: "How best can teachers manage change?"

The word "manage" has a variety of uses in ordinary language. A common meaning is that of dominating or controlling; to be in charge of something as in the case of a manager managing a business. The word "manage" also conveys the meaning of being able to accomplish something or bring something about, as in managing to get a job. Yet another meaning of the word "manage" is to function or to get along, to cope, as in managing without a car. Further, manage also can mean helping to direct an individual's career (e.g., an agent) or even a team of athletes (e.g., a team manager).

Historically, "manage," as applied to the contexts of classrooms and schools, is linked to the first of these meanings. During the early 1900s, assembly lines achieved enormous success in meeting the aim of efficient industrial production. This success prompted the extension of the idea of the assembly line to the context of school. The assembly-line metaphor of education is captured in a statement made by Bobbitt in 1918: "education is a shaping process as much as the manufacture of steel rails" (p. 11). The metaphor of schools as assembly lines brought a focus on the power of managerial technologies to gain control over educational "processes" and "products." Although schools and classrooms have changed dramatically over the past century, and the assembly-line metaphor has fallen into disrepute, a widespread belief in technological control and power remains. As Egan (1988) describes,

> The assembly-line analogy is not usually so explicit today, but its persisting influence is seen when we hear people talk of "process" and "product" in education, when we hear education compared to an applied science like engineering, when teaching is represented as a technology, and when we see planning frameworks which differ from the assembly-line model only in details of their wording. (p 73)

More recently, alternative conceptions of what it means to manage have surfaced not only in the world of business, but also in education. These alternatives can be seen as attempts to replace the underlying metaphor of the assembly line and move beyond the traditional view that managing equates with dominating and controlling. One possibility is classrooms and schools as communities of learners. In many ways, the metaphor of community seems better than the metaphor of factory for describing classroom contexts where "productive" learning and teaching can take place.

As we already have mentioned, Lave and Wenger (1991) offer a view of learning based on the notion of a community of practice. In this conception, new members undergo a graduated process of participation as they proceed toward the status of full-fledged member. From this perspective, educational change is a transformation in the level of one's participation in a community. As learners participate in the socio-cultural activities of their community, they transform their beliefs, values, knowledge, understandings, roles and responsibilities. Socio-cultural theory poses that these transformations occur through complex traditions of relationship and means of expression that are products of the histories of societies and cultures. To reiterate, the richness of mental life may be seen as a consequence of participating in historical traditions of socio-cultural practices and incorporating them as forms for thought.

In this light, the managerial task for teachers is to provide opportunities for learners to come to appreciate and care for, in increasingly more sophisticated ways, those forms and practices of intellectual and socio-cultural life sustained by their communities. Underscoring this view is the belief that human learning, knowledge and understanding are distributed throughout communities by interactions amongst their members. In other words, as socio-culturalists argue, the nature of our relationships mediate both how and what we learn. Perhaps the creation of safe and productive classroom environments requires an appreciation and understanding of this insight.

We believe that it is important to consider issues of classroom management in light of this broader socio-cultural, developmental context. Our position is that the fundamental challenge of individual educational change is a developmental challenge facing our educational and broader communities (Martin & Sugarman, 1996). Clearly, we cannot promote positive individual change and development unless we understand the kinds of relationships we create through various practices. We cannot educate successfully where there is blatant disregard for individuals' rights and responsibilities. At the same time, education is founded on the accomplishments of intellectual inquiry. How can education be successful in schools where critical, intellectual life is absent? We need to reflect critically on the kinds of communities we want, and consider our relationships accordingly. In our view:

> *The general and particular relations that pertain between our socio-cultural practices and individual development and learning, demand that we see ourselves in the communities we inhabit, and that we work consistently to improve that vision. (Martin & Sugarman, 1996, p. 315)*

References

Anderson, J.R., Reder, L.M. & Simon, H.A. (1996). Situated learning and education. *Educational Researcher, 25*(4), 5-11.

Anderson, R.C. (1959/1963). Learning in discussions: A résumé of the authoritarian-democratic studies. In W.W. Charters & N.L. Gage (Eds.), *Readings in the social psychology of education* (pp. 153-162). Boston: Allyn & Bacon.

Bakhtin, M.M. (1986). *Speech genres and other late essays.* (V. W. McGee, Trans.). Austin, TX: University of Texas Press.

Baumrind, D. (1967). Child care practices anteceding three patterns of pre-school behavior. *Genetic Psychology Monographs, 75*, 43-88.

Baumrind, D. (1971). Current patterns of parental authority. *Developmental Psychology Monographs, 4*, 1-103.

Baumrind, D. (1972). From each according to her ability. *School Review, 80*(2), 161-197.

Bobbitt, F. (1918). *The curriculum.* New York: Houghton Mifflin.

Bruner, J. (1987). Life as narrative. *Social Research, 54*, 11-32.

Burgess, R.G. (1986). *Sociology, education, and schools: An introduction to the sociology of education.* London: B. T. Batsford.

Clifton, R.A., & Roberts, L.W. (1993). *Authority in classrooms.* Scarborough, Canada: Prentice-Hall.

Egan, K. (1988). Metaphors in collision: Objectives, assembly lines, and stories. *Curriculum Inquiry, 18*(1), 63-68.

Egan. K. (1997). *The educated mind: How cognitive tools shape our understanding.* Chicago: University of Chicago Press.

Eisenberg, A.R. (1985). Learning to describe past experiences in conversation. *Discourse Processes, 8*, 177-204.

Fivush, R. (1994). Constructing narrative, emotion and self in parent-child conversations about the past. In U. Neisser & R. Fivush (Eds.), *The remembering self: Construction and accuracy in the self-narrative* (pp. 136-157). Cambridge, NY: Cambridge University Press.

Fivush, R. & Reese, E. (1989). The social construction of autobiographical memory. In M.A. Conway, D.C. Rubin, H. Spinnler & W.A. Wagenaar (Eds.), *Theoretical perspectives on autobiographical memory* (pp. 115-132). Dordrecht, NL: Kluwer Academic.

Foucault, M. (1967). *Madness and civilization: A history of insanity in the age of reason.* London: Tavistock.

Foucault, M. (1979). *Discipline and punish: The birth of the prison.* Harmondsworth: Penguin.

Foucault, M. (1981). *The history of sexuality: An introduction.* Harmondsworth: Penguin.

French, J. Jr. & Raven, B. (1960). The bases of social power. In D. Cartwright & A. Zander (Eds.), *Group dynamics: Research and theory* (2nd ed., pp. 607-623). Evanston, IL: Row, Peterson, & Company.

Gnagey, W.J. (1981). *Motivating classroom discipline.* New York: MacMillan.

Gergen, K.J. & Gergen, M.M. (1988). Narrative and the self as relationship. *Advances in Experimental Social Psychology, 21,* 17-56.

Getzels, J.W. (1978). Paradigm and practice: On the impact of basic research in education. In P. Suppes (Ed.), *Impact of research on education: Some case studies* (pp. 477-515). Washington, DC: National Academy of Education.

Grossman, H. (1995). *Classroom behavior management in a diverse society (2nd ed.).* Mountain View, CA: Mayfield.

Howard, G.S. (1989). *A tale of two stories: Excursions into a narrative approach to psychology.* Notre Dame, IN: Academic Publications.

Hudson, J.A. (1990). The emergence of autobiographic memory in mother-child conversation. In R. Fivush & J.A. Hudson (Eds.), *Knowing and remembering in young children* (pp. 166-196). New York: Cambridge University Press.

Lave, J. (1988). *Cognition in practice: Mind, mathematics, and culture in every-day life.* Cambridge, England: Cambridge University Press.

Lave, J. & Wenger, E. (1991). *Situated learning: Legitimate peripheral participation.* New York: Cambridge University Press.

Leriche, L. (1992). The sociology of classroom discipline. *The High School Journal, 75*(2), 77-89.

Lippitt, R. & White, R.K. (1958/1963). An experimental study of leadership and group life. In W.W. Charters & N.L. Gage (Eds.), *Readings in the social psychology of education* (pp. 141-153). Boston: Allyn & Bacon.

Martin, J. & Sugarman, J.H. (1996). Bridging social constructionism and cognitive constructivism. *Journal of Mind and Behavior, 17,* 291-320.

McAdams, D.P. (1988). *Power, intimacy, and the life story: Personological inquiries into identity.* New York: Guilford Press.

Mead, G.H. (1934). *Mind, self and society.* Chicago: University of Chicago Press.

McCaslin, M. & Good, T.L. (1992). Compliant cognition: The misalliance of management and instructional goals in current school reform. *Educational Researcher, 21*(3), 4-17.

McFadden, A.C., Marsh, G.E., Price, B.J. & Hwang, Y. (1992). A study of race and gender bias in the punishment of school children. *Education and Treatment of Children, 15,* 140-146.

McNamee, S. & Gergen, K.J. (1992). *Therapy as social construction.* Newbury Park, CA: Sage.

Mitchell, D.E. & Sprady, W.G. (1983). Authority, power and the legitimation of social control. *Educational Administration Quarterly, 19,* 5-33.

Neill, A.S. (1960). *Summerhill: A radical approach to child rearing.* New York: Hart.

Pea, R.D. (1993). Practices of distributed intelligence and designs in education. In G. Salomon (Ed.), *Distributed cognitions: Psychological and educational considerations* (pp. 47-87). New York: Cambridge University Press.

Polkinghorne, D.E. (1988). *Narrative psychology.* Albany: State University of New York Press.

Ryan, F.J. (1994). From rod to reason: Historical perspectives on corporal punishment in the public school, 1642-1994. *Educational Horizons, 72,* 70-77.

Solomon, G. & Perkins, D.N. (1998). Individual and social aspects of learning. *Review of Research in Education, 23,* 1-24.

Steinberg, L., Lamborn, S.D., Dornbusch, S.M. & Darling, N. (1992). Impact of parenting practices on adolescent achievement: Authoritative parenting, school involvement, and encouragement to succeed. *Child Development, 63,* 1266-1281.

Steinberg, L., Mounts, N.S., Lamborn, S.D. & Dornbusch, S.M. (1991). Authoritative parenting and adolescent adjustment across varied ecological niches. *Journal of Research on Adolescence, 1,* 19-36.

Tauber, R.T. (1995). *Classroom management: Theory and practice (2nd ed.).* Orlando, FL: Harcourt Brace.

Tavares, H. (1996). Classroom management and subjectivity: A genealogy of educational identities. *Educational Theory, 46,* 189-201.

Vygotsky, L.S. (1986). *Thought and language* (A. Kozulin, Trans.). Cambridge, MA: MIT Press. (Original work published 1934)

Vygotsky, L.S. (1978). *Mind in society: The development of higher psychological processes.* Cambridge, MA: Harvard University Press.

Chapter Nine
Building Your Own Approach

In the preceding chapters, we explored the theoretical foundations, techniques and applications of specific classroom management models. While these models make intelligible significant portions of classroom phenomena, no one model would seem to capture sufficiently the broad and intricate manifold of classroom environments and situations, to avail consistently ironclad and efficacious prescriptions. Multifarious and interacting factors such as teaching styles, individual characteristics of learners (e.g., grade levels, abilities, skills, personal identities), and specific environmental and social contexts (including community and socio-economic factors, availability of resources, organizational factors in the school, and the political structure of the local school system) bear in varying degrees upon the etiology of classroom problems and the suitability of courses of action open to teachers. The enormous complexity of this picture would seem to render any single model inadequate for generating solutions to all classroom concerns.

The foregoing scenario suggests that teachers need to be flexible, aware of their own strengths and weaknesses, sensitive to contextual particularities, and able to view and evaluate situations from a variety of theoretical perspectives. Thus, we advocate that teachers build their own approaches to classroom management by thoughtfully assessing pertinent factors and then selecting, adapting, combining and modifying methods from several theoretical models depending on the particular circumstances and context. If this process of localized strategy development is conducted systematically and purposefully, and is based upon a serious attempt to match teaching methods to specific teacher and learner characteristics, and specific environmental and social factors, it is possible to speak of such teacher-developed approaches as *eclectic* models. Effective eclectic approaches to classroom management do not result from the simple and capricious "throwing together" of a variety of elements from established theories and methods. The construction of eclectic strategies is a time-consuming process that demands careful analysis, sensitive implementation, and constant monitoring and evaluation.

While the various models studied in this book espouse vastly different philosophies and often seem to reflect divergent values and attitudes, there are some central notions or core ideas to which almost all models subscribe. By a careful juxtaposition of these "shared-belief" practices, a *consensus* model may be constructed that can act as a further guide in building eclectic approaches.

In addition to the theoretical and technical considerations of various models of classroom management, teachers ought to be aware of two other distinct domains of concern that cut across the spectrum of models and have considerable implications for building an eclectic approach to classroom practice. One of these domains is comprised of *pragmatic* concerns such as making referrals and working with others concerned with students' difficulties, coping with the demands and stresses of teaching, and understanding relevant legal and ethical matters. The second domain falls under the rubric of *developmental* considerations, important issues pertaining to child and adolescent development.

This chapter begins with an explication of building eclectic approaches to classroom management. Subsequently, the notion of a consensus model will be elaborated. The chapter then moves to a brief treatment of developmental considerations, followed by discussion of the pragmatic concerns mentioned above.

Building Eclectic Strategies

Essential to a sound eclectic approach is the belief that there is some truth in each of the major theoretical models dominating the literature in classroom management. The task of the eclectic is to determine which theoretical approach, or combination of theoretical elements, works best with which type of situation and problem. The sound development of an effective eclectic management program has potential for working through an almost infinite series of classroom problems in a manner often prevented by unilateral adherence to, and exclusive faith in, one favorite theoretical system or set of methods to the virtual ignorance of all others. What is lacking for most would-be eclectics, however, is an adequate integrative framework for thinking and working across diverse theoretical perspectives. What follows in this section is a discussion of eclectic principles and their use in delineating a systematic model capable of serving the integrative, eclectic function of providing optimal matches between specific techniques and specific problems and situations.

Eclecticism, applied to classroom management, is the determination and implementation of a method best suited to a specific situation and problem. Eclecticism may involve the use of different theoretical and methodological approaches to classroom management (such as the different models covered in this book) depending upon the exact nature of the problem at hand; it may involve an integration and combination of elements from different theoretical perspectives in dealing with a specific problem; or it may involve both the problem-specific use of different approaches and the integration or combination of these approaches. Whatever the nature of the eclectic orientation and practice adopted, it should be systematically planned and purposefully implemented. Eclecticism does not result from being indecisive or "wishy-washy." The practice of eclecticism, properly understood, necessitates clear analyses of problem situations and a decisive ability to make specific judgments concerning a host of factors that impinge upon these situations. While it may be true that many teachers who are unable, for whatever reasons, to adopt a sound management and discipline policy erroneously label themselves as eclectics, true eclecticism demands a careful and painstaking weighing and sifting of the multitude of variables active in any problematic classroom situation.

There are at least five general factors that need to be considered carefully when planning eclectic interventions: teacher characteristics, learner characteristics, teacher-learner interactions, school and community variables, and intended outcomes (compare to Centra & Potter, 1980).

1. *Teacher Characteristics* – Individual teachers have their own specific strengths and weaknesses. These are better matched to some management methods than to others. Also, the individual strengths and weaknesses of teachers may show demonstrable change during their inservice career. Stylistic characteristics such as enthusiasm, need for structure, introversion/extroversion, democratic/authoritarian, teacher-centered/learner-centered, boisterous/reticent and degree of anxiety equip different teachers with different abilities to perform effectively within the context of different management methods. The teacher who, at a certain point in his or her career, is teacher-centered and enthusiastic may have difficulty successfully employing Dreikurs' democratic classroom concept, or granting learners the freedom re-quired by Rogers' communication approach. This does not necessarily

imply that this teacher is doomed to be ineffective in the classroom. Indeed, such characteristics may be well-suited to other management methods. It simply means that this teacher, at this point in time, should adopt management strategies that conflict less with his or her current methods of operating in the classroom. Teachers should carefully and continually reflect upon the current characteristics of their teaching practice as part of the overall decision involved in the formation of problem-specific eclectic methods.

2. *Learner Characteristics* – Like teachers, different learners have different personal identities, abilities, skills, interests and behavioral repertoires. In considering learner characteristics, a teacher should become aware of both individual learner variables and the composite character of the classroom group. Where the classroom group is relatively homogeneous, this task is simplified. However, where great ranges in learner abilities and interests are present, the teacher's task is much more complex. In the latter case, it is quite likely that different management strategies (or at least strategies that permit extensive individuation of instruction) will need to be developed for different learners or subgroups.

Perhaps the matter of learner characteristics may best be illustrated in relation to the extent to which different learners can take differing degrees of responsibility for their own learning. Learners who are clear about their own learning objectives and have mastered some rudimentary skills to teach themselves may benefit greatly from the cognitive self-control strategies described in chapter six. For other learners, who have yet to internalize such self-instructional skills, the use of the same cognitive methods might prove to be relatively futile.

We are at a time of rapid social change. Drug use in schools has increased, poverty is increasing and may affect as many as one in every four children, and single-parent families are facing great challenges (Charles, 1996). In addition, teachers must now be sensitive to increasingly diverse cultural backgrounds and contexts of learners, colleagues and parents. Children in contemporary classrooms exhibit differing cultural, social and linguistic characteristics that may affect school achievement.

The question of learner characteristics is very complex given the myriad ways learners may differ from one another. Nonetheless, the effective teacher must be able to determine which learner characteristics are important with respect to specific learning tasks, and to match these characteristics with an appropriate classroom management strategy.

3. *Teacher-Learner Interactions* – A composite factor that brings learner and teacher characteristics together is the nature of the social relations and interactions between teachers and learners. Different teachers interact differently with different students (see, for example, Cooper, Burger & Seymour, 1979). Some interactions are warm and friendly, while others are formal and hostile; some are helpful, some are discouraging; some are stimulating, others are boring. While it is a teacher's responsibility to attempt to ensure that positive, productive interactions occur with all learners, this attempt often can be fraught with grave difficulties. In this regard, it can be helpful for a teacher to be familiar with the variety of classroom interaction systems that underlie various models of management. In cases where classroom interactions between the teacher and a specific learner are unproductive, the teacher may want to consider the use of a problem-solving strategy such as that described in chapter six. Where interactive difficulties are more pervasive and involve many classroom participants, the teacher should be aware of the potential of classroom discussions and meetings (see chapters three and seven) for resolving such difficulties. Just as a careful examination of teacher and learner characteristics should influence the selection and use of eclectic management strategies, so the nature of teacher-learner interactions should become an integral part of this same equation.

4. *School and Community Variables* – As discussed in the previous chapter, what a teacher does to promote the learning and social well-being of learners cannot be considered outside of the larger school and community context within which the classroom is embedded. There is no easy way to describe all of the school and community variables that need to be considered, but a few illustrative relationships can be drawn that should underscore the importance of social and cultural factors outside the classroom. Such factors may at times operate as constraints upon the selection of viable classroom management strategies and, yet at other times, act as supporting resources. In specific cases, school policies or legislated school acts may curtail the use of certain procedures or

facilities (e.g., time-outs). School principals may or may not be willing to cooperate with programs involving the coordinated use of office areas outside the classroom. Parents, directly through Home and School Associations or Parents' Advisory Committees, and indirectly through Trustee Associations, may demand to be kept informed of management practices affecting their children. (In all cases, whether or not such formal mechanisms exist, it is generally a good idea to keep parents informed, involved and to solicit their cooperation. Remember, the rights and responsibilities of parents are extensive and on moral grounds alone, should be respected and safeguarded by the classroom teacher.) In some communities, volunteers may be readily available to act as unpaid teaching assistants, thus permitting greater individualization of management programs. In high school and junior high school settings, curriculum constraints may exist that necessitate the continuous movement of learners from one classroom to another throughout the school day. The selection of management procedures in such cases should clearly involve a decision about the extent to which other teachers are willing and able to assist in the execution of consistent school-wide management methods.

5. *Intended Outcomes* – It sounds rather simplistic, but no attempt to arrange eclectic management strategies should be made without first ascertaining, as clearly as possible, the intended outcomes to which such strategies are addressed. As the old cliché goes, "If you don't know where you're going, you may end up somewhere else." The potential problem is accentuated if that "somewhere else" turns out to be undesirable and counterproductive to the effective learning and social development of learners. Before selecting an eclectic strategy, the teacher must determine what it is that the strategy is intended to accomplish, and whether or not the accomplishment of the management objective is in the best interest of effective and positive teaching and learning.

From the plethora of considerations and decisions conveyed by careful reflection on the preceding five general factors, it should be obvious that the development of sound eclectic management strategies must be undertaken in a systematic, logical fashion that ensures that relevant information is not overlooked or ignored. What is required to safeguard against such exclusions is an adequate integrative model capable of providing a framework for thinking and working across diverse theoretical perspectives in relation to the practicalities of a specific classroom within the context of the broader social structures of school and community. As you might well imagine such frameworks are not easily found.

One model that can help provide such a framework is the *systematic instruction model* developed over the last three decades by educational psychologists working in the area of "the psychology of teaching and learning" (Charles, 1996; DeCecco & Crawford, 1974; Dick & Carey, 1978; Gredler, 1992; Popham & Baker, 1970). The systematic instruction framework helps to ensure that the factors of teacher and learner characteristics and interactions, relevant school and community variables and intended outcomes are all given adequate consideration. In this sense, it can act as a useful aid to the development, implementation and ongoing evaluation of eclectic management strategies. The basic components of the systematic instruction model are illustrated schematically in Figure 9:1.

Figure 9:1

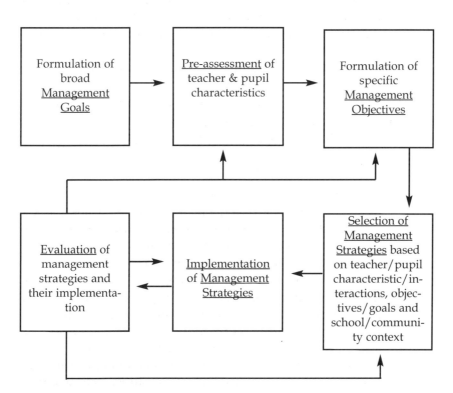

When the eclectic strategies that have been formulated and implemented are not optimally effective the teacher should proceed by reexamining the preassessment procedures, the specific management objectives, and the selection and implementation of the eclectic management strategy (or strategies) in question.

To illustrate the use of the systematic instruction framework, the following section of the chapter is devoted to a detailed description of one teacher's use of this framework in developing eclectic management strategies appropriate to her own specific instructional context.

An example

The management problem that faced Mrs. Day (a grade eleven mathematics teacher in a suburban high school), and the methods she employed to resolve it, provide a good illustration of the practical application of the systematic instruction model. Although Mrs. Day had Bob in her classroom for only 50 minutes of mathematics instruction each day, she had become very concerned about Bob's withdrawn and hostile classroom behavior, and his lack of progress in the mathematics curriculum. Bob wasted his time during math class and his homework was never completed. He seldom spoke, and when asked a direct question, his typical response was to scowl and shrug without saying a word. He seemed to view the actions of his classmates and class proceedings with contempt and disdain.

What follows is a step-by-step description of the management program that Mrs. Day devised with Bob's assistance.

1. *Formulation of broad goals* – Before she began to work more systematically with Bob, Mrs. Day asked herself what was bothering her about the present situation, and what she thought would be a reasonable improvement benefiting Bob and the classroom group as a whole. Since Mrs. Day perceived her role as assisting all her students to learn effectively in the context of a positive learning environment, she concluded that she must help Bob to become more active in the mathematics class and to exert greater effort in mastering the grade eleven mathematics curriculum. If, in the process, Bob became less hostile in his reactions to her personally, and the class as a whole, this would be considered an added bonus. It was with these broad, general goals in mind that Mrs. Day began to gather more information that she thought would be

useful in designing an eclectic management program well-matched to her own capabilities and the teaching context, and to Bob's present abilities, attitudes and interests.

2. *Preassessment of teacher and pupil characteristics* – In order to double-check her perceptions of Bob's classroom behavior, Mrs. Day decided to observe carefully and note the number of times Bob completed homework and class assignments and the number of times he entered into classroom discussions (either volunteering information or responding to direct questions). When her observations confirmed her perception that these events rarely occurred (she noted no assignment completions or classroom responses, other than "I don't know," over a four-day period), she decided to examine her own classroom behaviors in relation to Bob. After all, it was just possible that she was not providing the opportunity for Bob to participate and/or was not encouraging him to master the subject matter. Although she felt she liked Bob (despite his lack of response), she was not sure that this feeling was ever communicated to him. What she discovered surprised her. She found that she rarely interacted with Bob, and in actual fact seemed not really to notice his presence for the vast majority of class time. Casual conversation with some of Bob's other teachers revealed that the classroom demeanor she knew was not reserved for the math class alone. Indeed, it was only during his "technical automotives" class that Bob seemed to be enthusiastic and successful as a learner. When Mrs. Day observed Bob in the automotives class (during her daily spare period), she was amazed at the interest he showed, the skill he demonstrated and the positive nature of his interactions with the teacher and his classmates. A final bit of information that Mrs. Day obtained during a brief talk with Bob during the noon lunchbreak (initiated by Mrs. Day asking Bob if he could look at her car to see why it was always stalling) was that Bob's parents wanted him to be a medical doctor and someday to take over his physician father's extensive medical practice.

3. *Formulation of specific management objectives* – By this time, Mrs. Day was really becoming interested in Bob as an individual with complex concerns and an intriguing variety of productive and unproductive learning and social behaviors. Indeed, she had to force herself to remember that her specif-

ic role in relation to Bob was to help him succeed at mathematics in a way that enhanced his view of himself as an effective learner. It was tempting to try immediately to become Bob's friend, counselor and big-brother all rolled into one. Fortunately, Mrs. Day realized that she couldn't be all things to Bob. However, she thought that if she could help him within the specific context of the mathematics class, a positive change here might "tip-the-balance" in favor of other desirable learning outcomes. To this end, Mrs. Day determined that the specific management objectives to which she would help Bob direct his efforts were: a) to respond positively to classroom discussions (at least 1 or 2 times per class) and b) to complete the majority of classroom and homework assignments (at least 2 or 3 each week). If Bob was to succeed in mastering the grade eleven mathematics curriculum, he would need to become more active as a learner. Both of the specific management objectives formulated by Mrs. Day had the aim of assisting him to do exactly that.

4. *Selection of management strategies* – It was now time for Mrs. Day to sit down and do some careful planning. What instructional methods could she employ, based on the information she had collected during the preassessment, that would help Bob achieve the specific management objectives? It was clear that if Bob was to change his classroom responses and become more motivated to achieve in the mathematics class, she would need to do some changing too. In this regard, she decided to concentrate on improving some of her own teaching skills. Using Kounin's (see chapter four) descriptions of group management skills, she began to pay much more attention to her use of the "group-alerting" skills of "positive questioning technique," "positive recitation strategy" and "alerting cues" in particular. By improving her own performance in these areas, she felt that she could ensure that she did not forget about Bob during class time; and that when she did call upon Bob, he (1) would be ready to answer (alerting cues) and (2) would be given the opportunity of doing so (positive questioning technique). In addition, she decided that she would treat any response from Bob with respect, perhaps using descriptive praise (see chapter five) when appropriate, thus modeling (see chapter six) to

the class as a whole that Bob and his contributions were an integral part of the class proceedings.

Once she felt satisfied about planned improvements in her own general teaching performance, Mrs. Day turned to a consideration of the management objectives in a more direct manner. With respect to assignment completion, she decided that she would apply an idea from behavior modification (see chapter five) and try to arrange (together with the automotives instructor) some special, extended work in the automotives shop contingent upon Bob's successful completion of a minimum of two assignments per week. In formulating this plan, Mrs. Day was careful to ensure that such extended work privileges would be in addition to Bob's present access to the automotives shop. She knew that it would only punish Bob for cooperating with the management program if she attempted to make his current automotive shop time contingent upon work in mathematics. With respect to his in-class responses, Mrs. Day determined to follow any attempted response with descriptive praise and to avoid punishing any failures to respond. She also realized that she would need to be careful not to overdo the descriptive praise bit, since she was aware that any hint of "gushiness" would simply turn Bob off.

Mrs. Day also decided to take some time each week to talk with Bob outside regular class periods. In these conversations, she hoped to be able to employ Rogers' notions of empathic responding (see chapter two) and perhaps eventually, once rapport was firmly established, to move into discussions based on D'Zurilla and Goldfried's cognitive problem-solving approach (see chapter six). The aim of this last idea was to help Bob formulate a realistic view of his own career aspirations and how to achieve them.

Finally, Mrs. Day added an idea of her own. During class periods she determined to attempt to make some of the mathematics problems more meaningful for Bob by using problems derived from mechanics and mechanical engineering.

5. *Implementation of management strategies* – Before launching the management program she had planned, Mrs. Day arranged meetings first with Bob, and then with Bob and his parents, to discuss her proposed actions. A major accomplishment from these meetings was that both Bob and his parents agreed that the specific management objectives made sense, and that they would try to cooperate. From Bob's parents, Mrs. Day succeeded in getting a promise that they would not "nag" Bob about his school work, but would

attempt to encourage him whenever he showed any signs of improvement.

After these initial meetings, Mrs. Day and Bob went into action. Mrs. Day worked hard on her teaching skills and reactions to Bob's classroom behavior. Bob, for his part, made a serious effort to complete assignments and take advantage of the bonus automotive shop times. Outside the classroom, weekly conversations between Bob and Mrs. Day began to occur on a regular basis but were not so frequent as to attract peer jealousies or ridicule.

6. *Evaluation of management strategies and their implementation* – As the eclectic management program continued in operation, Mrs. Day continued her daily monitoring of Bob's class participation and assignment completions. Within a month of the inception of the program, Bob was consistently meeting the specific management objectives to which he and Mrs. Day had agreed. Most assignments were completed and Bob had become a more frequent classroom contributor. An added bonus was the extent to which Bob's interactions with his classmates had begun to improve. The withdrawn, sulky Bob seemed to have disappeared almost overnight. Happy with Bob's improvement, Mrs. Day (with Bob's involvement) began to make further plans for helping Bob to generalize his new found learning potential to other areas of the high school curriculum. She realized that she couldn't tell other teachers what to do, but she was always available for consultation if they asked her for assistance in helping Bob. She also began to invite other concerned teachers into her math class for casual observation.

A Consensus Model

Several of the most important ideas, methods and strategies of classroom management and discipline examined in the previous chapters can be cast in the framework of a *consensus model* that can guide the eclectic practitioner. Despite theoretical and philosophical disparities among the various models, there are several commonly-held assumptions about effective practice. The collection of ideas and procedures that emerges from this synthesis is itself a viable general model of classroom management and discipline – one without a unitary philosophical base, but one with a great deal of potential pragmatic utility.

Since most of the principles fundamental to the consensus management procedures to be discussed have already been presented in previous chapters, they will not be reiterated here. There are, however, three general assumptions or attitudes that may be seen to underlie almost all effective classroom management strategies. These beliefs appear essential for teachers at all levels.

1. *All students are first, and foremost, learners* – Every student has the basic right to learn fundamental academic skills and knowledge, and the social behaviors necessary to learn effectively in classroom situations. Students should not be treated primarily as "problems," "handicapped," "stupid," "lazy" or "difficult." They should be treated primarily as learners who have significant potentials for positive growth and development.

2. *All learners should be well informed about classroom policies and practices* – To facilitate learners' academic and social development, it is important that classroom rules, teaching methods and their purposes, and consequences of misbehavior be made known to all learners. It is a teacher's responsibility to ensure that each learner clearly comprehends the rules of the classroom. As participants in any human enterprise, we all tend to perform better and have more positive attitudes when we understand the nature and procedural rules of the enterprise in which we are actively engaged. It is a great handicap to be asked or expected to participate in events that are strange or unfamiliar to us. Like a stranger in a new culture, our actions and their consequences are removed from our direct control through ignorance of the social conventions and moral orders that govern matters of behavior and social interaction. If learners are kept in ignorance of procedures, policies and practices, they will be severely handicapped in their efforts to learn and develop academic skills and knowledge.

3. *Clarify needs of students and teachers* – As Glasser (see chapter seven) points out, effective classroom procedures should reflect the needs of teachers and students. Teachers can facilitate a discussion about their needs and the needs of the students. Behavior limits can be set that reflect both sets of needs. Teachers should firmly assert their most strongly-held views and desires, but at the same time should be flexible and willing to show compromise.

4. *Successful classroom management cannot be separated from effective teaching* – Teachers who do not possess basically sound instructional skills will inevitably fail in their attempts to achieve management strategies that result in positive and productive student classroom behavior. No amount of specialized management technique can substitute for good sound instructional planning and execution. If the teacher is unprepared, disorganized, uninterested or confused in his or her basic instructional role, management methods in and of themselves are of little use. Only when teachers are skilled in, and consistently practice, effective strategies for planning and implementing instruction will they have the opportunity of participating in a well-managed classroom with few discipline problems (Lemlech, 1979; Martin, 1983).

In addition to these three general assumptions, there are ten central ideas about effective classroom management practices shared by almost all management and discipline models.

1. *Become a good organized teacher first* – As Kounin (see chapter four) has so often pointed-out, good teaching *prevents* the vast majority of problems from occurring in the first place. Since many management difficulties arise from learner confusion, boredom, lack of attention and general apathy or indifference, teachers are well-advised to ensure that their lesson planning and execution skills are effective in promoting organized, interesting and well-paced instructional periods. Further, teachers' own attitudes toward knowledge, learning and social interactions may be more or less conducive to modeling and promoting desired approaches to classroom learning and behavior. Self-examination of such attitudes by teachers always is in order.

2. *Become involved with your students* – It is imperative that teachers get to know their students' likes, dislikes, abilities, skill deficiencies, attitudes and opinions. The "flip-side" to this record is, of course, that learners should also be given the opportunity of getting to know their teacher. This essential two-way communication between teachers and learners can be facilitated in numerous ways (see chapters two, three, five, six and seven). Classroom meetings and discussions (see chapters three and seven) provide a particularly useful format for meaningful teacher-learner exchanges. Whatever the methods employed, teachers must learn to be straight-

forward and honest in their dealings with learners. Teachers should involve learners directly in the setting of classroom rules and limits, in decisions about consequences for misbehavior and in the general instructional program of the classroom.

3. *Apply consequences consistently* – Once classroom rules and consequences for upholding or breaking them have been agreed upon, the teacher must ensure that consequences are fairly and consistently applied. Productive academic and social behavior should be encouraged and disruptive behaviors should be weakened systematically. While the types of consequences, and the labels associated with them, differ subtly across different models of classroom management, it is generally important to follow student on-task behaviors with stimulating and encouraging interactions that carefully describe what the student has done and why it has been effective, and to follow students' off-task behaviors with consequences that are logically associated with specific types of misbehavior and that increase the offending learner's awareness of his or her responsibility for behaving productively. Whatever the system of consequences employed, it should be administered fairly and monitored carefully to ensure that it is producing desirable effects.

4. *Be non-punitive* – Strong forms of punishment for classroom misbehavior do not result in effective teaching-learning relations. Strong punishment doesn't teach what to do. It simply fosters a negative avoidance of the teacher and classroom activities on the part of the punished student, and it models an aggressive method of solving problems (see chapters two, three, five, six). Methods of dealing with misbehavior such as the application of logical consequences (chapter three), temporary loss of privileges (chapter five), time-out from classroom activities (chapter five) and (if misbehavior is very mild) total ignorance (chapter five) are much more efficient, effective and productive than are harsh, punishing consequences.

5. *Be calm* – If a teacher is to apply consequences effectively and to manage an organized, stimulating learning environment, she or he must remain calm. Teachers should model a well-controlled, efficient style of coping with life's situations. Soft reprimands and the calm administering of classroom rules

and consequences are extremely powerful teaching methods when compared to the anxious, hassled, panicky style of the poorly organized teacher.

6. *Don't threaten* – There is no quicker or surer way to produce a tense, aversive classroom situation than consistently to threaten students with "what you'll do if they don't smarten up." There are many problems with threats, but two of the most important are that they are seldom implemented and succeed only in creating a negative climate in the classroom. The common combination of severe threats with no follow-through makes the teacher a nagging, ridiculous figure who never means what he or she says. One of the best ways to avoid the "threat trap" is to develop (in consultation with learners) a well-stated and easily understood list of classroom rules and consequences, and to stick to this framework (see chapter seven). This should prevent a teacher from constantly picking away at minor irritations and annoyances. The guideline here should be that if a situation is truly problematic, it should be covered in classroom rules and the teacher should be prepared to follow through with negotiated consequences. If classroom actions are minor irritants, they should probably just be ignored. If a teacher does respond to misbehavior, however, he or she must be prepared to follow-through (see chapter seven) with an intervention and ensure that the situation is resolved.

7. *Individualize* – Since learners differ in many ways, it is important that the instructional program employed provides opportunities for learners to work at tasks appropriate to their own skill levels and successfully to increase their academic capabilities "one-step-at-a-time." With respect to management, many potential problems are intercepted by a careful matching of appropriate instructional programming to individual learners. While limits to individualizing instruction are related to the size of the student-to-teacher ratio, use of tutoring and/or instructional grouping methods (see chapters five and six) can help a teacher ensure that instruction is appropriately matched to each learner's academic needs.

8. *Develop an effective one-to-one problem solving strategy* – While many classroom management and discipline problems can, and should, be dealt with in the classroom context itself,

some problems arise from personal confusion, anxieties and crises that are better discussed in one-to-one encounters outside regular class periods. Every teacher should be prepared to handle such encounters in ways that promote positive resolutions. The D'Zurilla and Goldfried problem-solving strategy described in chapter six provides an overall strategy for structuring one-to-one interviews, while the interpersonal style described by Rogers (see chapter two) can inform teachers about interactive teacher characteristics that can facilitate the implementation of problem-solving interviews. Whatever approach a teacher adopts, it is important that such a contingency plan be available, and that the teacher is sensitive to the feelings, as well as the thoughts and classroom behaviors, of learners experiencing personal anxieties and difficulties in coping.

9. *Evaluate actions, not learners* – This is a point that has been made repeatedly throughout this book (see chapters two, three, five, six and seven). Teachers must learn to distinguish between learners and their actions. Actions may be productive or unproductive, good or bad, clever or foolish. However, learners themselves should not be labeled in similar ways. Through their interactions with (and feedback to) learners, teachers should indicate to each learner that, while some of the things the learner does may be right or wrong (good or bad), the learner is always worthy of love and respect as a human being. (See discussions in chapter two on "unconditional positive regard," chapter three on "encouragement vs. praise" and chapter five on "descriptive praise.")

10. *Always work toward the goal of learner self-control* – Ultimately, one of the primary goals of education is that learners should be taught to control their own actions and to direct their own learning. Before learners can be held accountable, and be responsible, for their own actions, they must be given the opportunity to exercise such responsibility. Teaching learners to evaluate, monitor and motivate their own learning behaviors (see chapter six) is an essential part of effective pedagogy. While learners at different developmental and behavioral levels may require varying degrees of external structure and discipline, teachers should never lose sight of the fact that their ultimate responsibility is to equip learners

with the knowledge, skills and attitudes necessary to control their own actions (Coates & Thoresen, 1980).

Developmental Considerations

Any discussion of classroom management would be incomplete without a consideration of the impact of developmental factors. As learners change from young children to adolescents, and finally to adults, a number of crucial alterations occur in their physical, cognitive, emotional and moral characteristics. Without some understanding of the essential nature of such changes, and how they interact with learning environments to render some instructional processes effective and others ineffective at different developmental stages, a teacher cannot mount a truly successful management program.

What follows in this section is a cursory introduction to major developmental theories. We will begin with the theory of cognitive development proposed by Jean Piaget (Piaget, 1952, 1954, 1957, 1968; Piaget & Inhelder, 1969). Next, the work of Lawrence Kohlberg (Kohlberg, 1963, 1969) in the area of moral development is presented. Additionally, a contrasting theory of development posed by Lev Vygotsky (1978, 1986) is discussed. The section will conclude with some direct implications of developmental theory for classroom teaching methods and management strategies.

Piaget

Piaget's work in developmental psychology has had a tremendous impact on contemporary education. His theories provide a view of how a child incorporates experiences into an egocentric conception of the world, how one behavior must develop so as to set the stage for another to follow, how scientific thinking develops, how moral values develop sequentially, how symbolic systems of language and communication emerge, and how abilities to generalize, categorize and discriminate grow with a child's experiences. In general, Piaget saw intellectual (cognitive) development as occurring in four major stages: sensorimotor (approximately corresponding with chronological ages 0 to 2), preoperational (which he subdivided into preoperational – 2 to 4, and intuitive – 4 to 7), concrete operational (approximately 7 to 11) and formal operational (11 to 14 to adulthood).

1. *Sensorimotor Stage* – During the first developmental stage, the child moves from a newborn's reflexive activity to a more highly organized kind of behavioral repertoire characteristic of the two year-old. During this stage, children gradually perceive themselves as different from surrounding objects, seek stimulation from lights and sounds, try to extend interesting experiences and define things by manipulating them. Piaget's careful, painstaking observations of children between birth and the age of two have highlighted the developmental importance of *object permanence* (the knowledge that objects don't cease to exist when they suddenly go out of one's direct observational field), child babblings in relation to the development of comprehensible speech, and the repetitive nature of children's behavior for the development of skilled motor performance.

2. *Preoperational Stage* – The second major stage in the child's cognitive development traces the gradual shift in a child's cognitive operations from total reliance on the perceptual field (preoperational phase – 2 to 4), to more logical, rational and verbally-mediated forms of cognition (intuitive phase – 4 to 7). In the preoperational stages of development, the child tends to be very self-centered and incapable of adopting another person's point of view. The child is able to classify objects on the basis of a single conspicuous feature, but is unable to see that objects similar in one respect may differ in another. Preoperational children can arrange things in series, but cannot draw inferences about things that are not adjacent to each other in the series (e.g., Sue is shorter than Pam, and Pam is shorter than June – is Sue shorter than June?).

In the *intuitive* stage (ages 4 to 7), the child learns to form classes of objects, see relationships and work with the idea of number. The stage is called intuitive because the child is not *conscious* of the categories he or she is using. During the preoperational stages, children are able to understand logical relationships of increasing complexity, begin to comprehend the idea of number and acquire the principle of conservation. One important kind of conservation is the notion that the amount of a thing is constant regardless of changes in its shape or the number of pieces into which it is divided (e.g., an amount of liquid remains the same despite being poured from a tall, thin container into a short, broad container).

3. *Concrete Operations Stage* – From the ages of roughly 7 to 11, the child becomes capable of various logical operations involving concrete things. An *operation* is a type of cognitive manipulation of objects or their internal representations. For example, children at the stage of concrete operations can respond to questions like "What does the other side of the moon look like?" by cognitively turning the moon around and telling you that it looks just like this side of the moon. During the concrete operational stage, the child is able to handle more complex logical ideas and systems of classification such as *composition* (the idea that whenever two elements of a system are combined – e.g., pens and pencils – we obtain additional, higher-order elements of the system – e.g., writing instruments), *associativity* (for example, that sums are independent of adding order – e.g., A + B = C and B + A = C) and *reversibility* (for example, that if we combine A and B to create C, that we can also subtract A from C to obtain B). The child, while still not fully aware of the principles involved, now can think through a number of problems independent of their perceptual dimensions. Nonetheless, the 7 to 11 year-old still has problems with highly abstract thought.

4. *Formal Operations Stage* – In most instances of normal development, the child between the ages of 11 and 14 becomes capable of logical thinking with abstractions. The realm of the "here and now" is supplemented with the realm of the "possible." This final developmental stage marks the beginnings of scientific thinking of the hypothetico-deductive type, propositional thinking and combinational analysis. The child now can draw conclusions, offer interpretations and develop hypotheses. The child's thinking has, by the age of 14, usually become flexible and powerful, requiring only additional use and practice to shape it in increasingly more sophisticated manners.

Since he was originally trained as a biologist, it was natural for Piaget to view human development as a *process of adaptation*. In adapting to environments, the human learner strives to maintain an equilibrium between what he or she currently perceives, knows and understands, and what he or she sees in any new situation, problem or experience. If present conditions of understanding can handle new situations, equilibrium is undisturbed. If present conditions are inadequate, intellectual effort must be expended to restore the equilibrium. (Note that a theory of the cognitive processes and elaborations necessary to support such thinking operations is presented in chapter six.) In other words, when equilibrium is temporarily destroyed, some adaptation of the organism to its environment must occur.

For Piaget, there are two basic mechanisms of adaptation. Both these forms occur simultaneously and are referred to as (1) *assimilation* and (2) *accommodation*. Assimilation is the process of changing what is perceived so that it fits present cognitive structures (see chapter six). Accommodation is the process of changing existing cognitive structures so that they fit what is perceived. Thus, for Piaget, cognitive development is a continual process of interaction between organisms and environments assisted by the key adaptation (developmental) operations of assimilation and accommodation.

Kohlberg

Lawrence Kohlberg's work in the area of moral development generally supports Piaget's cognitive development stage theory. In Kohlberg's description of moral development, we find a progression from a simple, egocentric, highly unstable stage to a period of mutual cooperation, and finally to a stage in which the legal aspects of rules are clearly and logically comprehended and rationally abided. Kohlberg's theory of moral development encompasses three levels – (1) *preconventional-premoral level*, (2) *conventional-morality of conventional role conformity* and (3) *postconventional-morality of self-accepted principles* (see Lefrançois, 1977).

1. *Premoral Level* – At the premoral level, the child's judgement of right and wrong takes one of two orientations or types. Type 1 is a *punishment and obedience orientation* in which the child's sole notion of right and wrong is that evil behavior is punished and that good behavior results from obedience, or, at least avoidance of disobedience or evil behavior. Type 2 is a *naive instrumental hedonism* in which what is good is that which is pleasant, and what is evil is that which has undesirable consequences. At the premoral level, children have little notion of right or wrong in terms of the objective consequences of behaviors or the intentions of actors. Children will go out of their way to do something good for someone only if they themselves will benefit from the deed.

2. *Morality of Conventional Role Conformity* – At this second level of moral development, two additional orientations to, or types of, morality are possible, each of which reflects the increasing importance of peer and social relations to the developing child. Type 3 (*the good-boy/girl morality* of maintaining good relations and the approval of others) moral behavior is behavior that receives wide approval from significant others (parents, teachers, peers) and society at large, and is engaged in for this reason. Type 4 morality (*authority maintains control*) involves conformity to social rules and laws because of the child's desire to maintain adults' approval and a friendly status quo.

3. *Morality of Self-Accepted Principles* – At the highest level of morality, the adolescent child begins to view morality in terms of *individual rights and liberties* (Type 5) and in terms of *individual principles of conscience* (Type 6) that have value as rules or laws apart from their influence on social approval. At the third level, the person's individual notions of right and wrong begin to take precedence.

Kohlberg's system of moral development, like Piaget's system of cognitive development, views the developmental sequences across stages or levels as invariant. All learners go through the same sequence of stages although they may progress with different rates, have different starting ages, or may become fixed at different levels. There are no fixed chronological age ranges attached to Kohlberg's moral development levels. Even in considering Piaget's cognitive development levels, it is important to understand that there is a wide range of individual differences with respect to the chronological ages at which different people achieve different developmental levels. The ages that Piaget gives are at best only rough approximations of average developmental changes. Further, different individuals may become fixed at different levels of cognitive or moral development. There is absolutely no assumption on the part of either Piaget or Kohlberg that all individuals will proceed through all developmental levels. Indeed, the final level of Kohlberg's system of moral development frequently may not be reached.

Vygotsky

A contrasting view of psychological development is that of Soviet psychologist Lev Vygotsky (1978, 1986) whose socio-cultural perspective was mentioned in the preceding chapter. Unlike Piaget,

Vygotsky alleged that culture, not biology, is the primary consideration in explaining human psychological development. Vygotsky was inspired by the Marxist claim that the fundamental condition of human existence is socially organized labor activity, founded on the use of technical tools. His theory centers on the underlying premise that if you want to understand the nature of psychological development, you have to understand the historical, social and cultural relations in which human individuals exist. Vygotsky saw the resemblance between socio-cultural interactions and individuals' mental functions as the key to understanding psychological development.

Vygotsky distinguished between two types of mental functions. *Elementary mental functions* are the natural, unlearned ways infants have of attending to, perceiving and remembering something of their encounters in the world. Psychological development is marked by the transformation of these basic elementary functions into higher mental functions. *Higher mental functions* develop from learning to use language to bring our thoughts (attention, perception, memory and imagination) and actions under increasingly sophisticated forms of control. The transition to higher mental functions consists in learning to direct our thoughts and actions primarily with words. This link between thought and language highlights the importance of societies and cultures in human development. According to Vygotsky, language and other forms of historical socio-cultural relations are the point of origin for the development of all higher mental functions.

Vygotsky applied the analogy of tools to account for the ways in which language and other symbolic means mediate thought. Tools are *mediational means*. The tools of labor (i.e., technical tools) mediate our relationship with the world, enabling greater control in transforming environments to suit our purposes. Vygotsky argued that, similarly, the communicative tools used by people to relate to one another also are mediational means, but in this case, they are directed inward to transform thought, action and experience. Vygotsky referred to communicative tools such as words, gestures and numbers as *signs*. According to Vygotsky, the young of a culture become thinking individuals by *appropriating* (taking up) and *internalizing* signs such that they become psychological tools (i.e., tools for thought).

Vygotsky argued that in order to understand the way in which a sign comes to play an instrumental role in an individual's thought, action and experience, it is necessary to trace its history back to the original context of its communicative function in the public domain of socio-cultural relations and practices (i.e., interactions between and among people). The meanings of signs first are learned as a result of the ways in which they influence the behavior of others. Subsequently, signs are internalized as ways of influencing oneself. Vygotsky illustrates using the gesture of pointing. The gesture of pointing begins with a infant's failed attempt to grasp an object. Responding to the infant, the caregiver interprets the infant's movements as a sign of desire for the object. By treating the movements as a sign, and coming to the infant's aid by providing the object, the caregiver transforms the child's reaching into a meaningful social act of communication. It is not long before the child learns that his or her reaching movements control the caregiver's behavior. The reaching becomes a gesture, a sign, a way of responding to needs. As the caregiver begins to point to objects, the child refines reaching as pointing.

The child's use of words follows word use by others. Words are at first a substitute for gestures used by the caregiver to indicate objects. The child appropriates and begins to use words to direct the actions of the caregiver towards desired objects. Gradually mastering the shared meaning of words, the child learns the value of speech in influencing others and manipulating features of the environment. Eventually, speech begins to precede actions as the child makes plans, reflecting on previous experiences. In this way, speech becomes internalized as the medium of thought.

Vygotsky's theory of development can be seen as comprised of four stages, marked by the changing nature of the relationship between the child and the child's environment through the appropriation, active use, and mastery of mediational signs (Díaz, Neal & Amaya-Williams, 1990). During the *first* developmental stage, the child's experience is controlled by the nervous system, and behavior is governed by basic stimulus-response environmental contingencies. The child's caregiver can only direct the child's behavior by manipulating concrete, external stimuli.

In the *second* stage (emerging usually at two to three years of age), the child becomes able to use external signs (e.g., gestures and words) as tools in responding to the environment. In this initial and external use of mediational signs, the child recognizes the link between the sign and the concrete external stimulus. With further attention to and use of signs, the child begins to remember and recognize them, gradually becoming aware of their place and function in experience. It is this awareness, that signs help in satisfying needs, that provides conditions for the third stage of development.

In the *third* stage (three to seven years of age), the child begins to generate and manipulate signs to organize aspects of the environment in producing a desired response. It is important to note, however, that during this stage the child still relies on arranging or organizing concrete external stimuli.

The *fourth* stage (seven to nine years of age) involves the internalization of the external relations among stimuli, signs and behaviors, such that the child no longer requires the aid of concrete external stimuli in generating responses. At the point where children are able to present to themselves the same sign for an object that they present to others, they have made the passage to using signs to regulate their own thoughts and behavior. This fourth stage marks a new relation between the child and her or his environment in which signs are used internally to plan, direct, monitor and evaluate the child's own activities. The internalization of signs and their relations provides for mature individuals' psychological organization.

A critical distinction between the developmental theories of Vygotsky and Piaget concerns their explanation of *egocentric speech*. Egocentric speech is observed in play as the way young children speak aloud to themselves, as if they are speaking to someone else. Piaget interpreted this to be an expression of the highly egocentric nature of the preoperational child. He believed that egocentric speech did not serve any useful function, and that it eventually disappeared, eroded by the process of socialization and the emergence of logical operations. In contrast, Vygotsky believed that egocentric speech is an important intermediary stage in development in which the child is using language to guide his or her own behavior. Egocentric speech is a bridge between initially using speech to guide the behavior of others and the transition to using speech to guide one's own behavior. Vygotsky argued that egocentric speech does not disappear. Rather, it becomes sub-vocal. The child no longer utters the words aloud, but silently to him or herself. Vygotsky called this use of speech in thinking *inner speech*.

An important aspect of Vygotsky's theory for education is the concept of the *zone of proximal development*. Vygotsky (1978) asserted that a child has an *actual developmental level*, in a particular content domain, that can be determined by testing the child's problem-solving ability. Vygotsky termed the difference between the actual developmental level (as determined by the problem-solving test) and the *level of potential development* (the problem-solving ability of the child while being guided by an adult or more capable peer/s), the *zone of proximal development*. It is collaboration with an adult or a more knowledgeable peer in the zone of proximal development that permits the child access to the mediational means for psychological development. In the zone of proximal development, the child does not passively adopt the instruction of the adult or peer. Activity in the zone of proximal development is social interaction where the child comes to view the problem in the other's (adult or peer/s) terms (goals and perspectives). Adults or more capable peers provide aspects of their own thinking to the child as mediational means of support.

By providing these supports in the creation of a zone of proximal development, the child's conversational accomplice plays an essential role in creating the conditions that make psychological development possible. An illustration is provided by Tharp and Gallimore (1988):

> A 6-year-old child has lost a toy and asks her father for help. The father asks where she last saw the toy; the child says, "I can't remember." He asks a series of questions: "Did you have it in your room? Outside? Next door?" To each question, the child answers no. When he says, "In the car?" she says "I think so" and goes to retrieve the toy. (p. 7)

In this example, the father engages his daughter conversationally, guiding her step by step through the memory strategy of self-questioning. As Wertsch (1991) argues, in this instance it would be misleading to assign the act of remembering to only one of the individuals. The remembering takes place as a function of the interaction. In this case, the remembering is ostensibly something shared, emerging through the participants' co-constructed conversation. Further, through relationship in the zone of proximal development, the memory strategy is made available to the child, and by appropriating and internalizing the strategy, she is equipped to trace similar steps on her own when there is a need for her to do so.

Based on his observations of interactions in the zone of proximal development, Vygotsky noted certain transitions in instructional relationships. These transitions are concerned with the distribution of responsibility and control, and the division of labor, in performing an activity. Initially, the child's conversational partner takes a leading role while attempting to regulate the child's mental processes. However, as the child gains competence in the activity, the adult or more competent peer gradually transfers increasing responsibility for performing the activity to the child. With the guidance of others, children are able to engage in activities which they would not be capable of performing on their own. This is because the more able partner also takes on the self-regulatory role of the child, explicitly providing psychological tools that are needed for self-regulating the activity, tools the child has yet to grasp.

The zone of proximal development has important implications for the sequence of development of learners' self-regulation (Díaz, Neal & Amaya-Williams, 1990). First, the learner's activities are initially regulated by 'the other' in the context of their social relationship. Second, the learner adopts the regulatory role of the other, becoming more responsible for the process by actively redefining the activity in the other's terms. Third, the transformation by which the learner's activity becomes self-regulated (as opposed to other-regulated) occurs by virtue of the kinds of teaching interactions and directions provided by the other.

Implications for classroom management

Developmental psychology in the areas of cognitive and moral development can provide teachers with strong indications of what they need to emphasize or provide in their classrooms for learners of different developmental levels. Here are a few of the implications for teaching derived from Piagetian and Vygotskian theories of cognitive development (adapted from Gage & Berliner, 1992).

1. A teacher must not assume that children's thinking processes and understandings are similar to his or her own. Through interviewing, questioning and careful observation of students' learning performances, teachers should develop an *intellectual empathy* with their students. Children at different stages of development can be expected to act and respond differently. Teachers must be sensitive to the nature of the "cognitive or psychological tools" a child possesses for grasping the information or problem being presented.

2. Children in the early elementary years learn particularly well from concrete instructional materials and aids. Giving children firsthand opportunities to *experience and manipulate objects* with their senses is likely to be a more effective general teaching strategy than is abstract discussion of things and events.

3. Even for older learners, instructional sequences that begin with hands-on experiences with objects or events, move on to instructional directions as to the important characteristics of the objects or events, and end with verbal discussions of the objects or events in more general terms seem to make sense. This kind of *inductive approach to sequencing instruction* can be a powerful instructional strategy for all age levels.

4. Since new experiences interact with existing knowledge to arouse interest and to develop understanding, it is essential that instructional experiences be novel enough to extend current understandings, but not so novel as to be completely incomprehensible given present cognitive capacities. Teachers should attempt to provide instructional experiences that take place in a learner's zone of proximal development. *"Moderate novelty* helps, while zero novelty bores, and radical novelty bewilders" (Gage & Berliner, 1992).

5. Children should be permitted to proceed through developmental sequences at their own pace. This suggests that individualization of instruction and *learner self-regulation* should be emphasized within feasible classroom limits.

6. *Social interactions* in the classroom are integral for cognitive as well as affective learning. Through discussions and cooperative projects with other learners, each learner can be helped to grow more fully to comprehend himself or herself in relation to other people and events.

7. It is important to instruct learners about acceptable classroom behaviors. Such instruction provides a discourse that allows students to develop (or appropriate) the conceptual tools needed for thinking about and regulating their own behaviors.

Instructional development in schools should be directed toward the overall educational goal of producing self-directed learners who can plan, execute and take responsibility for their own lives as adults in society. Implicit in the developmental theories discussed in this chapter, and in many of the discussions in preceding chapters, is the central notion that instructional development is a matter of internalization of control. As a learner grows and develops, he or she gradually comes to incorporate, understand and apply the relationships between environment and behavior that control and determine learning, to the purposeful attainment of the learner's own instructional goals. This gradual movement from dependence on external control for instructional progress to independence through internal control and self-directed learning, can be facilitated by teachers at all levels if they are aware of the various aspects of this developmental evolution. Hopefully some of the developmental notions presented here will serve to increase such awareness.

Working With Others

Despite a teacher's best efforts, there are some students' difficulties that exceed a teacher's capacity, and demand attention from resources outside the classroom. Students manifesting unmanageable difficulties can undermine the positive, instructive climate of a classroom and can cause teachers to question their own competence. It is important that teachers be able to acknowledge the limits of their expertise and recognize situations that warrant consultation with, or referral to, specialized resource persons. As with any profession, a teacher's expertise is not all-encompassing. However, as Porter (1996) points out, teachers are in an ideal position to identify at-risk children and adolescents, and to refer them to appropriate specialists. In this section of this final chapter, we discuss the issue of dealing with problems that require working with others. We shall address referrals, the role of different school resource personnel, parental involvement, and the planning and managing of parent conferences.

Referrals

A referral is warranted if a teacher judges a student's difficulties to be beyond the teacher's own personal expertise, and to be interfering greatly with the student's academic or social development. The more deviant, disruptive or frequent a misbehavior, the more likely a referral should be made. Additionally, there are problems not necessarily manifested as disruptive behavior, but that warrant referral because they may signal serious underlying difficulties such as sexual or physical abuse, anxiety, depression, learning disability, suicide, family strife, physical dysfunction, substance abuse or gang involvement. Levin and Nolan (1991) present the following list of signs to which teachers should be sensitive.

1. *Changes in physical appearance* – Posture, dress and hygiene often reflect mood and self-image. Marked weight gain or loss is of particular concern given the dramatic increase of

eating disorders. Bruises, scarring or unusual soreness can be signs of neglect, abuse or self-injurious behavior.

2. *Changes in activity level* – Absenteeism, excessive lateness, lethargy and falling asleep in class may be indicative of depression or substance abuse. Hyperactivity, impulsivity, a lower threshold for frustration and aggressiveness may signal emotional disturbance.

3. *Changes in personality* – Emotional disturbances are sometimes shown in direct forms of expression and behavior. Unusual or excessive displays of anger or agitation should be noted.

4. *Changes in achievement status* – Deteriorating grades, an increase in uncompleted work or an inability to focus on tasks may also be indicative of emotional predicament.

5. *Changes in health or physical abilities* – Complaints of visual or auditory deficiency, headaches, stomach aches, dizziness, rashes or sores or frequent bathroom use are health concerns that warrant referral.

6. *Changes in socialization* – Students who become withdrawn or unusually quiet should also be cause for concern. Such behavior is often ignored by teachers as it does not pose a disruptive influence on classroom events.

It is important that referrals are not seen as a way of "passing the buck" – making the problem somebody else's. Teachers should view referrals as an opportunity to improve their knowledge and skills by collaborating with other professionals (Long & Frye, 1977). When referral becomes necessary it is important that the teacher be aware of the referral system in the school, and the trained resource persons available to help. Although each school may have its own procedures for referral, there are several general considerations.

In requesting assistance from a resource person, the teacher should take time to explain fully the nature of the problem, being clear and specific about details. Nonspecific, nebulous complaints contribute little to gaining solutions. It can be valuable for the teacher to keep documentation regarding the problem as this may help to ensure important factors are not overlooked. It also is valuable for a school to have a policy about how to use consultants and specialists (how and to whom to refer students for help, and under what circumstances) (Porter, 1996). Teachers will be more likely to make appropriate referrals if they have clear procedures for doing so. Subsequent to contacting the school resource person, parents should be notified if any individualized intervention is being considered for the student. In fact, some school districts require written parental consent before changes are made in a student's program, or specialist evaluations are conducted. School-based solutions to problems should be explored first. If parents need to be notified, they are more likely to be responsive and cooperative if presented with a record of school-based personnel's attempts to deal with the problem (Levin & Nolan, 1991).

Faced with a particular concern, a teacher may be unsure as to the correct resource person to contact. We suggest that it is better to make a referral on the basis of a "best guess" than to delay indefinitely. Specialized resource persons are most often trained to recognize problems that should be treated by other specialists. While it is important that the student does eventually have contact with the correct resource person, this may only occur after a short series of referrals as the problem is uncovered (e.g., the root of Danny's inattention may be a learning disability compounded by a hearing deficit).

There are a number of different kinds of specialized resource persons. First referrals often are made to the *school counselor*. The school counselor can bring a fresh perspective to and supply a second opinion about the gravity of a problem. Often it may be that the teacher simply has become stuck, responding consistently in an ineffective way to a particular problem. In such cases the counselor can provide the teacher with valuable feedback or suggestions for a new approach. A counselor can also assist in ameliorating troubled relations between the teacher and student. Seeing both sides of the problem puts the counselor in a position to act as an intermediary. The counselor can play a major role in exploring more deeply the source of the student's difficulties, and work one-on-one with the student in developing solutions. Additionally, the counselor can provide support to the teacher who is experiencing stress in dealing with a chronic, emotionally-draining situation. When problems cannot be dealt with adequately by the school counselor, others may need to be consulted.

Decisions to suspend or remove a student from the classroom, shift a student to another classroom or refer a student for evaluation by a specialist, usually require the approval of an *administrator*. As discussed in the previous chapter, administrators also can play a key role in the enforcement of disciplinary consequences. If a teacher suspects that a student is experiencing difficulties prompted by serious personal or family disturbance, the clinical expertise of a *school psychologist* should be sought. The school psychologist can conduct an in depth diagnostic evaluation, recommend specialized treatments or refer to other specialists external to the school system if warranted.

Involving parents/guardians

Research findings consistently underscore the pivotal importance of parental influences on students' educational achievement and classroom behavior (see Eitzen, 1992; Fullan & Stiegelbauer, 1991). It is generally the case that most parents are interested and willing to assist in ensuring their child's education. However, parents are often not consulted unless their child is misbehaving, truant or failing to meet academic requirements (Long & Frye, 1977). Jones and Jones (1998) cite four reasons why teachers ought to work at establishing a positive involvement with parents. First, if parents maintain a positive image of the teacher, children are more likely to receive encouragement and reinforcement for their accomplishments. Second, parents are legally responsible for their children and ought to be kept informed about their children's behavior and academic progress. Third, parents can be a valuable resource for the teacher. Parents can not only provide helpful information about their children to teachers but also can be brought into the classroom to tutor students, share their expertise on particular topics or assist with practical chores (e.g., copying materials, organizing field trips). Fourth, parents can be involved in the consistent application of rewards or consequences (as described in chapter seven).

Gaining parental support is aided by communicating clearly to parents instructional aims, classroom rules, procedures and methods early in the school year. Teachers may adopt a policy that includes a systematic procedure for involving parents in academic and behavioral issues, both positive and negative. Such procedures might focus on providing a positive basis for later routine communication and joint problem-solving (Porter, 1996). Parents are more likely to be supportive of a program they understand and have had an opportunity to discuss. Establishing open communications early in the school year allows teacher-parent relationships to begin on a positive note, and eases future interactions necessary in dealing with a student's difficulty. Further, the more frequent interactions with parents occur, the more comfortable and familiar teachers and parents will feel with each other.

Conducting *parent conferences* requires preparation. Careful preparation both reduces a teacher's anxiety and enhances the likelihood that parents will be cooperative. There is little point in contacting parents unless the teacher has considered a plan for how parents can contribute effectively in dealing with their child's difficulties. In involving parents, teachers should be prepared to offer specific suggestions (e.g., the application of consistent predetermined consequences, supplying encouragement for tasks completed). Merely informing parents of the problem can simply give parents the impression that they are expected to "do something," to punish or threaten the child (Good & Brophy, 1997). As discussed throughout the various chapters of this book, the focus should be on promoting positive reinforcement, not punishment. A well-planned meeting should encourage parents' cooperation, and ensure that the teacher and parent can support each other's efforts. Jones and Jones (1998) suggest three basic steps to a successful parent-teacher conference. First, teachers should adequately prepare student and parent(s) for the conference. Preparing students includes discussing the purpose and goals of the conference and allowing the student to ask questions and express concerns. Students need to know what will happen at the conference. Preparing parents involves reminding them about the conference one week beforehand, and providing them with an agenda for the conference. Second, teachers should acquire and clearly organize important and relevant information about the student. Third, teachers should create a comfortable and relaxed environment for all parent-teacher conferences.

When conditions require that parents be contacted regarding students' misbehavior, it is important that phone calls to parents and parent conferences be conducted with a view towards inspiring cooperation and preventing hostility or defensiveness. Albert (1989) offers the following suggestions for cultivating positive communications with parents.

1. *Discuss misbehavior in objective terms* – Labeling a students' misbehavior using subjective, judgmental terms is more likely to elicit defensiveness from parents than clear, precise, qualified statements. Providing parents with data about a specific misbehavior and the actions the teacher has taken in attempting to deal with it, demonstrates professional com-

petence, clearly illustrates the nature of the teacher's concern and shows the need for parental involvement.

2. *Limit complaints to three or four specific misbehaviors* – Listing *ad infinitum* every minor transgression is unlikely to garner parental cooperation. Providing a few examples of the misbehaviors causing the most concern is sufficient for parents to comprehend the nature of the problem and the teacher's concern.

3. *Avoid predicting future failures* – The fact that their child currently is having problems is difficult enough for parents to accept let alone having to abide a teacher's prognostications of doom and despair.

4. *Anticipate success* – It is important that parents not lose confidence in themselves, their children or the teacher. Presenting concrete suggestions about how parents can best assist their children and instilling a belief in the increased likelihood of success of parental actions is empowering for parents and can have dramatic positive repercussions.

5. *Don't take defensive reactions personally* – A defensive reaction to upsetting news is not unnatural. Being informed about their child's misbehavior may reflect parents' feelings of guilt, powerlessness, fear or being overwhelmed.

6. *Don't ask for the impossible* – It is important in making suggestions to parents that what they are being asked to do is in fact doable (e.g., that parents have the time and/or financial resources that may be needed for a particular intervention).

When meeting with parents, listening to parents' concerns is as important as making sure that teachers communicate their concerns. Being a competent listener is absolutely essential for developing positive, productive communicative relations with parents. Listening begins with conveying the impression that one is ready and willing to listen (Bonney Rust, 1985). An impatient or rigid demeanor will greatly impede garnering the parental support that may be critical to alleviating a problem. In addition, providing positive closure to interactions with parents is important. Statements like, "I'm glad we had this opportunity to talk about Brenda today" or "You've helped me gain a better understanding of her difficulties" help to provide parents with a sense that their participation is valuable.

Personal Coping

There has been increasing recognition of the stress experienced by teachers burdened with increasing responsibilities and conflicting demands associated with the rapid change of school conditions (Dunham, 1984; Friedman, 1991). *Teacher stress* and *teacher burnout* are terms that have become commonplace in both professional and public domains. Students' disruptive behavior and disciplinary concerns are often listed among the major sources of teacher stress (see Baker, 1985; Kyriacou, 1987; Veenman, 1984). Curwin (1992) found discipline problems to be responsible for 40 percent or more of teacher departures during the first three years of professional life.

Teachers' responses to stress can be manifested as mental symptoms (e.g., anxiety, depression, frustration, anger, fear, irritability), muscular symptoms (e.g., tension in shoulders and limbs, headaches, backaches), visceral symptoms (e.g., cardiovascular problems, ulcers, colitis), drug and alcohol abuse, or suicide (Curwin & Mendler, 1988). In learning to cope with stress it is crucial that teachers become sensitive to their own physical, emotional and cognitive states, and learn to recognize their own particular, individualistic reactions to stress. Regularly monitoring one's physical health, feelings and the thoughts that accompany stressful feelings provides cues to a teacher in determining when active measures are needed to reduce stress.

There are three major routes to diminishing stress. One way is to work actively to change the features of the environment that are stress evoking. Teachers' own application of problem-solving techniques in generating solutions to difficulties (see chapter six), the kinds of skills acquired through assertiveness training (see chapter seven) and the classroom management techniques described throughout this book can assist teachers in altering their surroundings to reduce the influence of external stressors. Unfortunately, however, not all external circumstances and individuals are subject to change, and it may be more realistic to adjust one's own response to external stressors.

A second route to reducing stress is directed inward and involves self-change activities. In addition to following the current wisdom regarding regular exercise and a healthy diet, a very useful way of dealing with stress is by employing relaxation techniques. Learning how to relax has the twofold benefit of reducing current stress-induced feelings, while preparing the way for positive actions.

In a calm state, it may be easier to generate rational solutions and to imagine dealing with a situation more successfully. While there are numerous relaxation methods available (see Bernstein & Borkovec, 1976; Goldfried & Davidson, 1976), a simple method cited by McManus (1989) is as follows: take deep breaths for a couple of minutes, breathing in deeply while slowly counting to five (or more if you can); exhale slowly, counting again, and press the air right out of your lungs; tense the muscles, while imaging you are very cold, then relax and feel yourself becoming warm. With practice of this or a similar technique, a relaxed state can be attained with decreasing effort and less time spent on the induction procedure.

A third route to reducing stress comes from making a commitment to becoming an effective classroom manager (Brophy, 1996). Teachers who have not learned to effectively manage their classrooms and students often are authoritarian and punitive, yet at the same time are ineffectual and frustrated. Under stress, teachers often revert to authoritarian discipline. Effective classroom managers are authoritative but also socially adept, in control but not controlling, firm with respect to articulating inappropriate behavior yet perceived as caring. These teachers spend less time reprimanding and punishing, and more time teaching and praising. They also experience a feeling of greater control and satisfaction.

As discussed in chapter six, feelings and thoughts are integrally related. Another self-change tactic for coping with stress is by changing the kinds of beliefs experienced in stressful situations; beliefs that impact upon the ways individuals think about, perceive and label stressful events and experiences. A general stress-reduction strategy described by Martin (1983) targets the *defeatist internal self-talk* made manifest by adverse beliefs. Martin (1983) lists a number of stress-inducing beliefs and defeatist self-statements common among teachers.

1. *"If you're the anxious type, teaching isn't your game."* Stress is a common experience. However, there is much variation in how individual teachers learn and practice effective coping skills. The ability to deal with professional stress is more a matter of learned capability than a preordained personality trait.

2. *"It is a bad sign if you experience any stress at all."* Stress is a natural reaction and coping, rather than complete mastery or total elimination, is the realistic goal to be kept in mind. Dealing effectively with stress requires recognizing (rather

than denying) the initial signs of stress as a cue to begin exercising a coping strategy.

3. *"Every student, colleague and parent must like me and approve of everything I do as a teacher."* Although this appears to be extreme and irrational, the degree of upset experienced by many teachers when being criticized would indicate the prevalence of this belief in many situations. The diversity and plausibility of opinions regarding issues of instruction and classroom management precludes total agreement in all matters. It is simply not possible or reasonable to expect to please everyone all the time.

4. *"It's a terrible shame that I can't teach in the ideal situation."* A consequence of this belief may be that a teacher spends so much time dwelling on inadequacies and problems that positive aspects are ignored and little effort is expended on improving matters.

5. *"The whole teaching system needs to be changed, and until it is there is little I can do."* Similar to the previous defeatist belief, this kind of thinking poses a severe limitation to constructive action and easily can lead to a sense of powerlessness and/or apathy. Placing blame on external factors may be reassuring temporarily. However, it can become a denial of a teacher's immediate professional responsibility to provide the best instruction possible given present constraints.

6. *"I must never make a mistake."* Every teacher makes mistakes. No single instructional error is likely to "ruin" a student. The real danger of this belief is that it may restrict any experimentation or creativity on the part of the teacher to develop new and more effective instructional methods. The point is to be able to learn from mistakes, not to be preoccupied with committing them.

7. *"I'm not a born-natural teacher."* While it may be true that some individuals are better suited to teach than others, ruminating over whether or not you are a "natural" teacher is unproductive and needlessly stressful.

The general stress-reduction strategy described by Martin (1983) highlights three basic steps comprising a simple and effective approach to managing stress: (1) recognizing defeatist self-talk and beliefs (such as those described above), (2) using relaxation to inter-

rupt such self-talk and the stress it provokes and (3) promoting constructive action through the use of positive, enhancing self-talk.

1. *Recognizing defeatist self-talk* – Recognizing self-defeating
   beliefs and self-talk of the kinds depicted above can best be
   accomplished by observing stress-evoking situations and
   noting the internal dialogue occurring before, during and
   after such events. Often, stressful experiences are dominated
   by feelings that seem to obscure any discernible self-talk.
   However, by focusing on internal dialogue, it is possible to
   probe the major themes and self-statements that seem particularly debilitating (those statements that accompany the
   kinds of stress-related symptoms mentioned previously).

2. *Stopping defeatist self-talk* – There are essentially two components to eliminating defeatist self-talk. The first is to establish an internal cue that can be self-delivered at the first sign
   of debilitating self-talk. This cue serves to interrupt the
   defeatist thought pattern momentarily. One way to establish
   such an internal cue is to use the word "STOP" as a *thought
   stopping* technique. Whenever you are alone and recognize
   defeatist self-talk, yell "STOP!" Gradually reduce the volume of the STOP cue over successive uses until it is effective
   simply being uttered at a sub-vocal level (internally). Using
   the STOP cue to interrupt negative thought patterns allows
   one to refocus, and engage in a relaxation technique and/or
   more positive self-talk.

3. Promoting positive self-talk and action – If negative forms of
   self-talk evoke stress, positive forms of self-talk should promote stress reduction (Meichenbaum, 1977). By examining
   the self-talk that occurs during activities in which one experiences a sense of efficacy, it is possible to gain an understanding of the forms that positive, coping self-statements
   take. Positive, coping self-statements can be used to prepare
   for stressful situations (e.g., "Now that I'm relaxed, I can
   think about what I need to do."), handle situations as they
   are occurring (e.g., "O.K., here we go. I'm relaxed, the lesson
   is prepared, and I'm just going to take it one step at a time."),
   cope with the feeling of being overwhelmed (e.g., "I'm feeling anxious but I can manage. I'm just going to focus on the
   present and what it is that I need to do now.") or self-rein-
   force ("Hey, it worked. I'm on top of this.").

It's important to practice these procedures so that they become virtually automatic. While gaining these skills requires time and effort, it takes little time to use them, and they can be applied in almost any situation (e.g., classroom, staff meetings or parent conferences).

Another consideration regarding teacher stress is that teachers may feel that classroom difficulties imply incompetence and that therefore, problems must be kept hidden from others. Consequently, many teachers attempt to cope with their distress in an unbearable isolation. Hargraves (1982) also points out that there is an apprehension among teachers to offer unsolicited help to colleagues for fear of being accused of suggesting incompetence or of violating another's professional autonomy. Unless they are extremely lucky or wildly self-deluded, all teachers experience difficulties. Teachers can be an invaluable support to one another. It is up to individual teachers and the school staff collectively to take steps (e.g., establish a support group) to create and facilitate avenues for open communications and mutually supportive and collaborative staff relations. It is tragic when a teacher suffers in silence needlessly while colleagues are willing and able to provide peer support and assistance.

Legal and Ethical Considerations

Teachers are mandated legal authority and given considerable latitude to enforce and administer rules in maintaining students' acceptable conduct in classrooms. Teachers have a duty to regulate students' behavior in protecting the interests and educational progress of other learners and in safeguarding school property. However, this does not mean that teachers can set any rules or administer any punishment they wish. Teachers are, in fact, employees of their local school boards and are constrained in their actions by other authorities (e.g., constitutional and statutory provisions) (Province of BC Ombudsman, 1995). A generation ago, expectations were such that teachers exerted control over students on the basis of a largely unquestioned authority. Current expectations for teachers and students are dramatically different. Students are no longer expected to comply unquestioningly with teachers', or for that matter, parents' demands. Disciplinary policies have been struck down on the grounds that they are unconstitutionally vague or because acceptable behavior has not been specified precisely (McCarthy & Cambron-McCabe, 1992). There is increasing concern for the right of students to *due process of law* and that students' constitutional rights "not be left at the schoolyard gates" (see Fischer, Schimmel & Kelly, 1981). In this section, we shall discuss some important legal considerations. Our purpose is not to prepare you for the intricacies of litigation. Rather, it is to sketch briefly the nature of some important legal restraints and some of the attendant ethical considerations. In so doing, we attempt to underscore the importance of employing a "judicial temper" in matters of classroom management.

Teachers are empowered to make rules and regulations and to impose legitimate sanctions in dealing with students' misbehavior. However, teachers may incur legal action if rules or disciplinary activities impede students' constitutional or charter rights, particularly the right of students to due process. Saunders (1993) states that parents are becoming more demanding of schools and are increasingly willing to sue administrators and teachers for violating students' rights and freedoms. Therefore, it is important that teachers take the time and effort to familiarize themselves with the relevant legislation affecting their particular school and its operation. In this way, teachers increase the likelihood of their making informed, rational and legally prudent disciplinary decisions. One general guideline is to know where your sources of support are located. This includes knowing where and how to contact professionals who have expertise in specific problems (Jordan, 1994).

While parents (or guardians) bear the responsibility for the care and supervision of their minor children, parental authority is supplanted temporarily by school authorities during school hours. The legal principle is that the teacher stands *in loco parentis* (in place of the parent) to discipline children during those hours children attend school. Although *in loco parentis* is still often invoked, its applicability has become more limited (Fischer, Schimmel & Kelly, 1981). For example, it is clearly inappropriate for a teacher to make an appeal on the basis of *in loco parentis*, when parents have made an explicit request that corporal punishment not be used in disciplining their child.

It would be impractical, if not totally impossible, to specify in full detail the rules of conduct for parents in disciplining their children. It is assumed that parents use their best judgement to do what is necessary. The same is presumed of teachers. Teachers are expected to use their discretionary judgement in disciplinary matters. Although it is required that a teacher's disciplinary policies be specified as clearly as possible, it is not necessary that all criteria be stringently detailed (as is necessary in criminal statutes). When matters of regulating student conduct come before a court, each case is evaluated with regard to its own unique circumstances. For example, in determining whether or not a particular punishment has been warranted, courts consider the age, gender, mental condition and past behavior of the student, together with the extent of the penalty and its relation to the seriousness of the offense (McCarthy & Cambron-McCabe, 1992). In such cases, it is the discretionary judgement of the teacher that is called into question. Past judicial decisions have upheld the denial of privileges, suspension, expulsion, detention and corporal punishment (see McCarthy & Cambron-McCabe, 1992). It is important to emphasize, however, that decisions regarding these punishments vary widely. Judgments rendered in individual cases appear highly dependent upon the precise nature of the particular circumstances.

As mentioned, there has been increasing attention given to the right of students to due process. *Suspensions* and *expulsions* from classes or school are serious events in a student's life. The inclusion of such events in school records can have severe consequences for students' opportunities to receive higher education or gain employment. On this basis, schools and individual teachers are obligated to provide for students' right to due process in disciplinary matters that might result in suspension or expulsion. In such cases, excepting greater specificity in statutes or administrative regulations, students have the constitutional right (prior to the suspension or expulsion) to: oral or written notification of the offense and the consequences, an opportunity to dispute the charges before a fair adjudicator and an explanation of the evidence on which the decision is being made (see McCarthy & Cambron-McCabe, 1992).

While there are differences among school districts across North America (Provincial and State School Acts specify the procedures for suspension and expulsion of students), generally speaking, teachers have the power to suspend a student from class. As Giles and Proudfoot (1984) point out, however, it is generally the case that the teacher must report the circumstances of the suspension or expulsion to the principal. Also, it may be required that the school board be notified. (This is usually done through the school superintendent.) As a rule, the board of trustees has the final say about a student's expulsion and it is observed that students invariably are re-admitted (at least once). For this reason, teachers are cautioned to refrain from painting themselves into a corner by stating a refusal to allow a student back into their classes (Giles & Proudfoot, 1984).

The protection of students' right to due process is not intended to turn classrooms into courtrooms. Rather, it is to help safeguard against unfair or oppressive, authoritarian procedures such as arbitrary suspensions or expulsions. It is important to note two conditions in which teachers may proceed without adhering to the formalities of due process. The first pertains to the routine handling of minor rule infractions where lesser consequences are administered. The legal principle *de minimus non curat lex* (the law does not deal with trifles) applies and is intended to authorize teachers to deal with such situations on the basis of their expert knowledge and discretionary judgment. The second condition refers to emergencies in which immediate action is required to protect the safety of students. There is, however, the requirement to provide equitable procedures as soon as it is safe to do so (after the emergency has been dealt with).

Laws governing the use of *corporal punishment* also vary among schools across North America. That corporal punishment is legal in some school districts does not imply that the Court recommends or condones it. The question of whether or not children should be physically punished is not fundamentally a legal matter. Physical punishment is considered more a matter of local policy. Thus, even in school districts where corporal punishment is legally sanctioned, some schools retain policies forbidding its use (Fischer, Schimmel & Kelly, 1981). Notwithstanding, there is judicial concern in cases of excessive punishment. If corporal punishment is administered, it must be *reasonable*, by which it is meant, that the punishment must have an educational purpose, fit the gravity of the offense and take into account of the capacity of the student to withstand it.

Teachers have the right to impose *academic sanctions* (e.g., failing grades, academic probation, retention and exclusion from programs) for poor academic performance. However, with respect to grading practices, academic work and behavior are to be treated separately. The courts do not sanction lowering grades or withholding diplomas for disciplinary reasons. It is generally held that disciplinary problems should not be conflated with academic matters.

Previous judicial decisions on disciplinary matters support the following generalizations (McCarthy & Cambron-McCabe, 1992).

1. Disciplinary actions must be defensible on reasonable grounds and shown to be necessary for the management of the school and for the welfare of learners and/or school employees.

2. All regulations should be stated in terms as precise as possible and communicated clearly to learners and parents.

3. Consequences for rule infractions should fit the nature of the offense and take into account the characteristics of the offender.

4. Students should not be punished for the acts of others (e.g., parents).

5. Due process should be afforded to students prior to the administering of punishments.

6. Suspensions and expulsions must be handled using appropriate procedural safeguards and should not be unfairly or arbitrarily administered.

7. Students being transferred to different classes or schools for disciplinary purposes must be afforded due process procedures.

8. Teachers can search a student's locker or personal effects given that there is reasonable suspicion that the student possesses contraband that can disrupt the educational purposes of the school.

9. Personal searches should be avoided unless there is substantial evidence of a dangerous situation.

10. If students are unlawfully punished, they must be reinstated (without penalty) to their status prior to the imposition of the punishment. Further, any documentation of the offense should be removed from their records.

Just as citizens are subject by law to pay compensation for intentionally injuring another or for injuries caused through negligence, teachers are *liable* for injuries suffered by students in their charge. Teachers must exercise *reasonable care*, that is, the degree of care that a reasonable and judicious teacher would be expected to take under the particular circumstances. If conditions present greater cause for concern (e.g., a workshop, chemistry lab), a reasonable teacher would be expected to exercise greater care. A teacher who does not use reasonable care is being negligent and can be held accountable. Further, although it is often difficult to prove in court, teachers who intentionally inflict mental suffering or psychological injury (e.g., in providing punishment) may be found personally liable and required to pay compensation. In addition, such improper teacher conduct can lead to penalties imposed by teachers' professional associations.

It is important to remember earlier points made in this book regarding the use of punishment only as a last resort. Besides legal and ethical questions regarding the use of punishment, it is more sound pedagogically to implement disciplinary procedures that provide a positive learning situation wherever possible. Actions likely to provoke fear or hatred can have far reaching consequences. As Giles and Proudfoot (1984) point out, learners grow up, marry and have children of their own, and a parent who vividly recalls cruel treatment as a student and harbors resentment is not likely to be supportive and cooperative.

Ban (1987) indicates that the best guard against legal liability is to adopt a pro-active management system. This will help to ensure parental support for discipline. Many parents have a lack of knowledge of how schools and classrooms are run. Such knowledge among parents will decrease the likelihood of misunderstandings about how your classroom is managed, and about how inappropriate behavior is dealt with.

Another important legal and ethical issue concerns the reporting of *child abuse and neglect*. In addition to physical and sexual assault, child abuse also includes emotional abuse. Offenders may be parents, guardians, relatives, neighbors, baby-sitters, teachers, principals, clergy or other individuals with whom a child comes in contact. Jones and Jones (1998) suggest it is essential that all educators become familiar with the child abuse laws in their state or province, and the reporting and follow-up procedures used by their school district. It is important that teachers understand that it is not their duty to adjudicate matters of suspected abuse. Their primary responsibility is to report. Teachers may be subject to prosecution, civil action for damages or professional disciplinary proceedings for failing to report suspected abuse to the appropriate bodies specified in relevant State or Provincial statutes dealing with these matters.

Further, there are important ethical facets relating to child abuse and neglect in addition to the laws covering mandatory reporting. Their relationships with their students place teachers in a key position not only with respect to detecting instances of abuse, but of assisting a child through what may be a difficult and emotionally painful bureaucratic and personal process. There is an obligation as the primary contact person, as well as being someone the child knows and can trust, to provide support for the child throughout the process, and not abandon the child subsequent to making the report. Remember that the legal process will demand the child come into contact with a number of grownups that the child does not know and who have various agendas that the child will not understand.

Obviously, teachers' first responsibility is to familiarize themselves thoroughly with the specific acts of legislation, school policies and professional guidelines relevant to their conduct in the local, provincial/state and national context in which they work. We have provided only a brief sketch of some of the more general considerations likely to be reflected in these more specific documents. Specific questions and concerns should be directed to local school administrators, appropriate government officials and representatives of professional associations.

Finally, we want to emphasize that what is ethical may not always be synonymous with what is legal. Although it is extremely important for teachers to know intimately their mandated legal responsibilities and limitations, it also is important that teachers attempt consistently to reflect on their own sense of what is right and wrong, appropriate and inappropriate with respect to their reactions to their own and students' conduct in the classroom and school. For example, being the "best model" possible for students may not be mandated by law, but it may be adopted as a moral imperative based on a teacher's thoughtful self-reflection concerning the nature of teaching and himself or herself as a teacher.

References

Albert, L. (1989). *A teacher's guide to cooperative discipline: How to manage your classroom and promote self-esteem*. Circle Pines, MN: American Guidance Service.

Baker, K. (1985). Research evidence of a school discipline problem. *Phi Delta Kappan, 66*, 482-488.

Ban, J.R. (1987). Discipline literacy for parents: An imperative for the eighties. *NAASP Bulletin, 71*, 111-115.

Bernstein, D.A. & Borkovec, T.D. (1976). *Progressive relaxation training: A manual for the helping professions*. Champaign, IL: Research Press.

Bonney Rust, W. (1985). *Management guidelines for teachers*. London: Pitman.

Brophy, J. (1996). *Teaching problem students*. New York: Guilford Press.

Centra, J.A. & Potter, D.A. (1980). School and teacher effects: An interrelational model. *Review of Educational Research, 50*, 273-291.

Charles, C.M. (1996). *Building classroom discipline (5th ed.)*. White Plains, NY: Longman.

Coates T.J. & Thoresen, C.E. (1980). Behavioral self-control and educational practice, or, Do we really need self-control? *Review of Research in Education, 7*, 3-45.

Cooper, H.M., Burger, J.M. & Seymour, G.E. (1979). Classroom context and student ability as influences on teacher perceptions of classroom control. *American Educational Research Journal, 16*, 189-196.

Curwin, R.L. & Mendler, A.N. (1988). *Discipline with dignity.* Association for Supervision and Curriculum Development.

Curwin, R.L. (1992). *Rediscovering hope: Our greatest teaching strategy.* Bloomington, IN: National Educational Service.

De Cecco, J.R. & Crawford, W.R. (1974). *The psychology of learning and instruction.* Englewood Cliffs, NJ: Prentice-Hall.

Díaz, R.M., Neal, C.J. & Amaya-Williams, M. (1990). The social origins of self-regulation. In L.C. Moll (Ed.), *Vygotsky and education: Instructional implications and applications of sociohistorical psychology* (pp. 127-154). Cambridge, MA: Cambridge University Press.

Dick, W. & Carey, L. (1978). *The systematic design of instruction.* Glenview, IL: Scott, Foresman & Company.

Dunham, J. (1984). *Stress in teaching.* London: Croom Helm.

Eitzen, D. (1992). Problem students: The sociocultural roots. *Phi Delta Kappan, 73*, 584-590.

Fischer, L., Schimmel, D. & Kelly, C. (1981). *Teachers and the law.* New York: Longman.

Friedman, I.A. (1991). High- and low-burnout schools: School culture aspects of teacher burnout. *Journal of Educational Research, 84*(6), 325-333.

Fullan, M.G. & Stiegelbauer, S. (1991). *The new meaning of educational change.* New York: Teachers College Press.

Gage, N.L. & Berliner, D.C. (1992). *Educational psychology (5th ed.).* Boston: Houghton Mifflin.

Gardner, H. (1985). *Frames of mind: The theory of multiple intelligences.* New York: Basic Books.

Giles, T.E. & Proudfoot, A.J. (1984). *Educational administration in Canada (3rd ed.).* Calgary, AB: Detselig.

Goldfried, M.R. & Davidson, G.C. (1976). *Clinical behavior therapy.* New York: Holt, Rinehart & Winston.

Good, T.L. & Brophy, J.E. (1997). *Looking in classrooms (7th ed.).* New York: Harper Collins.

Gredler, M.E. (1992). *Learning and instruction: Theory into practice (2nd ed.).* New York: Macmillan.

Hargraves, D.H. (1982). *The challenge for the comprehensive school.* London: Routledge and Kegan Paul.

Jones, V.F. & Jones, L.S. (1998). *Comprehensive classroom management: Motivating and managing students (5th ed.).* Boston: Allyn & Bacon.

Kohlberg, L. (1963). The development of children's orientations toward moral order: I. Sequence in the development of moral thought. *Vita Humans, 6,* 11-33.

Kohlberg, L. (1969). Stage and sequences: The cognitive-developmental approach to socialization. In D. Gosslin (Ed.), *Handbook of socialization theory and research* (pp. 347-480). Chicago: Rand and McNally.

Kyriacou, C. (1987). Teacher stress and burnout: An international review. *Educational Research, 29*(2), 146-152.

Lefrançois, G.R. (1977). *Of children.* Belmont, CA: Wadsworth.

Lemlech, J.K. (1979). *Classroom management.* New York: Harper & Row.

Levin, J. & Nolan, J.F. (1991). *Principles of classroom management: A hierarchical approach.* Englewood Cliffs, NJ: Prentice Hall.

Long, J.D. & Frye, V.H. (1977). *Making it till Friday: A guide to successful classroom management.* Princeton, NJ: Princeton Book Company.

Martin, J. (1983). *Mastering instruction.* Boston: Allyn & Bacon.

McCarthy, M.M. & Cambron-McCabe, N.H. (1992). *Public school law: Teachers' and students' rights (3rd ed.).* Boston: Allyn & Bacon.

McManus, M. (1989). *Troublesome behavior in the classroom: A teacher's survival guide.* New York: Routledge.

Meichenbaum, D. (1977). *Cognitive behavior modification: An integrated approach.* New York: Plenum Press.

Moll, L.C. (1990). *Vygotsky and education: Instructional implications and applications of sociohistorical psychology.* Cambridge, MA: Cambridge University Press.

Ombudsman, British Columbia. (1995). *Fair Schools.* Province of British Columbia.

Piaget, J. (1952). *The origins of intelligence in children.* New York: International Universities Press.

Piaget, J. (1954). *The construction of reality in the child.* New York: Basic Books.

Piaget, J. (1957). *Logic and psychology.* New York: Basic Books.

Piaget, J. (1968). *On the development of memory and identity.* Worcester, MA: Clark University Press.

Piaget, J. & Inhelder, B. (1969). *The psychology of the child.* New York: Basic Books.

Popham, W.J. & Baker, E.I. (1970). *Systematic instruction.* Englewood Cliffs, NJ: Prentice-Hall.

Proudfoot, A.J. & Hutchings, L. (1988). *Teacher beware: A legal primer for the classroom teacher*. Calgary, AB: Detselig.

Saunders, T. (1993). *Providing for the health, safety, and well-being of students: A legal guide for school administrators*. Surrey, BC: Indigo Press.

Tharp, R.G. & Gallimore, R. (1988). *Rousing minds to life: Teaching, learning, and schooling in social context*. New York: Cambridge University Press.

Veenman, S. (1984). Perceived problems of beginning teachers. *Review of Educational Research, 54*(2), 143-178.

Vygotsky, L.S. (1986). *Thought and language* (A. Kozulin, Trans.). Cambridge, MA: MIT Press. (Original work published 1934).

Vygotsky, L.S. (1978). *Mind in society*. Cambridge, MA: Harvard University Press.

Wertsch, J.V. (1991). A sociocultural approach to socially shared cognition. In L.B. Resnick, J.M. Levine & S.D. Teasley (Eds.), *Perspectives on socially shared cognition* (pp. 85-100). Washington, DC: American Psychological Association.

A Final Word

To paraphrase the words of the distinguished psychologist, Abraham Maslow (1966), "If the only tool you have is a hammer, it is tempting to treat everything as if it were a nail." This book is largely an attempt to help equip the reader with an assortment of conceptual and theoretical tools representative of a broad understanding of the nature of classroom management. To this end, we have presented theoretical principles and applied techniques from a diverse array of models of classroom management. However, a book of this kind does not guarantee that readers will acquire the actual teaching skills and attitudes necessary to enact effective classroom discipline and management programs in real-life instructional environments. Conceptual and analytic abilities with respect to management models are necessary, but not sufficient, bases for the development and refinement of effective teaching and classroom management. While this book has explicated many management skills and strategies, it has not afforded readers essential opportunities to practice such skills in actual classroom contexts and to receive valid informational feedback about their skill practice. Without actual practice and feedback, it is difficult to acquire and refine useful skills or develop an acute sense of discretionary judgment. Thus, those of you who are, or wish to become, classroom teachers in full possession of effective management skills, should make arrangements to translate immediately your newly-acquired conceptual knowledge of management and discipline models into useful teaching methods through actual classroom experiences.

The reader should also remember not to assume that any of the procedures and techniques advocated in this book are infallible across the full range of teachers, classrooms, learners and situations. This point is difficult to overemphasize in the increasingly diverse, and multicultural context of most contemporary classrooms and schools. Teachers must learn to match their management strategies to their own teaching styles, to individual differences in learners and to classrooms, schools and socio-cultural contexts. Moreover, few of these relevant considerations are static. Consequently, effective classroom management requires ongoing, dynamic assessment and adjustment as time passes and conditions change.

In general, a good classroom manager is a good teacher. Instructional skill and capability contribute significantly to management skill and capability. Therefore, we re-emphasize the importance of developing sound instructional practices for organizing and implementing classroom curricula. Without a good basic ability to teach, any classroom management approach becomes meaningless and empty. However, instructional competence and management savvy are only two of the necessary ingredients for good teaching. Teaching involves more than imparting knowledge and developing skills. A good teacher is committed to acts of caring. The good teacher cares not only about the intellectual lives of learners, but also about their emotional and physical well-being, and about those traditions of knowing and living together that constitute the very best that humankind has managed to develop at this stage in its evolution.

A final point concerns the invaluable time and effort teachers expend reflecting upon and clarifying their positions regarding their own teaching practice. Consider carefully your instructional and management theories, your philosophy of teaching, and your educational aims. Are they coherent and consistent with your teaching practices? If, for example, your goal is to create a cooperative, communitarian, democratic moral order in your classroom, are your students involved in solving disciplinary problems? What kind of teacher do you wish to become? What sort of relationship do you want to have with students? How are you going to achieve that sort of relationship? What is important in your role as teacher? Furthermore, do you act in ways that are consistent with your answers to such questions? These are fundamental questions that pertain not only to the sort of teacher you wish to become, but to the sort of person you believe yourself to be. It is your willingness and the extent to which you thoughtfully delve into these questions, unravel issues and make commitments that will determine your substance, merit, success and fulfillment as a teacher.

Reference

Maslow, A.H. (1966). *The psychology of science: A reconnaissance.* New York: Harper & Row.